GRACE LIKE A RIVER

Christopher Parkening

WITH KATHY TYERS

Tyndale House Publishers, Inc.
Carol Stream, Illinois

Library of Congress Cataloging-in-Publication Data

Parkening, Christopher.
    Grace like a river / Christopher Parkening with Kathy Tyers.
      p. cm.
    Includes bibliographical references (p.), discography (p.).
    ISBN-13: 978-1-4143-0046-7 (hc)
    ISBN-10: 1-4143-0046-8 (hc)
    ISBN-13: 978-1-4143-0047-4 (sc)
    ISBN-10: 1-4143-0047-6 (sc)
    1. Parkening, Christopher. 2. Guitarists—United States—Biography. 3. Christian biography—United States. I. Tyers, Kathy. II. Title.
    ML419.P42A3 2006
    787.87092—dc22   2005036077

Printed in the United States of America.

12   11   10   09   08   07   06
 7   6   5   4   3   2   1

GRACE LIKE A RIVER

DEDICATION

To my son, Luke:
My heart's desire for you, Luke, is that you will love the Lord Jesus
with all your heart and that whatever you do in life, you will do with
excellence for His glory.
I will love you always,
Dad

And this I pray, that your love may abound yet more and more in
knowledge and in all judgment; that ye may approve things that are
excellent; that ye may be sincere and without offence till the day of
Christ; being filled with the fruits of righteousness, which are by
Jesus Christ, unto the glory and praise of God.

Philippians 1:9-11

CONTENTS

FOREWORD BY JOHN MACARTHUR

Christopher Parkening's life has been filled with amazing experiences in two very different worlds—classical guitar and fly-fishing. He is a master of both the closed concert hall, with its skeptical audience, and the open stream, with its uncaring isolation. He moves from the public performance, which demands disciplined perfection, to the rippling water where in the midst of failures, one hopes for success.

Both are solo experiences. In one you are alone in a crowd. In the other you are absolutely alone.

Each has captured Chris's heart and taken him to world-class opportunities. He has known the fulfillment of the highest awards in classical music and in fly-fishing.

Though the two seem so far apart, they each require unusual athletic ability, manual dexterity, mastery of equipment, and—more critically—relentless discipline and hard practice. To be able to capture an audience with breathtaking artistry on six strings and also be able to capture a wild trout with the same delicate skill on one string are wondrously related in the extraordinary life of Chris Parkening.

This is the riveting story of the experiences of a man who has conquered his two worlds. More important, it is the story of how the grace of God has conquered him.

God has used Chris to grace my life for many years—Chris is about to do the same for you.

John MacArthur
July 2005

FOREWORD BY JONI EARECKSON TADA

It was a delightful summer evening, and my husband, Ken, was standing outside over a barbecue, flipping steaks, and "talking fish" with his friend Chris Parkening. Ken would describe his latest ocean-fishing adventure of fighting tuna, and Chris would counter with tales about the trout he was able to hook and release from the stream by his cabin. Back and forth it went. From my view in the kitchen, I wondered when they would run out of stories.

The steaks were great that night, and I was hoping during dinner that the discussion might turn from trout and tuna to something more . . . refined. Like music. Surely Christopher Parkening would enjoy talking with me about thirty-second notes, transcriptions by Segovia, and his latest performance at the Hollywood Bowl. Fat chance. The two men were as animated as before, discussing the fine points of rods and hooks, and the time Chris jumped out of his boat and wrestled a tarpon into submission in the Florida Keys. No getting around it: Chris's stories were really fun. But I knew I would not hear—at least that night—about Bach or Bernstein.

Shortly after dessert, as we were moving into the living room, I confided to Chris that I had a dream of one day sitting close to him and watching him play "Recuerdos de la Alhambra," a beautifully sensuous guitar piece that was one of my favorites from his recordings. "We'll do that sometime," Chris said in a chipper voice. Then it was time for fish videos.

When Chris was about to put on his coat to leave, Ken said,

"Wait a minute, there's something I want you to see." He disappeared into the bedroom and returned with his old guitar from high school. It was dusty, and probably the last thing played on it was "Michael, Row the Boat Ashore." But Chris took it from Ken as though he were being handed a Stradivarius violin. He ran his hand over the dry wood of the face and then gently turned it over to inspect its back. The wood had a couple of small cracks. Chris rested the guitar on his knee and fingered the fossilized strings. He then leaned down to inspect the pitch as he tightened the strings. By this time, Ken had finished telling Chris about his teenage guitar-playing days. Now we were wondering what our friend was up to.

Without a word—and with me looking over his shoulder—Chris closed his eyes, nodded a few times as though he were reaching for something in his memory, and then launched into "Recuerdos de la Alhambra." I was breathless. Tears welled in my eyes as our friend wove a melody that turned our living room into a romantic Spanish hideaway. The night suddenly seemed filled with mystery, with stars above and a heavy scent of evening jasmine in the air. I smiled and sniffed.

It was a gift sent straight from heaven. I could hardly sputter the words "thank you," I was so overcome. Ken turned his guitar over in his hands to make certain it hadn't changed. Yet as quickly as the enchantment had come, it left. Chris and Ken slapped each other on the back, we said our good-byes, and then my husband walked Chris out to his car.

While they were gone, I stared at Ken's guitar sitting innocently on the couch. Was this the same instrument that had only known "Kum Ba Yah"? Yet it wasn't the guitar that was filled with surprises. It was Chris.

That's our friend—a package of surprises (like this book). I mean, how many world-class musicians are as comfortable in freshwater waders as they are in a tuxedo? How many can tie a fly as easily as they can tune an instrument? Maybe a few. But none can match Chris's winsome personality, his exuberant love of God, and his incredible penchant for a good story.

Things *happen* to Chris. To head out to dinner with him and his wife, Theresa, is to head straight into an adventure. And I know before the evening's over, I will have laughed uproariously and talked much about the Lord we love.

That's my hope and prayer for you as you turn the pages of *Grace Like a River*. Maybe you picked up this book at the table after one of Chris's concerts. Perhaps you were browsing through a music store and there it was. Or better yet, a friend gave you a copy with the promise, "It's a *great* read!" Whatever the case, you have a few surprises in store from Mr. Parkening. Because you will not only enjoy great stories—and nobody tells a story quite like Chris—but you will discover why the supreme and massive grace of God happily rests on him.

> Joni Eareckson Tada
> Founder, Joni and Friends
> Fall 2005

"Success"

1974

The center of a concert stage can be a lonely place. As I carried my guitar onto the stage at New York City's Lincoln Center in March 1974, I felt as if I were stepping onto a tightrope over the Grand Canyon. A solitary black piano bench and a footstool had been placed under brilliant stage lights. Other than that, the stage was empty.

I couldn't see the audience very well, but I knew it was a full house. I also knew that everyone out there expected something from me. Many had come hoping to enjoy the music and escape life's pressures for a while. A few were critics, who knew every measure of every piece. They would notice any mistake, and they would listen for what might go wrong.

The pressure on a classical soloist to play perfectly in front of a demanding audience is daunting. This tour had been relentless, and I was exhausted. The pace, the pressure, and the schedule seemed unending. I'd been on the road since mid-January, performing at venues in California, Washington, Wyoming, Tennessee, New York, Massachusetts, and Connecticut. I had played fourteen concerts and had five more to go on the first U.S. leg of this tour. I hadn't seen my home for four and a half weeks and was emotionally and physically drained.

But this was New York. I had to reach inside myself and find the strength to give it my all. To the public in 1974, I may have appeared to be at the top of my career: sold-out concerts, record albums on the classical charts, and widespread critical acclaim. But inside, something was missing. Something important. As I sat down to play, I felt empty but had no choice but to grit my teeth and plow ahead with the performance.

Just two years before, I had made my Lincoln Center debut, a pivotal moment in any musician's career. The *New York Times* concert critic had been gracious to me then, saying, "Christopher Parkening's New York debut recital on Thursday proved the 24-year-old Californian to be an impeccable classic guitarist, perhaps the finest technician this country has yet produced on his instrument. Mr. Parkening . . . could well become one of his generation's concert heroes." Those kind words only increased the pressure I was feeling for this appearance. For this tour, I'd put together another difficult program, with compositions by Dowland, Handel, Bach, Ravel, and Poulenc. The last piece on the program was the challenging "Rumores de la Caleta," by Isaac Albéniz.

Although it felt as if I were simply going through the motions, the performance went exceptionally well. At the end of the concert, the usually reserved New York audience gave several standing ovations, with one critic describing the performance as "incredible." It would have been a wonderful concert to end a tour with.

But it was not the end. I couldn't go home yet. I still had twenty-six performances to go.

My goal in those days was to retire at an early age. My father had retired at forty-seven, so I thought thirty would be a good age for me to retire. I was willing to work extremely hard to reach that goal. I endured the loneliness of hundreds of hotel rooms, the tension of endless, often nerve-racking airplane flights, the monotony and pressure of concert after concert after concert, persevering because I thought that if I could quit at thirty, I would finally be happy.

Knowing there was an escape route kept me going. If I just hung in there and took as many concert dates as I could get, then I could quit while on top, relax, and enjoy the "good life." It wasn't money, fame, or success that drove me back then. It was the dream of retiring to a Montana trout stream.

ৡ৹ ৡ৹ ৡ৹

I grew up in a family that put anyone with great talent or ability on a pedestal. My mother's brother, Bill Marshall, married the famous actress Ginger Rogers in 1961. Ginger was greatly respected in our family, as elsewhere, for her talents as an actress and a dancer. The Marshall family also included Mom's cousin Jack, staff guitarist for the MGM movie studios, and his sons, Frank and Phil. Frank Marshall is a successful movie producer, married to fellow producer Kathleen Kennedy, and Phil Marshall is a well-known film composer.

We all knew that achievement requires hard work and discipline. My father's early retirement was a tribute to his tenacity and perseverance. I also liked setting tough goals and working toward them, so I responded well to the challenges of mastering an instrument. As a young boy, I'd hear a piece of music and think, *With hard work, I'll be able to figure that out and play it.* It was exciting for me to learn a piece that had never before been performed on the classical guitar. Even more than that, I simply loved the music itself. It was thrilling to be the first classical guitarist to play Rick Foster's arrangement of Bach's "Jesu, Joy of Man's Desiring" on the concert stage. I did not enjoy being onstage, though.

When I was about twenty, I heard my mom talking to Ginger Rogers, who was explaining that for her, to be onstage was almost a high. She just ate it up. She adored the applause, the atmosphere, and the electric tension of a live performance.

I had been playing concerts for five years and didn't feel that way at all. It was a high for me when I was *off* the stage. I never looked forward to performing for its own sake.

In 1974, after that sold-out concert at Lincoln Center, I traveled on to Lexington, Kentucky; Johnson City and Nashville, Tennessee; and then back to New York to catch an international flight. My manager at that time, Sam Niefeld of Columbia Artists Management, had booked me on an immediate European tour: Amsterdam; Cambridge, Folkestone, and London; Barcelona; and Paris. My London concert would be a debut at Queen Elizabeth Hall. After the tour, I would fly back to the United States for seventeen more concerts in seven weeks.

In the world of classical music, that was success.

I just wanted to go home. I was so exhausted that I had nothing left to give. I stood alone that night in Kennedy Airport's cold international terminal, feeling completely burned out, discouraged, and empty. I did not want to go on, and those feelings were compounded by the fact that in Europe, I would be playing for a fraction of the fee that I normally received in the United States. Sam told me this was acceptable because playing in Europe was essential to building an international career. He didn't realize that this didn't fit in with my goal at all. I was knocking myself out, saving up enough money to say good-bye to my career. I didn't care about London reviews or international celebrity.

I was so distraught about heading overseas that I found a pay phone, set down my guitar, and called Sam's home to cancel the European tour.

I got his answering machine.

There seemed to be no point in leaving a message, so I reluctantly walked down the long terminal, found the right gate, and boarded the all-night flight to Amsterdam. After a sleepless trip, I landed on the other side of the ocean and plodded through immigration. The concert presenter didn't send anyone to pick me up, so I had to get a taxi and then point to the hotel's name on my printed itinerary. My bags were so heavy that my hands and arms ached. Checking into the hotel meant one more round of unpacking my suitcase, hanging up my coat and tails, and ordering room service.

The clock said I should be awake, but all I wanted to do was sleep, so I lay down to take a "short nap."

I woke up in the middle of the night, facing a concert that day. There was nothing else for me to do, so I got my guitar out and started to practice.

At that point, I noticed that the fingernails on my right hand were a little too long. A classical guitarist's fingernails are essential tools that must be protected at all times. The left-hand nails are kept extremely short so they won't get in the way of pressing down the strings on the fingerboard. The right-hand nails pluck, strum, and "slice" across the strings, so they must be longer and perfectly shaped, with their edges polished to remove any unevenness that might cause a scratchy, tinny sound or catch on a string instead of producing a smooth, beautiful tone.

When I wearily held up my right hand, I saw too much nail over my fingertips. I bent over and pulled my nail file out of the center compartment of my guitar case.

Then I clenched my jaw and looked at my nails again. *I'll file them all off,* I thought.

In what seemed like just a moment, it was over. I stared at my right hand in disbelief as the reality of what I had done swept over me. My right-hand nails were now as short as my left. That hadn't been the case since before I started to play the guitar fifteen years earlier.

I had chosen a devastating way to rebel against the pressures of the schedule, the expectations, the loneliness, and the disillusionment. What was done in a moment of frustration would greatly affect the next three weeks in Europe. With no nails to pluck the strings, I had set myself up for failure.

The tour was indeed disastrous, beset with technical struggles and memory lapses. Night after night, without adequate nails to pluck the strings, I felt as if I were trying to compete at Wimbledon with a Ping-Pong paddle. I was living a nightmare.

Each frustrating performance only added to my desire to be done with it all. I longed for peace and contentment, and I truly believed that if I could just make it to that cabin in Montana, I would be free. I couldn't have known at the time that God's hand was nudging me in another direction.

2

Perseverance

~~~~~~

1950–59

Early in my childhood, we lived in a two-story red house with white trim, on a cul-de-sac in Brentwood, just south of Sunset Boulevard. I loved the street's name, Terryhill Place, because it reminded me of my sister, Terry. My mom was sweet, supportive, and encouraging; my dad was a man of tremendous drive and energy who had the ability to focus that drive into any task he undertook. Before I was born, he was proficient on four woodwind instruments, practicing more than ten hours a day, hoping for a Benny Goodman–like career as a solo clarinetist. By the time I came along, he had gotten his real estate license in order to provide for his family, though he continued to play some professional jobs with his clarinet. I learned many years later that he had sold his bass clarinet to pay for Mom's hospital stay when I was born.

I was only two or three years old when I first experienced my father's quick temper. I'd been told not to touch the main thermostat in our house, but one morning when I woke up, I was really cold. I had seen my mom move the little lever on the thermostat in order to make the furnace turn on, so I crawled out of bed and went into the dining room. I pulled a chair over to the wall, right next to a plate-rail cabinet where my mother kept her beautiful English china teacups and saucers. I grabbed hold of the cabinet, stood up on my tiptoes, and stretched up to reach the thermostat.

That's when I lost my balance and pulled the entire china cabinet over. All my mother's favorite china came crashing down to the floor.

Suddenly, a towering figure appeared around the bend in the hall. "I told you not to do that!" My dad grabbed me by the pajamas and literally threw me through the air, like a football, back onto my bed. I lay there for a long time, crying and shivering.

I certainly wasn't a perfect little kid, and I had to learn my share of tough lessons. We didn't have a second car, so sometimes when my dad was at work, my mother would walk my sister and me a few blocks to the drugstore. On one visit to that store, I spotted a piece of bubble gum that looked very good. I grabbed it, along with several more pieces for later, and shoved them all deep into my pocket.

We walked all the way home, and then Mom saw me chewing gum. She asked, "Where did you get that?"

I reluctantly confessed that I had taken it from the drugstore. "We," she said in a firm voice, "are walking back there. You're going to bring the other pieces of bubble gum back to the store manager, and you're going to tell him what you did, and we're going to pay him for the one that you have already chewed. And we are going back right now."

I begged her to change her mind, but she took my hand and marched me back. I had to walk up to the store manager, look him in the eye, hand him the pieces of bubble gum I had stolen, and pay him for the one I had chewed. What a lesson. My mother's strong moral values—always taught in practical ways—made a strong impression that has stayed with me all my life.

Another hard lesson came when I was seven or eight years old, and we were living on Barrington Avenue in Los Angeles. I was playing catch with a neighbor boy. Johnny had his back to his house, and I was throwing the baseball toward him. I threw it too hard and too high, sending it crashing through a plate-glass window.

I was terrified. I ran home and told my parents that Johnny had broken a window. I knew lying was wrong, so for three days, I couldn't look either of my parents in the eye.

Finally, I couldn't stand it anymore. I broke down and confessed. To my surprise, they felt pity for me and didn't punish me; instead, they forgave me. Only at that point could I look them in the eye again. Of course, much later I saw the spiritual comparison to 1 John 1:9: "If we confess our sins, he is faithful and just to forgive us our sins, and to cleanse us from all unrighteousness." When we confess our sins, we can look the Father in the eye again. Our fellowship is restored. But when we're holding on to our sin, it separates us from both God and other people.

When I was eleven, on my first day of sixth grade at Brentwood Elementary School, the teacher walked around the room and asked us to introduce ourselves and say our first and last names—or, "If your last name is complicated, you can just say your first name and last initial."

I wanted so badly to make a good impression that I became

more and more nervous as the teacher walked around the classroom. By the time she finally reached my desk, I had decided "Parkening" was definitely too complicated.

I said "Chris P." a little too fast. Everyone in the class started laughing, including the teacher. I sat there, embarrassed and confused, until she explained, "For a moment, we thought your first name was Crispy!" I'm sure my face turned all shades of red.

Teachers always seated us in alphabetical order, and I nearly always ended up in the very back of the classroom. I rarely spoke up; I rarely raised my hand. I was just a shy little kid way back at the end of a long row of desks.

I had a great love of sports, however, and there were a few things I was good at. I could run quite fast, and I could also hit a ball a long way. In the elementary grades, we played a game called sockball, which is played like baseball but with a volleyball. We would stand at the plate and sock the ball with a fist into the outfield, then run the bases.

The first big game was mixed boys and girls. The first time up, I intentionally hit the ball short. The next time, everybody on the opposing team—including one little girl whom I thought was cute—called, "Easy out, easy out! Run in closer; he can't hit it far." The whole outfield ran into the infield, and then I socked the ball well over their heads, driving all the other runners in. Unfortunately, it didn't seem to impress the girl.

This was the late 1950s, when most of the girls in our school were carrying rectangular plastic purses. One day the girls were playing sockball on one diamond, and the boys were playing on another. One of the guys thought it would be "neat" if one of us could sock the ball far enough to reach the girls' bench, where there was a pile of about thirty of those plastic purses. It made a huge and inviting target. I got nominated.

I also got lucky. I hit the ball all the way from our diamond to the other diamond's bench, where it landed squarely in the middle. Purses flew like plastic confetti. The girls all stormed over together and demanded, "Who did that?" That time, I wasn't the least bit shy about confessing and felt rather proud of my accomplishment.

My favorite sport though, one that has given me lifelong pleasure, was fly-fishing for trout. When I was six, my dad started teaching me how to fly cast in our backyard. Although it was unusual for a six-year-old to take up fly-fishing, I liked it, mostly because it was something my dad and I could do together. Initially, we took lessons from Cliff Wyatt, who owned the Wilderness Fly Shop in Santa Monica. A few years later we met Jimmy Green, the international world champion fly caster, who also happened to be the designer for the Fenwick Rod Company. Fly rods for small mountain streams are quite different from the heavier ones designed for casting larger flies, used in fishing for big steelhead trout and salmon.

Whenever Jimmy came up with a new design, my dad and I put different weight lines on the prototypes to test them for distance and accuracy. Not only did we benefit from Jimmy's expertise, we also learned how he selected the exact rod to be manufactured for public sale. Sometimes the design changes were extremely small, having mostly to do with the rod's density, stiffness, and flexibility, but when Jimmy matched a rod to the weight of the line and the fly it was designed to cast, those small changes could make a big difference.

My family headed to the Long Beach casting pool almost every weekend. There we practiced our accuracy, casting into thirty-inch metal rings that floated at different distances, out to about sixty feet. The payoff came later, when we were out on a real fishing stream. It was exciting to try to place the fly at an exact spot, way across the stream in a little cove, where a big trout was rising to feed on a tiny insect.

It wasn't long before my whole family became very serious about fly-fishing. In the Mammoth Lakes area of northern California's High Sierras, about forty miles north of Bishop, was a spot that I loved more than any other place in the world: Hot Creek Ranch.

Hot Creek Ranch was my heaven on earth, a 220-acre property nestled in a valley at about seven thousand feet of elevation, with a winding stream meandering through it. I could look up from almost anywhere on the ranch and see the jagged, glistening Minaret peaks against the deep blue sky. For me, this magical place represented adventure, excitement, freedom, and challenges, with a little danger mixed in (my parents often warned us of the bogs— pockets of quicksand that could be anywhere along the streams). These were the happiest times of my young life; as my dad and I both learned to fly cast, it was almost as if we were equals.

Dad had a love of excellence, which he instilled in me. His heroes were people who had worked hard to master a skill at the highest level. He idolized the fly-casting ability of ranch owner Bill Lawrence, a true artist with the fly rod. Even if the wind was blowing twenty miles an hour, which it normally did in the afternoon, Bill could place a trout fly within a couple of inches of any spot on that stream. Additionally, he had developed a unique technique for fly-fishing in weedy, spring-fed creeks. He used a twenty-foot leader (the transparent section at the end of a fly line to which the fly is attached so that the fish cannot see it—normally only about ten feet long) and cast it so that it "piled up" in a loose coil, with the dry fly positioned to float down freely between the weeds on the surface. A dragging fly leaves a wake, an immediate signal to the fish that it's a fake, but this natural float fooled the trout every time. Every fisherman there, including my dad and me, tried to copy his technique.

We went to Hot Creek the first time when I was six years old, and my parents had bought me my own little cowboy hat and boots. My dad and mom told me that Bill was a *real* cowboy. He wore a cowboy hat and leather boots, and he rolled his own cigarettes. He had tanned, wrinkled skin from being out in the sun so much, and for me at age six, meeting a "real cowboy" was awe-inspiring. It all made going to Hot Creek an adventure, since I got to be a cowboy for a week.

Bill had two horses, Hot Shot and Rex, and a burro named Homer, who was amazingly smart. A swinging wooden gate separated the grazing area from the place where the nine guest cabins were nestled together. Rusted springs held the gate shut, and the horses couldn't get through, but Homer could! Almost every guest in the cabins sat on their porches in the morning when Homer regularly put on his little show. He pushed the heavy gate open and made a mad dash through, and when it swung shut and spanked his behind, he broke into a gallop. Guests yelled, "Yaaaay, Homer!" Then he slowed down and sauntered over to the cabins, where many of the guests fed him. His favorite treat was pancakes, which we fed him from our front porch.

ᏬᎤ ᏬᎤ ᏬᎤ

My mom's cousin Jack Marshall had started playing jazz guitar in his early teens. Although he earned an engineering degree at the University of Southern California, he spent only one day at a promising engineering job and hated it so much that he quit. He decided to try the long shot instead—playing guitar as a professional musician. "The one thing I got from my engineering degree," he told me, "was that when I wrote out the scores, my musical notation was so clear and precise, the musicians loved how easy it was to read." Over the years, he learned to play the guitar in many styles. He worked with the distinguished classical composer Igor Stravinsky and was often consulted by other Hollywood composers on technical aspects of guitar playing. In the early 1950s, he became a musical director at Capitol Records. He was also a gifted composer and arranger. His first of many Grammy nominations was for his arrangement of "Fever," done for Peggy Lee in 1958.

Jack and my mom were quite close, and he often came over to our house, always bringing his guitar. He could play any song in any key. I loved the way he played and the sound of the instrument. I decided I wanted to play the guitar.

My parents asked Jack if it would be okay for me to start taking lessons, even though I was only six. He told us, "His hands are too small. But if he wants to get his left hand used to playing some chords, you could start him on the ukulele."

I knew what a ukulele was; I had seen Kirk Douglas play one as he sang "A Whale of a Tale" in *20,000 Leagues Under the Sea*. My parents bought me a little Martin uke and some music books, including "A Whale of a Tale," and I couldn't wait to get started.

My grade school teacher soon found out that I was learning to play the ukulele, and she asked me to show the class. I wasn't a singer, but I couldn't just sit there and strum chords, so even though I was terrified, I ended up playing and singing for my whole class. Their enthusiastic response was encouraging to me. Performing for the first time had actually been enjoyable—after it was over!

When I turned eleven and my hands had grown, my parents decided it was time to find me a guitar teacher. Jack Marshall gave us more advice. "Start him on the classical guitar. He'll get a good foundation in technique and establish solid skills. If he learns classical, it will be easier to play other styles later." He added, "And get the records of Andrés Segovia. He's the greatest guitarist in the world."

My parents purchased some of Segovia's records, and my dad and I sat for hours in the living room listening to those LPs. We played a few pieces over and over. One was the Courante by Bach, from his Cello Suite no. 3, and another was the Prelude by Weiss/Ponce, from a recording entitled *An Andrés Segovia Recital*.

One night, my parents threw a big party for my Uncle Bill and Aunt Ginger at our house on Terryhill Place. Jack played any song Ginger wanted to hear, from any one of her movies, in any key she asked for—and to everyone's delight, she sang along. What Jack could do with the guitar was amazing, but he was perfectly casual and laid-back about it.

I was so impressed that I couldn't wait to get started. My dad called a music store in Hollywood, Wallach's Music City, and asked if they had a classical guitar teacher. The man who answered said, "Our classical guitar teacher is completely full. He can't take another student."

We were disappointed, but then he added, "There is a family who just moved here from Spain, and I've heard they're very good."

My dad and I drove to Wallach's, sorted through about fifty instruments—comparing the sound quality to the beautiful tone we had heard on Segovia's albums—and chose a nice little Goya guitar that cost one hundred dollars. On a fall day in 1958, Dad drove me to an old, Spanish-styled duplex on Melrose Avenue in Hollywood. That "family who just moved here from Spain" turned out to be the Romeros—Celedonio and his sons, Celin, Pepe, and Angel, who later became famous as the "Royal Family of the Spanish Guitar." I took my first classical guitar lesson from Celedonio.

In a plain, gray little room, Celedonio—who spoke very little English—taught me to play the guitar by having me mimic whatever he did. We started with a short melody that I still remember, though he never told me the name of it. He showed me how to prop up my foot on a footstool and hold my new guitar in the classical style.

The guitar is one of the easiest instruments to play, but classical guitar is one of the most difficult instruments to master. The Romeros wanted me to start on a good instrument, so when they found out we'd bought a guitar by ourselves, they said, "We'll take it back to Wallach's with you and help you pick out a better one. We're sure they'll exchange it."

To everybody's surprise, after playing all fifty guitars in stock, Celedonio and Pepe decided that we really had selected the best one in the store.

Just as Jack Marshall predicted, playing the ukulele made it easy for me to learn left-hand technique, so I could concentrate on my right-hand technique with Celedonio. At home, my father worked with me on reading music and practicing correctly.

Before I knew it, the experience I had thought was going to be a "fun little adventure"—like Jack Marshall's casual playing in our living room—started turning into a very serious endeavor.

FISH TALE

*Over the years, I've had many interesting experi-
ences, often when fishing. Although they might not
seem to have much to do with the classical guitar,
I believe they show how the river of grace has run
through my life.*

Go Back and Catch Him Again

One summer day after many fruitless hours fishing Hot Creek,
I learned a lesson about perseverance and realized that some
"impossible" things turn out to be possible after all.

I was just a beginner, but I could tell this trout I had hooked
was really big. Through that crystal clear water, I could see his
long body and big, broad back; he made a strong wake when he
swam upstream and downstream. He stayed in the deep section
of the pool for a long time, and he pulled hard. I was nervous and
excited. I had never hooked a fish this big before.

I didn't know how to reel in a big trout. I knew just enough
to be able to keep him on the line. After he swam around the pool
for about twenty minutes, the only thing I could think to do was
to keep the line tight and back away from the water. The stream
bank was more than a foot high at that spot. I ended up about
forty feet away, trying to drag the big trout through the moss and
the muck at the edge of the stream, up the tall bank, and onto dry
land. After tugging and pulling and lifting the rod high with all
my might, suddenly—*Snap!* My line broke. I couldn't believe it.
I'd lost him, the biggest fish I had ever hooked in my whole life!

My mom was fishing about a quarter mile away. Not knowing

what to do, I tearfully walked downstream to her for some consolation. I told her that I had just lost the biggest fish of my life.

She said, "Chris, you go back there and catch him again."

I thought, *Go back there and fish for the exact same fish? Why would a fish that's just been on a hook for twenty minutes bite on another fly? How could I fool him again? It's impossible.* But I walked back to the pool to give it one more try.

As I peered down into the weeds where I had lost the fish, I thought, *Do you suppose he might still be in there?*

This stream was called Hot Creek because of the geysers below the ranch, but spring-fed mountain streams are always cold, even when it's almost noon and the day is starting to heat up. I dreaded stepping off that bank into the ice-cold muck and weeds, not knowing how far I would sink in. (This wasn't a pristine, gravel creek bed but a deep, dark place where a big fish could hide for a long time.)

But I did it. In I went, and standing there hip-deep, I gathered my courage and reached into that gucky mess. I wanted that fish, and I had to find out if he was still there. I groped in the muck and weeds with both bare arms and couldn't believe it when my fingers hit something big, solid, and wiggling. That enormous fish was still there, trapped in the middle of the weeds. I plunged both arms up to my shoulders into the cold water, grabbed the big fish and a hunk of weeds, and threw it with all my might onto the bank. Then I climbed up out of the water and stared down in disbelief. There he was! I grabbed him and ran downstream again.

As soon as I got close enough for my mom to hear me, I yelled, "I got him! I got him!"

My mom's jaw dropped, and she hugged me, fish and all.

Experiments

1959–60

My dad had been a serious musician, and I believe he was deeply disappointed that he never had the opportunity to become a professional clarinet soloist. He knew what it demanded, though. As soon as I started taking lessons, he said, "Okay, you want to play the guitar? Then you need to get up every morning at 5 a.m. and start practicing at 5:30. Your mother will have breakfast for you at 7:00. When you get home from school, you will practice another hour and a half."

I was stunned. I thought, *Am I joining the army?* But at that point, the train had started rolling, and there was no stopping it. The instrument was purchased, lessons were arranged, and my dad was determined. All at once I went from being a carefree kid, excited to play the guitar like my mom's cousin Jack, to a very serious student of the instrument.

My dad was inflexible about that practice schedule. Every day I was up by 5 a.m.—or else—in a house that was totally dark and quiet. At first I set an alarm clock, but the sound of the loud alarm startled me, so I learned to wake up before it went off. The idea was to get up at 5:00 and get dressed, but that only took five minutes. I didn't have to start practicing until 5:30, so I would sit in my brown wooden rocking chair with the guitar case open, rocking and waiting until the very last minute. At exactly 5:30 I would pick up the guitar, turn on the metronome, and start my musical exercises.

The second-story hall floor creaked as my dad walked from the master bedroom to my bedroom, and from that point on, the pressure ratcheted up. I might have been trying hard before he got there, but I tried even harder after he arrived.

Occasionally on weekends, I practiced downstairs in the living room. My dad sat across from me and coached me. He would not tolerate anything short of absolute excellence, and I can still hear him repeating, "Do it again. Do it again. No, that's not right"—his teeth clenched—"*Do it again.*" I quickly learned that repeated mistakes meant something might get kicked, either the music stand or my shins. "Do it again."

This had gone on for about three months when my mom felt it was getting too intense. One Saturday morning she hurried into the living room and said, "Duke, that's enough."

He stood up. "You stay out of this," he said, taking her by the forearm and escorting her out. My mother is five foot four, and it must have taken courage to stand up to somebody six foot three with that kind of determination and temper. It's very hard, at twelve years old, to see tension between your parents, particularly when that tension involves you.

Once, when my father was teaching me dotted-note rhythms, he kept interrupting me with, "No. That's wrong! Do it again," he'd say. I'd try once more. "No. Do it again."

Finally, I started crying. But my father didn't tolerate tears. "If you cry anymore, you'll get it worse," he said. I was terrified to play that passage again, but I did. This time he looked at the music. "Oh no!" he said, "You were doing it right!" He stormed out of the room, distraught, because he had been punishing me for doing it correctly.

At our Terryhill Place house we had a detached room out back. About a third of it was my dad's workshop, where he kept his tools and built all kinds of things. The other two-thirds was an open room with no heat or water. I eventually began to practice there, where it wouldn't disturb anyone. I moved my practice chair into the room, along with an electric heater and a daybed. In the winter months, Southern California mornings can be damp, and the chill makes your joints stiff. When I first got up, I turned on the heater and waited as the coils slowly grew red. I held my hands next to them to warm my fingers before starting to play, and I always tried to pull the heater as close to me as possible without burning myself.

It was in that room that my dad became so angry with my playing that he grabbed the guitar and threw it onto the daybed. By then I was playing a Miguel Rodriguez guitar that had cost about five hundred dollars—the equivalent, I suppose, of three or four thousand dollars now.

My father was exceptionally hard on me, and I learned not to cry, no matter how difficult his teaching. He was a demanding coach because he knew a lot about music, self-discipline, and proper practicing techniques. I realize now that his high expectations laid a strong foundation for my future career, but as a young child I simply couldn't see that far ahead.

Each morning my father assigned exercises and goals, most of which I was to accomplish by the time he got home that evening. Practicing was never casual. There was always accountability. My father's goal for me was nothing short of perfection. At the end of the day, the only thing that mattered was what I had accomplished. If I performed well, the day was great. Otherwise, it was a failure.

Eventually, Jack Marshall came by and said to my dad, "You're pushing him too hard, Duke. He'll hate the instrument."

"He has some raw talent," was my dad's answer. "That's why I'm pushing him." He repeated certain axioms over and over: "Slow it down until you can play it right." "Isolate the difficult passages." "Play it beautiful, play it beautiful. If it's not beautiful, it's not music." Or he'd say, "Play it again. Again. If you can't play that passage correctly seven times in a row, seven times *in a row*, you'll never play it right on the concert stage." Then there was "Finish the job." It might be three in the morning, but if we started a project, we completed it.

Even now, when I teach guitar lessons—although hopefully with a lot more empathy—I pass on many of the practicing techniques my father taught me: Isolate the hard passages; play them seven times in a row; slow them down until you can play them right; and more than anything else, play them expressively and beautifully.

My father told the truth when he said, "I will be your toughest critic. Nobody will be harder on you than I am." But he also said, "If you're not one of the top four or five in the world, you'll starve with this instrument. You *must* be one of that group." Competition is fierce in the music profession, and my father knew it.

A sports coach probably would have been hard on me too. After I took up the guitar, however, I didn't get many chances to participate in athletics. Kids would ring my doorbell after school, but I knew I couldn't go out to play. Instead, with the metronome keeping time, I stayed inside playing a tough scale over and over—first slowly and then slightly faster, then even faster. I knew if I couldn't play those assigned exercises nearly perfectly, and fast enough, when Dad got home from work, I would be in trouble.

There were a few times after school when the temptation to have fun with the neighbor kids was too great, and I snuck out to play instead of practicing. One time, the fun came to an abrupt halt at the sight of my dad's white Falcon turning up the street earlier than expected. My heart sank. I sprinted home, dashed upstairs, and ran into my room, where I grabbed my guitar, turned on the metronome, and started playing in the middle of a piece, hoping my dad wouldn't question my heaving chest and sweaty, red face.

The neighbor kids eventually stopped ringing our doorbell. Oftentimes, I glanced out the window and watched them in the street, yelling and having fun, while I kept playing and the metronome kept ticking. My dad would say, "Someday you'll thank me for this. Someday you'll thank me."

Maybe he's right, I thought. But I was athletic, the fastest runner in my school, and here I was, stuck sitting still, forced into the role of a classical musician.

ᴏ╫ᴏ ᴏ╫ᴏ ᴏ╫ᴏ

It's not as if my dad never praised me. He did—when he thought I had done something well. Right from the start, he was proud of whatever talent he saw in me, and he wanted the best for me. He poured himself into my work, hoping to give me the solo concert career that he had wanted for himself.

I did take great pleasure in the music. In fact, I loved Segovia's records so much that I enjoyed the challenge of trying to analyze his pieces: *How can I play this passage? Do I need to change my left-hand position? Do I need to do something different with my right hand? How can I get that sound?* I listened to Segovia play Rodrigo's *Fantasía para un Gentilhombre*, particularly the slow, beautiful movement with the melody in the bass—the Españoleta movement—and imagined myself playing that piece with an orchestra. Little did I know that one day I would perform that piece at Royal Festival Hall in London with the Royal Philharmonic Orchestra and with the composer in attendance. Occasionally, I went into the backyard at night and played my guitar in the dark. Since I couldn't see the fingerboard, it helped me learn to "sing" a phrase, listening closely to the music.

❧ ❧ ❧

That was how my career started. My dad deserves much of the credit for my career, although it wasn't a happy beginning. One thing that saved me from buckling under the pressure was fly-fishing. When the day's work was done, my dad and I often sat in our rocking chairs in the living room, talking about fly-fishing and Hot Creek Ranch. That inspired me and reminded me that Dad and I did have a lot in common.

And I always had Terry. She was my friend and many times my confidante, because she understood. Not long after I started playing the guitar, Terry took up the piano. Our dad sat down on the piano bench next to her a few times to "help" her practice. I can still picture her concentrating, trying her best—and crying. Eventually, when she wanted to get into an expensive private school with her girlfriends, she gave up the piano and concentrated on her grades. "I'll make a deal with you," Dad had said. "If you get straight As, I'll send you there next year."

So while I practiced, Terry shut her door and studied. She did get those straight As, and Dad kept his promise.

My mom, a wonderful encourager, knew just how to balance the pressure I always felt trying to please Dad. When I became so frustrated that I wanted to put down the guitar and walk away, she always came alongside me and said, "It will be okay, Chris. You're doing well. You're trying your best."

By the summer I was twelve, she had already taught Terry and me Psalms 1, 23, and 100. Each night she would recite them to us, and then we would say them in unison. I remember them to this day. That summer she enrolled us in Vacation Bible School, where we were taught to share the gospel using a little storybook. The teacher told us all to go home one afternoon, pick out a friend, and share the story of Jesus. A boy about my age lived up the street. His name was Richard, and we often played together. I decided to share my little booklet with him.

I took him to a shady spot in the backyard, and after we both sat down cross-legged, I took the gospel tract out of my hip pocket. Page by page, I went through it with him. Richard must have thought it sounded good, and he prayed the prayer to receive Christ.

The next day our VBS teacher asked the class how many had shared their tracts with a friend. Out of about a hundred kids, not one other person raised a hand, so when I realized that I would be the only one, I kept my hand down as well.

Right about this time, my parents had me baptized at our church. I knew this was important because they took the occasion so seriously. Riding in the car a few days later, I stared out the window and wondered how I could use my life for God. The best idea I could think of was to become a preacher, even though that might conflict with my father's plans for me.

I believe God was pleased with that desire and that He did grant it much later, although in a way that I couldn't have anticipated then.

ᘐᘐ ᘐᘐ ᘐᘐ

When I turned twelve, my parents bought me the *Segovia Golden Jubilee* three-record set. It came in a beautiful red box with a special booklet insert full of pictures and stories about Segovia. I still have it. The inscription on the set reads, "12/14/59. Dear Chris, Our deepest affection on your 12th birthday. After one year, it is apparent to everyone who hears you play what a fine little artist you are. Mom and Dad."

Not long after that, I was thrilled to hear that Andrés Segovia was coming to Los Angeles. My whole family attended the concert, and I sat spellbound, watching him play fabulous music that sounded just as wonderful in person as it did on my records. My parents had told me that we could go backstage after the concert. I had prepared a little speech about how I was beginning to study the classical guitar and that he was my inspiration. After the concert, we stood in a long line outside Segovia's dressing room. I clutched my concert program, hoping for his autograph. When I finally reached the front of the line, I looked up at Segovia with admiration and awe. I made my speech, and he signed my program. Then he patted my cheek and said, "Very good, very good." I knew that as long as I lived, I would never forget that moment.

I was so inspired by the performance that I practiced more than ever. I was now studying with both Celedonio and his son Pepe, wonderful teachers who helped me lay a strong technical foundation. All the Romeros, but especially Pepe and Angel, could play lightning-fast runs and scales that I really wanted to emulate. My dad and I analyzed everything Pepe did, from his hand position to his sitting position to his techniques for increasing speed. I was already tackling some difficult music, but I just couldn't make my runs go any faster. It seemed like I'd hit a wall.

It was then that my dad decided we needed to focus on my right-hand fingernails. We knew they had to be shaped perfectly to "slice through" the string and produce a beautiful sound. We were already filing them correctly. After more hours of experimentation, we discovered that off the guitar—on a tabletop, for instance—I could move my fingers about as fast as Pepe. But when we compared our fingernail shapes, we realized that Pepe's fingernails, like my dad's, were quite flat. Mine had an arch, almost a half-pipe shape. They produced a good tone, but they had to travel farther, from one edge of the nail to the other, to get across the string. This was what kept me from playing notes as fast as Pepe did.

My dad believed that any problem could be overcome, and he was willing to try almost anything if it meant improving my playing. We had already tried hanging weights off my left arm to make my left elbow hang in the proper position when I held the guitar. And I had set up a hundred-watt light on my music stand to shine into my face, simulating stage lights. We knew there also had to be a way to resolve the fingernail issue.

My dad came up with an idea. An orthodontist could change the alignment of someone's teeth with braces, so why not change the shape of my nails in the same way? He decided to make me some braces, like orthodontics for the fingertips. He bought four aluminum splints—the kind people use for a broken finger—took them out to his shop, and hinged each one at the end, like a clothespin. Then he bought some rolls of half-inch bandaging tape. We wound the tape around the brace and my fingertip, close to the first joint on each finger.

It was typical for me not to wait patiently for results. I just wanted to get the job done. Hoping to reshape my nails in one night, I wrapped that white tape as tightly as I could.

At about one o'clock in the morning, I woke up with a dull, throbbing ache in my fingers, and I'd lost all feeling in my fingertips. I ripped the braces off.

I didn't give up though. I wore them every night for about five years, although I taped them less tightly. I did notice a change after a while. It improved the speed of my playing, but only until the nail's natural arch came back. I realized that an orthodontist could create a permanent change in the teeth because they grow in once and then stay in place. My fingernails, though, were constantly growing, so any correction to their shape was temporary.

For my dad, however, that was no reason to give up. The more hours each day I could stand to wear the nail braces, the more effective they would be. Years later, when I went into high school, he told me to wear them to class. So I walked into Buckley High School for the first time with splints on my right thumb and index, middle, and ring fingers. The other students stared. It was bad enough to have long nails on my right hand; it was even worse to be a spectacle with those Frankenstein-like splints.

Finally I learned to file my nails to compensate for their shape. Although it took me a good hour to file them correctly, it was a better option than the nightly pain of wearing the braces. I still have the splints in a box in a chest of drawers—a reminder that there are some things that can be overdone.

ᚼᚬ ᚼᚬ ᚼᚬ

I was twelve years old and had been playing the guitar for sixteen months when the music minister at church asked me to perform for a church dinner. Apart from performing at school, this was to be my first public concert. I put on a suit, and my parents drove me to the Westwood Hills Christian Church, near the University of California–Los Angeles, on June 8, 1960. About 150 people came. I'd never played for a "real" audience, so I was nervous before it started. I played four pieces: a Bach bourrée, an etude by Brazilian composer Heitor Villa-Lobos, "Gavotta" by Scarlatti, and a piece called "Leyenda" by Isaac Albéniz, which was originally written for piano but was transcribed by Segovia for the guitar. Everything went well, and I was relieved when I could stand up and take a bow. My mother saved a clipping from the next week's church bulletin for a scrapbook she was starting for me.

She also saved a handwritten program from a concert I gave two months later, in August 1960, at the Burbank Boulevard School. According to her scrapbook, I played for ninety-six children, and besides "Leyenda," there were six other classical pieces and two flamenco guitar pieces on the program.

Mom loved to save my clippings and programs. I was starting to get more invitations to play, and she saved notes and programs from them all: a 1961 appearance at the St. David Men's Club, a Pasadena Junior Philharmonic committee meeting, and an appearance as "guest soloist" at my sister Terry's piano recital. In 1962 I performed at a fashion luncheon, an Optimist Club meeting, and another Pasadena Junior Philharmonic committee meeting, and on April 8, I played for a Spanish-language program on radio station KTYM. Jack Marshall sent a Western Union telegram congratulating me. All mementos from these occasions went into the scrapbook, along with a set of instructions from my dad for performance preparation and a copy of my first check for performing, which came from the Friends of the Classical Guitar Society in Hollywood. It was dated September 8, 1962, and it was made out for fifteen dollars. Later in 1962, I played for the Rotary Club and another of Terry's piano recitals.

I was already tackling the famous Bach Chaconne, a long set of variations from his Partita no. 2 in D minor. Originally written for solo violin, then transcribed for the guitar by Segovia, it's about thirteen minutes long. I loved Segovia's recording of this piece, but it was an extremely hard piece to play. Celedonio stepped in, and instead of having me follow Segovia's printed transcription, he taught me a new set of fingerings that made it considerably easier to play. "Segovia jumps all the way up on the same string to play the note, when the same note is right over here on the next string," he pointed out.

So, using Celedonio's fingerings, I tried to copy Segovia's style off his record. I thought it was a good compromise. Surprisingly, though, at the end of one lesson, Celedonio said he wanted to speak to both my parents the following week.

I knew something was wrong, but I couldn't guess what. The next week both my parents made the effort to come. After I'd had my lesson and put my guitar into the case, he brought them into the room, sat them down, and gave a short speech. His English was still broken, but he basically said, "I have been working with Christopher, as you know, on the Bach Chaconne. He is playing the Chaconne too much like Segovia. So I don't want him listening to any more Segovia recordings."

To my parents, he couldn't have paid their son a higher compliment. With their full approval, I continued to listen to Segovia's records.

The long hours of practice seemed to be paying off, especially when, in the summer of 1962, Jack Marshall called to tell us that he had gotten me an invitation to appear on a TV show called *Panorama Pacific*. My performance would be broadcast live at 6 a.m. In order to be at the studio by 5 a.m., I slid out of bed at about four o'clock and practiced. My mom promised that after the show I could take the rest of the day off from practicing and that she would take me to the beach. That was a huge reward. I played a Bach prelude, a Villa-Lobos etude, and a flamenco piece called "Alegrías por Fiesta." Jack Marshall said he was proud of me, and Mom naturally saved the clipping from the *TV Guide*. Then came my first major career break. Reading the *Los Angeles Times* that fall, my mom spotted an advertisement announcing a classical music competition for young instrumentalists and singers. She quickly collected all the information she could find. The Young Musicians Foundation, which sponsored the competition, is an organization of music lovers and professional musicians. Since 1955 the YMF has encouraged young artists by holding annual competitions, helping them connect with musical organizations, and offering scholarships as well as debut concerts. Their 1962 competition would be held at UCLA before a panel of distinguished judges. First prize included cash and a 1963 debut concert at UCLA's prestigious Royce Hall. According to the information in the newspaper, the contest was open to all classical instrumental and vocal musicians under the age of twenty-five.

Since I was only fourteen (well within the age limit), we filled out an application and sent it in.

Almost immediately we received a letter back from YMF's founding director, Sylvia Kunin, which essentially said, "Thank you for applying, but classical guitar isn't included in the stringed instrument category." They wanted violinists, cellists—*orchestral* instruments. There was no category for classical guitar.

My dad wrote back. We had read that Andrés Segovia's personal friend Mario Castelnuovo-Tedesco, who wrote a concerto for guitar and orchestra that Segovia played, was going to be one of the judges for the piano competition, so it surprised us to find out that classical guitar would not be included as a stringed instrument.

Sylvia Kunin sent a gracious reply. "Every competition has its regulations," she wrote, and she repeated that I would not be eligible to compete but that I could come and play for the judges "out of competition," as a guest artist. She offered me the opportunity to play for the stringed instrument judges to get some feedback on my musical abilities before the real competition began.

We had to be satisfied with that—and grateful. Now my practicing had a focus and a major target date: Saturday, June 16, 1962, 1 p.m.

FISH TALE

Charlie and the Island

At Hot Creek Ranch, there was once a trout so large it was eating
the ordinary-sized trout that ranch guests were trying to catch.
When I was twelve, the ranch's owner, Bill Lawrence, told me the
story of how he had finally caught a huge, twenty-pound trout.
I hung on every word.

First, he caught a little trout and left it out on the bank for a
few moments until it was tired. Then he cast it back into the large,
deep pool where the big trout lived. With a whoosh, the huge trout
took the little trout. Bill had to let the big trout swallow the little
fish before the big fish would be decently hooked, so he waited
long enough to smoke a cigarette, and then tightened up on the
fish. The big trout took him a half mile downstream, where he
finally landed it. When it was dressed out, it weighed nineteen and
a half pounds.

One day when I was fishing in the same pool, I remembered
that story. The bank where I was fishing formed a point, and I had
cast my dry fly across the point, upstream, and hooked a small
fish. As I was pulling the fish toward the bank, I heard a tremendous thrashing and whooshing sound. Maybe this was a bigger fish
than I thought! As I stripped in the line and walked to the edge of
the bank, I saw a huge brown trout trying to eat my little trout!

I gave the little fish some slack line so it could swim away and
tempt the big fish, but he saw me and swam away. So I went back

to the cabin and told my young friend Charlie what had happened. He thought, just as I did, that it would be exciting to try to duplicate Bill Lawrence's story.

We waited for a lull in the afternoon, when nobody was out on the stream. Our goal was to catch a tiny trout. Finally, using a little number-sixteen dry fly, we hooked a fish that was about four inches long and let him keep swimming near the surface.

A broad, solid wake appeared about twenty feet away, like a torpedo pushing water. The water seemed to explode, and the little fish vanished. We remembered what Bill Lawrence had told us: We couldn't put any tension on the line at all if we wanted the big trout to swallow the little one. I began madly stripping my white-colored fly line off the reel to give the fish plenty of slack.

I could see from the curve of my fly line on the water that the big fish had gone way down to the base of the pool and was slowly working back up into the deeper section. Charlie and I were ecstatic! We had a monster on our hands—Bill Lawrence's story reenacted. It couldn't have happened better.

I asked Charlie, "How long does it take to smoke a cigarette?" That's how long we were supposed to wait, but we didn't have a clue how long that was. The seconds seemed like hours, but we must have waited three or four minutes, until we couldn't stand it any longer. This was the moment of truth. It was time to tighten up on the fish and see if we still had him.

I put the fly line through the index finger of my right hand and slowly started to strip the line in. It made a big, arcing circle, well downstream of the pool, because I'd stripped out so much line. I was cautiously stripping back the line—getting closer to the point of contact—and then, suddenly, there he was! The weight of the fish and the current rushing past created a throbbing pull on the line, a gigantic tug from the bottom of the pool.

The fish felt me now, and it started to swim erratically, upstream and then downstream. I had a very light tippet on, probably two-pound test, so I couldn't put much tension on the fish. He was in control. I was like a flea on the other end of the line, with this huge weight going back and forth in the pool.

I was trembling in my hip boots, and I hadn't even seen the fish yet. This mysterious force that I was attached to swam back and forth, and I was incredibly nervous that I was going to break him off. I kept gingerly trying to put enough tension on him to tire him out.

After about twenty minutes, as if to say, "I've had enough of you kids," he headed out of the pool and ran downstream. We followed behind him, and because I'd stripped out so much fly line, I had about thirty feet dragging behind me. He swam next to an island, and I told Charlie, "We'd better get out on the island, because we can fight him better from there."

So we splashed out onto the grassy little island, and as I was fighting the fish, I realized that downstream the water was too deep to wade, clearly over my head. I was trapped.

The fish stayed below the island for a little while and then headed downstream. I told Charlie, "Take the rod." I wanted to retrace our steps off the island and then cross the stream where it was wadable so Charlie could toss me the rod across the ten-foot channel.

So this trembling kid stood on the point of the island, with all this deep water out in front of him, letting line out through his fingers as the fish pulled.

I raced to the upper side of the island and splashed through the stream to get to the other side, worried every moment that Charlie might lose the fish. Finally, I reached the stream bank and ran down across from Charlie. He yelled, "The fish is running downstream again! I can't hold him!" I glanced behind him and saw something awful. The stripped-out line had picked up a tumbleweed-sized hunk of sagebrush, and this tangled mess was headed straight for the rod's guide. If it reached the small-diameter guide ring, where the line rides through, it would surely break and we'd lose the fish.

I ran at full speed, watching the weed heading toward the first guide, and yelled, "Charlie, sacrifice! Jump in!" So with all his might, Charlie jumped off the lower end of the island and immediately sank out of sight. I could just see his rod in the air, drifting downstream. I waded out as fast as I could, grabbed his arm and the fly rod, and pulled him out.

When I tightened up the line, to my amazement, the fish was still on! He was still moving downstream, approaching the area where all the cabins were. A few people had seen us from their porches, and a small crowd was starting to gather.

After a fifteen-minute struggle, I finally pulled the great big fish up on the grass. Everybody stood around cheering, saying things like, "Wow, what a trout! Must be a six-pounder! Way to go, you two!" Charlie and I were feeling a great sense of accomplishment as we soaked in all the praise. Someone took a picture before we released the trout back into the water, and that photo went up in the clubhouse lodge as the biggest fish taken that year.

4

Chaconne

~~~~~~

1962–64

The day of the Young Musicians Foundation
competition started out sunny, as did most spring
mornings in Southern California. My family was
up with the sun and on our way to UCLA by
11 a.m. Sylvia Kunin had directed us to arrive at
noon, but naturally we arrived early. Terry and
Dad walked straight into the hall and found seats.
Mom and I went downstairs into a small room
so I could warm up.

Sylvia came into the room, probably meaning
to make sure we all understood the situation. "I just
wanted to remind you that classical guitar is not
included in the stringed instrument category, so you
will be first to play for the judges."

My mom and I nodded.

"All right. We'll knock on your door in about five minutes."
Then she left. Mom and I sat there without saying a word for
quite some time, and then I told her, "You know what, Mom? I'm
going out there to show them what the classical guitar sounds
like."

"That's what we're here for, Chris." She gave me one last,
encouraging look before she went out and took a seat in the
back row.

The tap on the door came. I stood up, wrapped one hand
around the neck of my guitar, and followed Sylvia's assistant up the
stairs into the backstage area of Schoenberg Hall. The big curtains
were drawn back and hung along the wings of the stage. Stacks of
chairs stood here and there. On the wide, brightly lit stage, someone had set out a chair and footstool.

The assistant walked onto the stage. "This is the classical guitar," she said to the judges and those in the hall.

I followed her out and announced my piece. I had chosen to
play—very ambitiously—the Bach Chaconne. As I sat down, I
spotted my dad and Terry sitting close to the middle, but I only
glanced at them, because scattered in the front section of the hall
were the nine judges I'd come to play for. They were extremely
accomplished people. That year's judges included virtuoso violinist
Jascha Heifetz, the great Russian cellist Gregor Piatigorsky, violist
William Primrose, composer/conductor Lukas Foss, composer/
songwriter Johnny Green, film composer Miklós Rózsa, pianist
Emmanuel Bay, pianist/composer Ignace Hilsberg, and cellist
Joseph Schuster.

In the year since I had started learning the Chaconne, I'd practiced it hundreds—perhaps even thousands—of times, polishing the
difficult parts and striving for a beautiful sound during all those
hours before and after school. I was about halfway through the

long piece when I vaguely noticed some noise in the audience. Apparently, I found out afterward, I'd gone over my allotted time, and one of the organizers wanted to stop me so they could begin the real competition. The head judge, Joseph Schuster, decided to let me finish. I stayed focused and kept playing.

When I completed the piece, I stood up to acknowledge the audience and saw that all the judges were clapping and shouting, "Bravo!"

Mr. Schuster told my mom and dad that since the guitar composer Mario Castelnuovo-Tedesco was going to be judging the next day's piano competition, we should meet him. It was arranged for me to come back the following day and perform again, this time for the piano judges. I played "Leyenda," and at the end of that performance, I was thrilled to be introduced to Maestro Castelnuovo-Tedesco.

There were two spots available on the winner's debut concert program, which was to be held the following spring at Royce Hall, a larger concert hall at UCLA. One spot was given to the piano-competition winner, Paul Schenley, and to our amazement, the judges—breaking with precedent—gave me the other. It was a great honor and a tremendous opportunity.

The concerto chosen for me to perform was Mario Castelnuovo-Tedesco's Concerto in D Major for Guitar and Orchestra. At fifteen, I had never played with an orchestra. Working with a conductor, coming in at exactly the right moment after many measures of rest, and balancing the softer guitar's sound against fifty other classical musicians in the orchestra would be just some of the new challenges I faced.

Incredibly, Maestro Castelnuovo-Tedesco offered to help me in his home on a weekly basis while he played a reduction of the orchestra score on his piano. He coached me on the interpretation of the music—for instance, he showed me when a slight rubato (a momentary slowing down of the tempo) might be in order, when I might drop down to a pianissimo volume without getting lost under the orchestra, and particularly, how he wanted each section of the piece phrased.

Because he was a pianist, not a guitarist, one thing he could not coach me on was guitar fingerings. The published guitar music had no fingerings, and I'd never before learned a piece that wasn't already fingered for the left and right hands. Now, as I learned this music, the only clue I had was Segovia's recording of that concerto. As I listened to it over and over, I discovered that I could track his fingers on the fingerboard by the tone quality of the notes. When the sound was very dolce, or sweet, I knew he was playing higher up the fingerboard. The dry *ponticello* sound came when he played closer to the first position, at the first frets of the instrument. I could often hear when he changed strings. Figuring out where on the fingerboard Segovia played each note, trying to follow his wonderful musicianship, was a great learning experience.

In the days leading up to my debut concert, I sat in my rocking chair at night and visualized playing through the piece. The Romeros, my parents, and most important, the composer would be at the concert, and it was going to be recorded. This was not always done in the 1960s. My dad made sure I got my hair cut short enough that I wouldn't look like a "beatnik."

As the day approached, I rocked in my chair and wondered, *What if I forget the music? What if I don't play it well?* It felt as if my entire self-worth was on the line. I was especially afraid of disappointing my father.

The day of the concert, March 10, 1963, finally came. The YMF scheduled me to play the first half of the three o'clock matinee concert, with the piano concerto in the second half. We arrived at UCLA early. The presenters had assigned me a practice room in the basement of Royce Hall, so I sat down there and went through the piece over and over. I had practiced so much that I was playing very accurately from memory. The Romeros were escorted to my dressing room, and I played through the entire concerto for them. They left smiling, but I didn't feel nearly that confident. Soon I was going to walk out onto that stage for my official Los Angeles concert debut. I knew I was representing the classical guitar to the musical community, and the composer would be in the audience. The pressure felt overwhelming.

My dad stayed backstage and ran up and down the stairs, keeping me posted. "There are fifteen minutes to go before the concert," he said. Then he disappeared, and I practiced until he peered in around the door again. "Ten minutes to go. By the way, the house is packed." Finally, "Five minutes and you're on."

I went upstairs and stood with conductor Kenneth Klein at the edge of the stage, collecting myself and waiting to walk out in front of the Young Musicians Foundation orchestra. There were about sixty high school– and college-age musicians sitting onstage, all wearing black and looking very serious, very formal. My chair was set up in front of them, along with my footstool and a microphone. The young conductor straightened his tux coat and said, "Go on. I'll follow." So out we went.

My heart was pounding, and the lights were so hot that I started to sweat immediately. The spotlights were almost blinding, so I couldn't see any faces beyond the first few rows . . . but I could hear that there was a large audience. First they applauded. Then, as silence fell, there remained the crowd noise that an audience always makes: the rustling of hundreds of people settling down in their seats, setting their programs aside.

I spotted one recording mike set up just a few inches away from my hand, and I'd been told that there would be another one twelve feet away, hanging high over the first section of the hall, but I didn't look for it. I only had a few seconds to softly play each string and make sure it was in tune; then I nodded to the conductor.

The orchestra played the first thirty seconds of the concerto, before the music called for the solo guitar to come in. I sat there almost in a daze, waiting to start. What I had visualized so many nights in my rocking chair was actually happening—right now. Feeling practically numb, moving mechanically, and only moving at all because I had practiced so long and hard, I began to play.

The first section went well, and then there was another rest for the guitar while the orchestra played. When I came back in, I couldn't believe what happened. I recomposed the next few measures, playing the right rhythm but the wrong notes. I was jolted completely out of my fog. I'd played that passage hundreds of times! How could I have done that? Shocked back into reality, almost angry with myself, I dug into the next difficult run.

In hindsight, I realize that it was the mistake that got me back on track, put me in an aggressive mood, and actually let me relax. Now there was no chance of playing the concerto perfectly. *Okay,* I told myself, *you blew that section. So now, give it your all.*

When I finished there was a big ovation. I acknowledged the composer by pointing him out, and he stood up in the middle of the audience. When my dad came backstage at intermission, he was positively glowing with happiness. "Good job," he said. "Well done." It was such a relief to hear that, rather than criticism for my mistake. I was grateful that it was over and that I apparently met everyone's expectations.

Interestingly, we were able to listen to recordings made with both microphones—the one six inches from my hand and the one that had been hung twelve feet away. The distant mike had a glorious, concert-hall sound that delighted us all. The other mike was simply too close, like looking at a face with a magnifying mirror.

Having worked so closely with Castelnuovo-Tedesco, I could now call him my friend. At the end of the concert, he wrote on my copy of the music, "To Christopher, who played so well my concerto today. Affectionately, Mario." Today, that music hangs inside a frame in my office. He also sent me a unique gift, which he described in a letter:

> *Dear Chris,*
> *I just told you that I had "a surprise" for you—and here it is. Of course it is just a joke . . . or rather a hobby of mine. Schönberg had his "twelve tone system," I have my own "twenty-five tone system," which allows me (when I am in a good mood) to send "greeting cards" to my friends and interpreters. Whatever the value of the music can be (and it is certainly very little), I have written, in this way, pieces on the names of Heifetz, Piatigorsky, Gieseking, Iturbi, Segovia (perhaps you know the "Tonedilla" on his name, which he even recorded); so you can see that . . . you are in good company. And take it as an early Christmas card from your old friend,*
>
> Mario Castelnuovo-Tedesco
> November 15, 1963

Along with that letter, he sent a short piece in which each letter of my last name was represented by a note on his "twenty-five tone system." The Western ear is used to hearing twelve tones in an octave, so the piece sounds exotic when played—and to me, it was a treasure.

The YMF connection became my entrée to more concerts

and appearances. During the next year, I played for the Pasadena Symphony Association, a United Way conference, Hollywood's Los Feliz Jewish Community Center, Beverly Hills High School, and a concert given by Los Angeles's Friends of the Classical Guitar.

The famous film composer Elmer Bernstein was president of the Young Musicians Foundation at that time, and in February 1964 he and Johnny Green presented me on *The Tonight Show*, which was hosted by Steve Allen before Johnny Carson made it an institution. Gene Kelly was also featured on that broadcast. Later that year there was a YMF benefit concert hosted by Rock Hudson. I was also asked to play the last movement of Castelnuovo-Tedesco's concerto with the Los Angeles Philharmonic at Claremont College, on a live radio broadcast.

It was hard to believe all this really was happening. While I was playing all these concerts in 1963 and early 1964, composer Mario Castelnuovo-Tedesco was making good on a promise he had quietly made before the Royce Hall debut. Maestro Segovia was going to give his first master class in the United States, at the University of California in Berkeley, in July 1964. When my parents and I sent my application, we included a letter from Maestro Castelnuovo-Tedesco, recommending me as a student; he also sent his old friend a recording of my performance of his concerto at Royce Hall and suggested that I be offered a scholarship.

Later that spring my dad received a letter from Estelle Caen, head of the Music Extension campus at UC–Berkeley: "I have just received a letter from Maestro Segovia. I am delighted to tell you that he was well impressed with your son's performance and would like very much to have him as a member of the Master Class. On behalf of Music Extension I would also like to tell you that we will waive tuition for the class. . . ."

Thanks to Maestro Castelnuovo-Tedesco's gracious support, I was given a full scholarship to attend. I had been chosen—out of three hundred participants—as one of nine guitarists to perform onstage for Segovia and to be given lessons in front of the class. We were each sent a list of guitar pieces that we would be allowed to play for Segovia. To my relief, I had already studied nearly all of them. They even included Castelnuovo-Tedesco's concerto. Still, because I wanted to play them *perfectly* for the greatest guitarist in the world, I put in even more long hours of practicing.

When it was time for the master class to begin, my dad and I drove up to the UC–Berkeley campus, and I checked into the dorm room where I would live for the next month. I had never left home before, so it was a daunting experience. My room was a depressing little place with paper-thin walls and a tiny bed; it reminded me a little of a prison cell. My dad hugged me good-bye and said, "I'll see you in a month. Be a man."

I had practiced well, and I believed I was ready to play for Segovia, but the night before the first class, I dreamed that I performed well but the maestro simply did not like my playing. I woke up with a terrible headache, ate a small breakfast, and joined some other students who were walking over to the auditorium. The nine performing students walked onto the stage, where chairs were set on one side, away from the two center seats. Segovia and each student would sit there while he critiqued his or her playing in front of the other performing students and auditors. I was disappointed to realize that his back would be to us. Whoever performed would face us.

Segovia entered, a white-haired Spanish gentleman with thick glasses and an unmistakably aristocratic presence. Assisted by his wife, he slowly walked onstage and was introduced to the audience. Three hundred guitarists, who had sat in a reverent hush as he walked in, now jumped to their feet and applauded. He sat down and pointed to one of the other performers, who took his instrument out of the case, walked over to the performer's seat, and handed his music to the maestro. Segovia nodded for him to start. I was very glad not to go first.

The first time Segovia demonstrated a passage for that student, it was so beautifully played, echoing on the wide stage and throughout the cavernous auditorium, that I turned to the guitarist sitting next to me and said, "Oh my goodness. Can you believe that sound?" It was rich, warm, full of overtones, and expressive. It was the Segovia sound.

To sit so close to this man, as his student—after studying his recordings for so many years—was an amazing and humbling sensation. Soon it would be my turn.

The most difficult thing for me about that first day was that I was not used to playing "cold," without having warmed up my hands immediately before performing. I sat on my hands to keep them warm, and after several other students had taken their lessons, Segovia pointed to me. I felt as if I'd had a mild cardiac arrest. I'd been sitting motionless for a long time, and to make matters worse, my hands were still freezing.

To play cold for the first time, in front of Andrés Segovia, was extraordinarily difficult. I chose to start with the Courante from Bach's Third Cello Suite, as Segovia had transcribed it for the guitar. I didn't do badly, but it certainly was inferior to what I thought I could have done if I had warmed up. As I was playing, I thought, *I'm playing the guitar right now for the greatest guitarist in the world.*

He demonstrated a section of the piece for me, from just three feet away. It was startling to hear his sound so close, because it had a roughness to it—still beautiful but not the enchanting sound I was used to hearing on his recordings or at his concerts. It reminded me of the too-close recording made at my Royce Hall debut or of standing too close to a painting. All the beauty was there, but you needed to get a few feet away before it became magical.

The next day the class's support staff moved the performing students' seating to the back of the stage so that we sat in a semi-circle, facing the audience. By the third day we had started to settle into something of a routine, and I had developed a technique for playing cold. We were never given an official performing order, and I never knew when I was going to be called, so whenever I sensed that another lesson was coming to a close, I started to warm up my hands, interlacing my fingers like "the church and the steeple," massaging them, and moving them back and forth, in case Segovia called me next. It was like doing warm-up exercises but without the guitar. This helped me get through the first few minutes of playing.

Each time I performed for Segovia I played a different piece. Typically we'd play a piece one day, he would ask for changes in that piece, and we'd play it for him the next day with his changes. On the fifth day of the master class, I made the terrible mistake of playing the Bach Chaconne, using my teacher's fingerings instead of Segovia's.

About a third of the way through I was jolted out of my seat by Segovia, who was stomping his foot on the stage. I stopped playing, looked up in shock, and saw Segovia's hands over his head. His face had turned red, and all but shouting, he demanded, "Why have you changed the fingerings?" His wife, who was sitting close by, laid her hands on his arm as if she were holding him back. "Never in my life . . ." he exclaimed.

I melted onstage and meekly replied, "I didn't change the fingerings. My teacher did."

He scowled. "Who is your teacher?"

I told him, and he said, "Change it back tomorrow." That was the end of my session.

I left the auditorium feeling shattered and devastated. Segovia was my inspiration, the man I looked up to more than anyone else in the world, and I felt I had greatly offended and disappointed him.

Reflecting while I walked back to my dorm room, I realized that his body language had changed when I told him I hadn't been the one to change the fingerings. He *had* calmed down a bit when he realized that I wasn't some brazen California kid, indiscriminately tossing out his artistic, expressive, carefully thought-out fingerings. I had learned those fingerings from a fine guitarist, but Segovia played the guitar on a level above anyone else in the world.

I found a pay phone and called home. When I described what had happened, my parents were both surprisingly protective of me and completely supportive. They asked if I'd like to just come home.

I thought it over. I had worked so hard to get here, and so many others had helped. I had also developed a pretty thick skin from working with my dad. Still, criticism from the maestro was devastating. From Segovia's viewpoint, I had committed an almost unpardonable sin, tantamount to changing Holy Scripture. It would be simple to cut and run.

Perhaps God nudged me. "No," I said grimly, "I just need to relearn the fingerings," and I went back to that dank little dorm room. I had a lot of work to do that night. As soon as I ate a little dinner—my stomach hurt, I was so worried—I got busy relearning all those fingerings. It was almost like relearning the piece from scratch, measure by measure, hand shift by hand shift.

Immediately I started to hear a difference in the way each phrase rose or fell as a musical thought and led beautifully into the next phrase. I stayed up long after midnight, relearning and memorizing most of the thirteen-minute piece.

Over the years since that night, one rule I have always observed is to keep a phrase on the same string whenever possible, for the consistency of the sound. Many guitarists will finger a piece of music in the easiest way it can be played so that the next note lies as close as possible to the notes before and after it. Playing cross-string like this is easier, and it doesn't require the guitarist to jump around the neck of the guitar as much with the left hand, but that inconsistent tone just isn't as beautiful.

When I played the refingered Chaconne the following day, Segovia smiled and immediately seemed to relax. I am grateful to my dad—a thick skin isn't a pleasant gift to receive, but it certainly is necessary for a concert performer.

When I finally played the Castelnuovo-Tedesco concerto, which I had fingered by listening to Segovia's recording, he seemed genuinely pleased to see how well I'd done.

An Italian guitarist roomed next to me, and he practiced ten hours a day. I would lie on my bunk bed and think, *He's playing the same thing over and over again, but it's not getting any better.* In fact, it became almost hypnotic, and I found I could fall asleep to his music. This reinforced something else my dad had been teaching me: I had to practice with purpose. It didn't matter if I played ten hours a day. If I didn't have goals and didn't improve, I was only reinforcing bad playing. Practice doesn't always make perfect, but it does make permanent.

One of our formal class sessions was televised nationally, and I was chosen as one of three students to play a solo. I wish there had been VCRs back then, because a tape of that broadcast would have been priceless to my family.

My parents wrote to me a couple of times a week, as did Terry.

Halfway through the month, she sent a letter that contained sand from the beach and said, "Just two more weeks, and you'll be able to have some fun too." The sand jiggled in the envelope when I held it up. That was encouraging. I couldn't wait to get back home!

As the month ended, I was exhausted but satisfied and grateful. Segovia told me that I had the potential for a wonderful career. That was a startling honor. At this point, I was simply focused on playing well, not on making it a career. I was encouraged by Segovia's enthusiastic support of my playing—his singling me out—yet I saw how far I still had to go.

At the end of the month Segovia gave a concert, and my dad drove up to hear it with me. I had spent a month with the maestro and learned many new techniques, yet witnessing his profound artistry with the guitar inspired me to work harder. That month was the beginning of a lifelong relationship with Segovia, based on a shared passion for the instrument that he described this way: "The beauty of the guitar resides in its soft and persuasive voice, and its poetry cannot be equaled by any other instrument."

FISH TALE

Lessons from the Master

One day when I was sixteen years old, I was fishing in a beautiful riffle upstream from the famous McDonald Hole at Hot Creek Ranch. Big trout in that hole had been known to feed on small snakes or mice that had fallen into the water. Here, I had been told, lived a fifteen-pound brown trout that was so big he had actually been seen eating a baby duck.

When you're fly-fishing a stream, oftentimes the lead fish in a group of feeding fish will be the biggest. He takes the lead spot in the run to intercept the insects—the hatch—coming downstream. When I saw the head of a big rainbow trout feeding voraciously on insects below a weed in the current, I snuck up to the edge of the bank, knelt down, and studied the situation.

It was interesting to see this fish move from side to side in a six- to eight-inch swath, gulping down insects as they floated on either side of the weed that was shifting back and forth with the current. In order to cast to where the trout would be, I would almost have to time my cast to be on the dry part of the weed, so the current would take the fly off as it drifted from side to side, mimicking the way the natural insects were approaching the big fish. It would be a very complicated cast, just as hard to time as it would be to place.

On my first cast, I piled the leader at the top edge of the floating weed. No good. I kept trying. Finally, I placed just the right cast, up on the edge, and the current carried the artificial fly to the relaxed rise of this big fish. He rolled up and out and back down over my fly.

I struck, and the big trout headed downstream for the deep, safe water of McDonald Hole. He swam like a freight train, taking all my slack line down to the reel. I had set the drag too tight. As soon as the slack line hit the reel, *snap*—the leader broke.

Disheartened, I walked to another spot and continued fishing, but I kept thinking about that big fish. I decided to make him my goal, my project for that summer vacation. Every morning I would leave the cabin early, sneak up to the edge of the bank on my hands and knees, and kneel, waiting for the hatch to start. I spotted the big fish, working again, but now he was educated. I fished for him that day and didn't get a strike. He didn't even look at my fly. This went on for two days until, to my surprise, I hooked him again.

This time he raced upstream, twisted around the edge of a weed, and broke me off. Certainly I wouldn't have another chance at him. Two days later—amazingly—I saw the fish feeding again. When I made the third cast, I saw him roll up on the fly, but I got so excited that I struck too hard and broke him off.

I had lost him three times! I couldn't believe it. Later that day I saw the ranch owner, a master fly fisherman and fly caster, and I told him my story. To my delight, he said, "Let's go down there. We're going to see if we can catch this fish."

Wow! The great Bill Lawrence was going to help me catch that fish. We walked down, and sure enough, we could see that the fish was working again, feeding in the same spot. I said, "There he is. Just below that weed, on the far side of the stream." I couldn't believe my hooking him hadn't curbed his appetite.

Bill started casting. He was a master, but by now, the fish was working on its doctorate. Fly after fly, drift after drift, he refused to take anything, but Bill was determined. He'd make a few casts with one fly, and the fish would come up and take a look but refuse it, slightly dimpling the surface. Bill would put on another fly.

Finally, he picked the perfect fly. He cast it on the lip of the weed, and it drifted off.

The big trout rolled up on the tiny dry fly. Bill took his time, struck, and set the hook.

Then he handed me the rod. "Take him," he said. "Now you land this fish!"

Bill stayed in the general area. I was nervous and excited. I finally had the big trout on, and he was going back and forth, circling the pool, and swirling around. Finally, after about twenty minutes, I pulled him in to shore.

We looked at the beautiful rainbow trout, with the sun glistening off his side against the cool weeds on the stream bank, and there—like a picture, all on the same side of his jaw, in a triangular shape—were all three of my flies, which I easily removed. Bill guessed that this fish, which wasn't the fifteen-pound monster, still weighed in excess of six pounds. As I watched Bill release him back into the stream, I couldn't help but think how much I had learned from this master fisherman.

5

"Professor"

1964–68

According to old-world tradition, studying with a tutor creates a lasting loyalty. Unfortunately, my month of study with Andrés Segovia seemed to displease the Romero family, and when I returned, I was limited to one lesson a month, and that was with Pepe. The Romeros had given me a solid technical foundation, and I continued to work just as hard for Pepe as I had before. Although the amount of time I spent taking lessons had decreased, my performances were increasing.

As the next year went by, I played outdoors for the San Francisco Classical Guitar Society. I performed at an all-girls school in Monterey, California, with two other young musicians. I played with the Pasadena Symphony, the Downey Symphony, the Westside Symphony—my first time inside the Wilshire Ebell Theater—and gave smaller recitals for musical societies and other clubs. When I graduated from Buckley High School, I played for graduation.

I entered UCLA as a music major in the fall of 1965. It was a time when world events affected every young man over eighteen, because the United States was involved in the Vietnam War. UCLA encouraged enlistment in the ROTC program, which put off military service until after graduation, and I applied to be commissioned as a second lieutenant in the Special Services branch of the army infantry. That entertainment branch performed a vital service—keeping up the soldiers' morale—and it seemed like the best choice for my future. It would allow me to continue to play my instrument even if I were sent overseas.

During the summer of 1966, I found myself in Fort Benning, Georgia, for a six-week basic training camp. I brought my guitar, but it was impossible to practice. Suddenly I was in the army infantry, and that's the only thing I was doing. We were up at four in the morning for marches through swamps; we endured nighttime low-crawl exercises under barbed-wire fences with live machine gun rounds whizzing over our heads; and we learned to avoid booby traps.

For five and a half weeks I didn't have time to touch the guitar. Then our company commander informed us that there was going to be a talent show and he wanted our company to participate. A few of the guys in my squad knew that I played guitar, and they suggested that I enter the competition. At lunch break, I pulled my guitar out of storage and went back to the empty barracks, hoping to practice a little. First, I realized I'd better file my nails. They'd been neglected for weeks.

Just as I got involved, my sergeant walked in. A burly guy with a wide neck, he marched over, spotted me filing my nails, and demanded, "Boy, what are you doin'?"

Caught off guard and very embarrassed, I said, "Well, sir, I've been asked to enter the talent competition. I'm going to play classical guitar, and you use your fingernails to pluck the strings. Have you heard of Andrés Segovia? He's the greatest guitarist in the world."

The sergeant wrinkled his whole face. "No, he ain't," he said in disgust. "Chet Atkins is the greatest picker in the world." Then he added, "Boy, if you don't win that competition tonight, I'm going to cut off every one of your nails in front of the entire company."

I was genuinely alarmed by his warning, because I knew he had the authority to do it. I won't say that he put any more pressure on me than I felt playing for Segovia, but I was greatly relieved when I won the competition.

After basic training, it was a relief to return to civilian life. Following my 1963 Royce Hall debut, Mario Castelnuovo-Tedesco asked me to do a world premiere of his new major work, the Guitar Concerto no. 2, op. 160, for guitar and orchestra. We had become good friends, and I gave that January 1966 premiere with the California Chamber Symphony, Henri Temianka conducting. The premiere was well received, and the work was an admirable addition to the guitar repertoire.

Writing about a later performance of the Concerto no. 2, the *Los Angeles Times* reviewer said some gracious things:

> It is music by a virtuoso for a virtuoso, and Parkening, with an ability belying his youth, brought it off in a manner suggesting that other virtuoso, Segovia (to whom the concerto was dedicated).[1]

In between those two concerts, I participated in Maestro Segovia's second U.S. master class, this time in Winston-Salem,

North Carolina. By this time, my lessons with Pepe had ended. I was on my own, practicing and performing in earnest. I had learned by now that perseverance mattered as much as raw talent, and consistent practicing helped me overcome the gaps I perceived in my own abilities.

Again, the master class had moments of terror. During one afternoon session I sat relaxing among the auditors in the auditorium (I had already played that morning) when Mrs. Segovia arrived. The maestro called, "Christopher, come down here and play something for Madame Segovia!" My heart rate jumped from 60 to 120 in about two seconds. This time, although playing "cold" was still stressful, it came as less of a shock. I was learning to cope with real-world concert conditions, and by their smiles it seemed that Mrs. Segovia and the maestro were quite pleased.

It was still possible, however, to experience the maestro's genuine wrath. One day a guitarist played his own transcription of the Bach Chaconne. Segovia sat fidgeting, silent but noticeably angry, through the entire thirteen-minute piece. When the student finished, Segovia said just two words in Spanish, which translated, "Leave town!"

Sheepishly the student stood up and walked off the stage. He did not return. I certainly felt sorry for him.

Nevertheless, my second master class was an even better experience than my first. I was able to focus better and learn more quickly, and I also began to form professional relationships with people whose influence would stretch far into my future.

At this class I met Jim Sherry of Chicago, who became a friend and an ongoing presence in my professional life. Also, Maestro Segovia graciously wrote me a letter of reference, which read, in part:

Christopher Parkening is an extremely talented young guitarist
who, like all fine guitarists, is self-taught. Certainly, he studied

with me in two short courses at the University of California at Berkeley and North Carolina, where I observed both times his gradual development of technique and musical sensitivities with tremendous interest and a great deal of personal appreciation. Each time I observed him, he seemed to grow into a more refined and thoughtfully developed artist. In my courses, more than having just learned the mechanics of the guitar, he seemed intuitively to feel his way to the proper expression. . . .

Without being fully aware of it, because of his own special talents, he belongs to that special group of my disciples of which I am so proud, which includes: John Williams, Alirio Diaz, Oscar Ghiglia, Guillermo Fierens; and I am certain, because he is like them, the future holds for Mr. Parkening the success he so well deserves.

Los Olivos, January 1968
Almuñecar, Prov. de Granada, Spain

At the close of that class, Segovia embraced me warmly and gave me another bit of advice: "All great players are self-taught. Ultimately, you must be your own student and teacher, and teacher and student get in many disagreements."

Not long after this second Segovia class, I received an unusual invitation. Meredith Willson, who had written the famous Broadway musicals *The Music Man* and *The Unsinkable Molly Brown*, was working on a new production based on the life of Christopher Columbus. Mr. Willson asked if I would perform in it. I was offered what seemed to me a substantial sum of money, but it would have required me to drop out of UCLA and move to New York. My parents and I discussed the offer at length, but after much consideration, we decided that I really didn't want to drop out—and working on Broadway wasn't what I ultimately wanted to do with the guitar. I was able to record the guitar parts for Mr. Willson that I would have played onstage, and that turned out to have been the better choice, because *1491* went into production but closed on the road.

This was a time for many important decisions. At the start of my sophomore year, I transferred to UCLA's crosstown rival, the University of Southern California (USC), where the music school was geared toward performance. Jascha Heifetz was on the faculty at USC, as were Gregor Piatigorsky and some other amazing musicians who were primarily concert performers.

USC soon asked me to start a classical guitar department, which afforded me some great opportunities. As a nineteen-year-old sophomore, I received a faculty parking sticker, which was extremely useful for a campus located near downtown Los Angeles. I had two teaching assistants, gave master classes, and scheduled playing juries, which were the students' final exams. As a student, I worked with three incredible musicians—cellists Gregor Piatigorsky and Gabor Rejto, and harpsichordist Malcolm Hamilton—on musical interpretation. It was tremendous to work with these gifted and experienced performers. I would play a piece, and they would coach me on its musical nuances. They emphasized over and over to me that guitar transcriptions from other instruments must compare well with the original versions in all respects of musicality and excellence. When I played for these instrumentalists, the relative difficulty of guitar technique didn't matter. They guided me toward a greater awareness of all facets of classical music interpretation.

In June 1967 my mom's cousin Jack Marshall asked me to make a demo recording of his Essay for Guitar and Orchestra. A demo recording isn't for general release; Jack simply wanted to document his composition and have a record he could listen to, though it was his dream to have it released someday. Studio and orchestra time were prohibitively expensive without a recording contract, so Jack and my dad split the cost. Jack hired the best studio musicians in Los Angeles and booked a studio for three hours.

Working with Jack Marshall as a fellow musician was a dream come true. I'd never been inside a recording studio. That session let me experience the recording process and see how important it is to play cleanly, consistently, and expressively. It was then, too, that I understood something about the squeaks that often happen when a guitarist's left hand slides up or down the fingerboard. Guitarists tend not to notice them since we get used to hearing them when we play. But the public notices.

My dad suggested spreading olive oil or talcum powder on the strings and the fingerboard. Oiling the strings made them even squeakier, and applying talcum powder made them sound dead. Nothing seemed to work until my dad had the brilliant idea, which remained more or less our secret for years, of sanding the metal-wound lower strings. First we tried heavy-grit sandpaper on strings that had been taken off the guitar. When we put them back on, they sounded thuddy and dead. I almost abandoned the idea, but then I got to thinking: Why couldn't I try the refined sandpaper that I used to smooth the unevenness off my right-hand fingernails? I tried that, and the strings sounded a little better, although they still didn't have the lively sound we wanted. I put brand new strings on and tried sanding only the top portion of the bass strings, just on the top side. Again, it was better, but it still sounded slightly dead.

Each time I sanded the strings and started to play, my fingertips picked up a black line of grit from the metal filings I'd sanded off the string. *Well,* I thought, *that's what's making the string dead!* So the next time I sanded the top section, I took several tissues and wiped the tops of the strings. The tissue ended up crisscrossed with black lines, but the sound was perfect—no squeaks, but still nice and bright.

It's extremely unusual for a demo recording to be released, but Essay for Guitar and Orchestra, which we recorded in 1967, actually was released many years later, after Jack's death, when EMI included it on a recording in 2000 that featured Elmer Bernstein's Concerto for Guitar and Orchestra.

All the work I was doing—experimenting, analyzing, studying, practicing, and even making a demo recording—still did not, in my opinion, make me a "professional." To have a future as a musician, I needed to acquire two vital contracts: one with a major record company and the other with a management agency, to schedule concerts and organize tours. Since Jack Marshall had made many recordings for Capitol Records in Hollywood, he offered to speak with the head of Capitol's classical music division, Angel Records.

"I have a cousin who's a very good classical guitarist," Jack told him, "and I really think you should sign him." There seemed to be some reluctance at first, but we finally had an appointment to see Robert Meyers in his office. He told us, "We've just had a bad experience with a classical guitarist. We recorded an entire album, and at the end, the artist agreed with us that it wasn't musically good enough to release. We don't want to repeat that experience. I will give you one recording session. If we like your playing, we'll sign you. If we don't, we won't!"

The next few weeks were full of stress and excitement as I prepared for the recording session that might launch my career—one three-hour shot for all the marbles. I chose two pieces: the Etude no. 1 by Villa-Lobos and Albéniz's "Leyenda." Then I practiced nonstop.

They booked Studio B, in the basement of the Capitol Records building at the corner of Hollywood and Vine streets, and we were to record from 2 until 5 p.m.

I drove with my father into Hollywood. The Capitol Records tower, built in 1954 and shaped—deliberately, according to some people—like a stack of records, represented the big time to me. The Beatles were on Capitol Records, and I felt very intimidated as I walked into the building, past the guard gate, and down a corridor that so many famous artists, such as Frank Sinatra, Nat King Cole, Bobby Darin, and Judy Garland, had passed through. Dozens of publicity pictures and framed gold records hung on the walls. Studio A was being used when we arrived, and as we walked past its big double doors, the red recording light went on above them. I had butterflies in my stomach.

We made a right turn and proceeded down the corridor into Studio B, where we met Dick Jones, the producer; Carson Taylor, the engineer; and assistant Bob Norberg.

The recording studio was a huge room with a high ceiling and a piano in one corner. A wooden piano bench was set up for me to sit on, and several pairs of microphones were set up to test for the best sound. I played a bit of each of the pieces while they decided which mikes they preferred, set them several feet in front of me and somewhat up in the air, and adjusted their tilt. Then they closed the inner double door. Next, I heard the outside double door being closed. Locked into a bright, spacious vault, I looked through a thick glass window into the control room.

Dick's voice came through the studio monitors. "Okay, Chris. We're ready for the first take. We'll do four or five, but after the first take, you can come in and listen to it."

I started with Etude no. 1. After I finished, I walked into the booth and listened to it on the studio monitors. Dick and Carson had achieved a good sound, so on the next take I concentrated on playing accurately and musically at a fast tempo, because Etude no. 1—besides being a magnificent piece of guitar repertoire—is a speed study.

I tried hard to look confident, but in reality, I felt anything but sure of myself!

Dick called the next take, and I started the piece again. We made the rest of the three or four takes consecutively, and then he had me come in and listen to one. He then said, "Okay, let's do 'Leyenda.'" So I ended the session with this monumental piece for classical guitar, one of the most famous guitar transcriptions Segovia ever made.

As we packed up at the end of that recording session, I was encouraged to hear Dick, Carson, and Bob saying things like, "When can we do the next session? Let's plan your other studio dates."

Does this mean that they like it? I wondered. *Does it mean I'm going to get a recording contract?*

We received a call the next day from the head of the company. Capitol's reaction was absolutely shocking, even to my dad. Not only did they offer me a six-record contract, they also wanted to do something they had never before done with a new artist: release my first two albums simultaneously. They would eventually title one *In the Classic Style* and the other *In the Spanish Style*.

My dad and mom were as ecstatic as I was. There would be a professional soloist in the family, after all! My dad, an experienced realtor, looked over my contract and fine-tuned every clause. Today, more than thirty years later, I still use that contract as my base model.

As I wrote my name at the bottom of the page, I could hardly believe I was signing a contract with Capitol Records. I was nineteen.

FISH TALE

"Duke's Hooked Josephine Again!"

At Hot Creek Ranch, just downstream from a wooden bridge supported by two wagon wheels, there lived an exceptionally large rainbow trout that the owner, Bill Lawrence, had named Josephine. Josephine fed during the hatch, and Bill caught her a couple of times. Ranch guests often walked across the bridge, looked in the water, and dreamed of catching a trout that size. Many a fisherman had cast a fly for Josephine, but now she was "educated" enough to discern a real insect from an artificial fly.

My dad took the challenge. When other fishermen would get tired of fishing for Josephine, Dad stuck with it. He made it his goal, his ambition that summer, to catch and release her on a tiny number-eighteen dry fly with pound-and-a-half test leader. Finally, one early afternoon in July, he hooked her. A number of people who were staying in the other cabins came down to watch him fight this big trout. She ran downstream, below the bridge where she lived. There, the creek got weedy, which made the catch even more challenging. This was a large trout on a small fly and light tippet leader, which could easily be broken.

After about a twenty-minute fight, Josephine worked her way back upstream and buried herself in some thick weeds in the middle of the stream. It was a standoff. My dad was standing in the middle of Hot Creek with his line taut and his fly rod bent; he couldn't budge her, and she wasn't moving forward, so nothing happened for several minutes.

Watching from the stream bank, I yelled to Dad, "Do you want me to help?"

"Yes!"

Wearing my hip boots, I waded into the middle of the stream about fifteen feet upstream from my dad, where I could see his line entering the water. Carefully, I followed the leader down into the water, just lightly touching it as it disappeared into the weeds. I got right down to where the fish was—facing my dad, looking downstream, with the big trout almost between my legs. I reached down into the weeds with both hands, and about two feet underwater, I felt the fish as I came up under her belly. *Wow! This is a huge fish!* I thought. The length and the size of the big, slippery trout made me nervous. I started to slowly, carefully lift her upward, separating the weeds as I went. *Maybe*, I thought, *I can pick the fish up and out of the weeds and carry her to the bank.*

At this point, Josephine wriggled out of my hands and, with a burst of energy, darted upstream. I made a valiant attempt to swing one heavy hip-boot wader over the top of my dad's fragile leader, so he could resume fighting the fish, but I fell right on top of his line and broke him off. The fish vanished.

Dad was devastated. What could I say? There were a lot of people around, and he didn't say much either. I dejectedly walked back to the cabin. That fish epitomized his goal as a dry-fly fisherman, to catch a six-pound trout on a number-eighteen dry fly, with pound-and-a-half test leader.

Happily, all was not lost. Several days later, late one afternoon, I heard a yell from one of the fishermen at the Hot Creek bridge: "Duke's hooked Josephine again!" This time the fish took him way downstream, under a barbed-wire fence. Watching from the front porch of the cabin, I saw him beach her on the far side of the bank and hold up the big rainbow trout while my mom shot two quick pictures, and then he released Josephine unharmed. She eventually swam back to her spot under the bridge, and my dad was a happy man for the rest of the vacation.

6

Concert Artist

~~~~~~~~~~~~~~~~~~~~~~

1968–69

Having signed a contract to record two LP albums immediately, I was eager to get down to business. One of the first pieces I laid down after my audition was "Recuerdos de la Alhambra," by Francisco Tarrega. When the red recording light went on, producer Dick Jones allowed me five takes—no more.

"Recuerdos" is a difficult tremolo piece, and it was tough to walk in off the street and play it well when I was "cold" and a little nervous. During the first couple of takes, I tried desperately to do everything I'd learned, all at once. When playing the fast, repeated notes of a long tremolo passage, a guitarist is tempted to let the right thumb drop into a vertical position with the strings, which stabilizes the three rapidly playing fingers and smooths out the tremolo effect. But holding the thumb that way gives the bass line a harsh, ugly tone color. Segovia taught me to hold the right thumb at a particular angle, which creates a full, rich bass sound but puts the fingers in a more unstable position.

By the fourth and fifth take everyone seemed satisfied, and we went on to record several other pieces. At the end of the three-hour session, I was given a reel-to-reel copy of the tape, which I was pleased and excited to take home.

My dad got in from work at about seven o'clock that night, and naturally he wanted to hear "Recuerdos." We loaded up the reel-to-reel player, switched it on, and sat down in our rocking chairs.

At the end of the first take, he sprang out of his chair and shut off the tape. "That's terrible! It's uneven. The whole thing is a washout," he declared. I stared after him as he stormed out of the room.

I plodded upstairs to my bedroom and flopped facedown on the bed, too discouraged to move, too well trained to cry. In a family where success mattered so much, I felt I had failed.

I vowed that if I ever had children or taught guitar to others, I would never impose the pursuit of success without regard to effort or heart. I had done my best . . . and that should have been enough. I knew that my father's incessant pushing was designed to drive me to excellence, but I wasn't sure I was willing to pay the price. The next morning I went downstairs and listened to the rest of the session tape. The fourth and fifth takes of "Recuerdos," to my relief, were nearly flawless, and for the recording all we really needed was one good take.

Once the projects were finished, Brown Meggs—the head of Angel Records—invited my dad and me to join him in his office on the top floor of the Capitol Records building in Hollywood. Brown looked at us and said, in an effort to encourage us about the future, "You're nineteen years old. In five years, you'll probably want to sail these records out the top window of the Capitol Records tower. But that's just the way it is in this business."

I glanced at my dad, and he looked at me. A week previously, I'd taken home the first pressing of *In the Spanish Style* and played it for him. His response to "Recuerdos," the piece he had originally criticized so harshly, was, "That is good. That is really good"—and I honestly felt the same. It shocked me to hear Brown make such a negative blanket assessment about the recording business—and about the record we'd worked so hard on, a record that Capitol was excited to release.

Dad looked Brown in the eye and said, "We will never throw these recordings away." I knew what he was thinking: *Brown, you don't understand how good these are.* Dad's confidence restored my courage to believe in what I had done.

It turned out that my dad was right. Donal Henehan wrote in the *New York Times*, "The two debut disks . . . demonstrate the kind of impeccable musicianship that only greatly talented people achieve at any age. Parkening's musical grasp of broad ideas is as impressive as his utter technical security and control in shading, colors, and dynamics. His playing of Bach's Chaconne . . . is so intelligent, sensitive and adept that one can forget everything but the music." Years later, my new recording producer transferred the reel-to-reel tapes to CD and we went through them, looking for our favorite pieces from my twenty-five years of recording. The Bach Chaconne, laid down at Capitol Records when I was nineteen years old, stood the test of time and twenty-five years later was rereleased on the *Artistry of Christopher Parkening* album. "Leyenda" and the Villa-Lobos Etude no. 1 were rereleased on a double-CD set for EMI called *The Great Recordings*. All those cuts came out of those very first sessions.

The album's release in the fall of 1968 was oddly anticlimactic.

Capitol sent me a package of each of the LPs, wrapped in cellophane. I looked down at them and thought, *Wow! Well, here's a record you've made.* I didn't have time to do much more than that.

I did a few in-store record signings, but there wasn't really any other celebration. I was too busy taking classes, teaching at USC, keeping up with my ROTC obligations, and trying to get ready for another major event.

Maestro Segovia had invited me to participate in the international guitar competition in Santiago de Compostela, Spain, and I was running out of time. Each contestant was supposed to learn a group of qualifying pieces to enter the competition and then a second group of pieces for the final judging. I simply did not have time to learn the qualifying pieces, so Segovia generously waived them for me.

Unfortunately, a small group of other contestants found out that I had been excused from learning the first group of pieces. They circulated a petition and publicly asked Segovia to ban me from the competition.

Segovia was outraged—perhaps, at least in part, because they had questioned his judgment and authority. Still, he granted their request and banned me from the competition. Then he and the other judges, including two fine composers, Federico Moreno Tórroba and Federico Mompou, invited me to participate as a judge and asked me to keep it secret until the last possible moment. I followed Segovia and the other judges out, walking in single file, to sit down behind the judges' table. I glanced at the group of contestants and saw their expressions of surprise and shock. Segovia decided not to award a first prize that year. At his request, I played two public recitals, after which he asked the mayor of the city to present me with a silver plaque and a gold watch, the honors that would have been bestowed upon the competition's winner. Before I left Spain, he patted my cheek and said, "Remember, Christopher, you must work very hard."

When I returned to California, record critics were starting to respond to my recordings. My parents were delighted to read that the *San Francisco Chronicle*'s reviewer, Heuwell Tircuit, thought I had a chance to join that group—as my father had said—who would "not starve playing guitar."

"At age twenty," he wrote, "[he] is one of the five or six finest guitarists alive."

A few weeks later, I received a phone call from a gentleman by the name of Chris Schang. He identified himself as a vice president of Columbia Artists Management in New York. "I'm in LA on business, and I have been told about you by a friend of mine in Connecticut. She heard you at the Segovia Master Class in Winston-Salem, North Carolina, and told me that I should hear you play."

Gripping the phone, I said, "That would be wonderful! When would you want me to play for you?" In my mind, I was already planning out a practicing schedule.

"How about tonight?"

Oh, no! Another incredibly important audition, but this time I had no time to prepare. Looking back, I now recognize this as another situation where God's grace upheld me.

We lived on the west side of Los Angeles, and Mr. Schang was staying north of the city. My dad and I drove over to his friend's home, where I played in the living room for about thirty minutes. At the end of that time, he said, "I'll tell you what I'll do. Come to New York for our annual convention in November. You'll have to pay your own expenses, but I will put you on for twenty minutes in a showcase concert for new artists. If I get bookings for you, I will sign you to Columbia Artists Management. If I don't, I won't." Concert management was the other essential element to my career and would expand the potential audience for my recordings.

After ten weeks of intense preparation, I flew to New York. My hotel was old, and its musty smell was depressing. When I went down for dinner, the restaurant was dark, dank, and unbelievably expensive. My room was a relic and the bathroom was dirty, and all night long, cars and taxis were honking down below on Fifty-seventh Street.

I practiced a little, but I didn't sleep much. In the morning I was picked up and driven to the venue; then I played my twenty minutes for about two hundred somber-looking concert presenters, each of whom had the ability to book three to five concerts. When I walked off the stage, Chris Schang gave me a hug and assured me, "You did great."

Representatives from Columbia Artists Management took me out for dinner that night, although I still had no idea whether or not I had a future with their organization. I could only fly home and wait.

Two days later, Chris Schang called. "Chris, we've got you seventy-two bookings! You're going to tour America! We'll be sending a management contract soon."

So there it was: touring management, taking me places where my records would appear in the stores. I wish I could say that I fell on my knees and thanked God, but spiritually I was much farther from Him than the twelve-year-old boy who was such a willing witness at Vacation Bible School. Still, in His grace, He poured out blessing after blessing.

I came to know Chris Schang better as time went on. His father had founded Columbia Artists Management, Inc. Within two years of our meeting, Chris was forced to retire due to a serious illness, and shortly after that, CAMI assigned me to Sam Niefeld. Sam truly was the classy, quintessential old-time manager:

creative; concerned about an artist's stage presence, repertoire, and recordings; and always trying to build on a career.

❧ ❧ ❧

For years, my dad had been joking that he would retire early and leave my sister and me before we grew up and left him. He was forty-seven, I was nineteen, and Terry was just eighteen when he and my mom bought property in Idaho and moved out of Los Angeles.

Since my grandma Marshall's death, her home in North Hollywood had stood empty. So, wanting to be close to the music business, I rented it.

It wasn't until Dad retired that my own "life goal" emerged. Since he retired at forty-seven, I decided that thirty would be a good retirement age for me to aim for. If I wasn't going to starve playing the guitar, maybe I really could make a lot of money, retire early, and enjoy "the good life." I had about a year of studies left to go at USC, two records in music stores, and a touring contract. Because of my position on the USC faculty, I was given a teaching deferment, so I withdrew from the ROTC program.

In September 1968, I heard from the contract department at Columbia Artists Management. CAMI wanted to start fulfilling those seventy-two bookings and send me on a national tour. However, I still had twelve units left to complete for my music degree— non-music classes, as I recall, which didn't seem relevant to my profession. I had taken all the music courses USC offered, which benefited me greatly, but I was already having a tough time juggling a recording career with full-time courses, to say nothing of teaching. How could I add touring to that?

I talked it over with my parents, and we agreed that the touring contract I'd been offered was a rare, once-in-a-lifetime career opportunity. So it was decided: I would "go pro" early.

I withdrew from my classes, arranged a teaching schedule that would fulfill my obligations to my students, and set out on my first national tour: Globe, Arizona; Laguna Beach, Fullerton, Stockton, and Fort Bragg, California; Mount Vernon and Spokane, Washington; Coquille, Oregon; Pocatello, Idaho; and then back to Santa Ana, near Los Angeles. Although I asked the tour's organizers to block out a month for exams, they booked me in Flagstaff, Arizona, and Quebec during that time. Then I was to head out for Oskaloosa and Marshalltown, Iowa; Saginaw, Michigan; Oak Lawn, Illinois; back to Los Angeles; and off again to Atlanta, Georgia; Winston-Salem, Misenheimer, Laurinburg, and Hickory, North Carolina; Anderson, South Carolina; Albany, Georgia; Huntsville, Alabama; Naples and Avon Park, Florida; San Francisco; and finally, Fish Creek, Wisconsin.

There was no way to simplify or organize the schedule for convenient traveling, because the presenters had booked the dates so quickly. So in my first year of touring, I literally crisscrossed America.

Up until 1969, I'd had some pleasantly naive, if not glamorous, ideas of what concert touring might be like. All my preconceptions were wrong. For one thing, apart from that time in the evening when crowds of people surrounded me, I spent the rest of the day by myself. If I took a newspaper down to the restaurant, I felt a little less conspicuous, but it still didn't change the fact that I was eating alone.

Some concert organizers were kind and gracious, but others seemed not to care. At one concert during the first season, a man on the concert series committee promised to pick me up for my eight o'clock concert at 7 p.m. in the hotel lobby. That would give me less than an hour to warm up, but it would be just enough.

At 7:15, no one was there. At 7:20, no one was there. Seven-thirty came, but my ride did not.

Finally, out of desperation, I hurried to the front desk and asked them to call a taxi. I arrived at the hall five minutes before the concert was scheduled to begin. The committee member who had promised me a ride was there at the hall, and he simply shrugged and said he'd forgotten.

Before giving a concert, I found that it was helpful to spend at least a few minutes on the stage to hear the hall's acoustics. It was also preferable to avoid playing cold, without a proper practice session. Those routines help me do my best, but on that first tour I had to learn to be flexible.

Unfortunately, I also had to learn to be "wise as a serpent, and harmless as a dove"—streetwise, but cordial and polite. I learned that lesson while riding a bus into New York City, where I was supposed to catch a taxi from the bus station to LaGuardia Airport to fly to my next concert. After playing late the previous night, I'd arisen extremely early for the two- to three-hour bus ride, fallen asleep on the bus, and arrived at the bus station exhausted. Still groggy when I walked off the bus with my guitar, I stumbled around to the side of the bus, grabbed my big suitcase, and as they say in New York, "schlepped" the guitar and suitcase to the curbside so I could start looking for a taxi.

A young man on foot appeared out of nowhere, talking extremely fast. "Taxi? You want a taxi?"

"Yeah."

"Where you going?"

"LaGuardia."

"You want a taxi there?"

"Yeah."

"You'll pay a fortune to get a taxi to LaGuardia. Three blocks down that way," he said, pointing, "there's a bus that'll take you there for five dollars."

That sounded good to me. "Really?" I asked. The man grabbed my suitcase and took off. I must have had a bull's-eye on my back: a blond kid who plainly didn't know what he was doing, wandering on the sidewalk, looking for a taxi. This guy had taken off with my bag, and he was walking fast. I followed him with the guitar.

We walked a block, then another half a block, to a spot that was kind of isolated. I could see in the distance, about a block and a half away, a sign that said "Newark" on the side facing me. I assumed that was where we were headed. I knew there was another airport in the New York area, in Newark, New Jersey, so I thought maybe the other side of the sign said "LaGuardia."

The guy stopped and put down my suitcase. "Well, there it is, over there. That'll be five dollars." He held out his hand.

We had stopped near a fence, where another guy was standing. I believed they were partners and that this second guy was going to take me the rest of the way—probably for another five dollars—or else beat me up if I wouldn't pay. I said, "Five dollars? Forget it!"

When I started to walk off, he grabbed a switchblade out of his pocket and whizzed it open. "Am I going to have to get tough with you?" he said, pointing the knife at me.

I pulled out a five-dollar bill and handed it over.

He left. I plodded on to the Newark sign, burning up inside.

When I reached the sign, which was next to a small bus building with an outdoor ticket counter, I didn't see any other sign pointing to LaGuardia. I walked up to the man behind the counter and asked, "Do you have a bus going to LaGuardia?"

"No, this bus goes to Newark."

"You mean to tell me I walked all this way for a bus to LaGuardia and I can't get to that airport?" By now, I did not want to walk back up the street to the bus station, so I asked him if I could call a taxi.

Fortunately he let me, and I went back to plan A—taking a taxi—after all. But my New York adventures weren't over. After a forty-five-minute wait, a tough-looking taxi driver pulled up and threw my suitcase in the trunk as I jumped in the backseat with my guitar and told him, "LaGuardia, please." He pulled out of there in a fury, but five minutes later he said, "I need some gas." He pulled in to a gas station, where he left the meter running!

I thought, *I sure must look like an easy target. I'm getting taken advantage of again.* I finally got to the airport and was relieved to be leaving New York.

To be honest, I dreaded the start of every tour, even my first one. But when I returned home, I always felt satisfied and fulfilled. Every tour was a new adventure, and although there were times when the accommodations were cold and creaky, the weather was depressing, or the food was bad, I also went places that were breathtakingly beautiful and played for people who were warm, hospitable, and appreciative. I knew early on that the vignettes of life on the road would be worth holding on to.

Another critical purpose of touring, according to Maestro Segovia, was to "burnish in" a new set of pieces in order to record them at the end of the season. So all roads eventually led back to the Capitol Records studio.

FISH TALE

The Casting Tournament

In my family, whatever we did, we pursued with a steadfast commitment to excellence. From a young age, I enjoyed the challenge of learning to fly cast for both distance and accuracy, making subtle changes in my hand position, learning to hold the rod at precisely the right angle, knowing just when to stop the rod's travel forward and how to control the flight of the line with the index finger against the side of the fly rod. On weekends, my dad, mom, Terry, and I went to the Santa Monica casting pool to practice.

However, it was at the Long Beach casting club that we met Jimmy Green, the international world champion fly caster and the designer for Fenwick Rods. He encouraged my dad and me to compete in tournaments when I was in my mid-teens.

In the beginning, I would have preferred to be fishing instead of tournament casting, but I soon realized that if I wanted to improve my fishing skills, I needed to be able to cast accurately at varying distances.

As I grew a little older, we started to compete earnestly, including the Western U.S. All-Around Casting Championships. The competition involved four distance casting events and a number of fly-, bait-, and spin-casting accuracy events. To demonstrate accuracy, we cast into thirty-inch-diameter metal rings at various distances. Each contestant started with a perfect score of one hundred, and a judge wearing hip-boot waders stood in the casting pool to measure the distance from the target to where the fly landed. For example, if the contestant missed by two feet, the judge deducted two points from the starting score of one hundred. In the distance events—steelhead fly, trout fly, and the $\frac{3}{8}$- and $\frac{5}{8}$-ounce spinning plugs—the distances cast in all four events were totaled.

In 1966 my dad won the Western U.S. All-Around Championship. The next year, we both competed at an indoor sports arena in Oakland. This time we were up against our coach, Jimmy Green, and the top casters in the western United States. I had won the trout fly accuracy event and a couple of others, and much to my surprise, the all-around championship came down to one last event, the $\frac{5}{8}$-ounce plug accuracy. The only two casters left were the current world champion and me.

I waited beside the casting pool with hundreds of people standing along both sides of it. We both cast into ten rings. He went first and cast well. I knew the score I had to beat.

I started out all right—nervous but focused. Cast by cast, I stayed within his score. In the end, it all came down to my final cast. If I could put the plug in the center of the ring, I would be the champion.

I remember the cast. The plug flew straight toward the final ring, but I could see that I'd sent it in a dangerously low arc. If I hardly used any pressure at all with my thumb against the spool of the reel, I might make it to that distance. But without applying a little pressure, the line was dangerously close to backlashing.

The cast flew like a bullet through the center of the ring, and I can still picture my dad jumping high in the air with both hands raised as the audience erupted with applause.

I received the champion's trophy, a beautiful new reel, and two tickets to Las Vegas. I never took the trip, but I put line on the reel, and it's still in its original presentation case, on a shelf over my desk.

7

Quest for Excellence

1969–71

Even after preparing a concert program, taking it on tour, and living with it for almost a year, the thought of bringing it into a studio to set it down permanently was still daunting.

My third recording for Capitol Records, *Romanza*, would include several pieces I had been playing on my current tour: "Romance" as arranged by Jack Marshall, Castelnuovo-Tedesco's tender "Melancholia," the Albéniz "Rumores de la Caleta," and several pieces by the Brazilian composer Heitor Villa-Lobos, among others.

Until now, my recording producer had been Dick Jones, who had been assigned to me by Angel Records. Dick retired, and a woman named Patti Laursen was asked to produce *Romanza*. Patti had been working in the Angel Records office and was extremely knowledgeable about classical music. We got along well from the start. She advised me whenever I needed help choosing repertoire to record, and she had a knack for making the process easier. We did many albums together over two decades, and Patti had a keen, observant ear. She was the one, in fact, who suggested that we do an all-Bach album. We worked together to come up with Bach pieces that fit the classical guitar. I learned early on to trust her judgment, especially when it came to choosing album tracks.

The other change in the booth came when Carson Taylor retired and Bob Norberg took over as my engineer. Bob and Patti also seemed to understand the importance of creating a quality recording. We always worked within a rigid time limit, so when I arrived at the studio I needed to be ready to render a recording-quality performance in just a few takes. Occasionally, however, if I told Patti, "I know we've got this piece technically clean, but I think I have something musically better left in me," she always gave me the extra time I needed to produce a recording I felt good about.

With each new recording, we worked hard and made many small adjustments to obtain the best sound quality we could.

Keeping the guitar strings from squeaking was a constant struggle. Even after we sanded the bass strings, they often would start to squeak a little as I played. Patti was the one to notice that whenever I washed my hands, the next few takes were noiseless. Apparently, the warm water softened my fingertips and greatly reduced the left-hand string noise. So Patti bought a small cooler and brought it to the next recording session. She ran hot water into it and set it on the floor on my left side with a towel. I periodically dunked my fingertips into the warm water to soften them and dried them on the towel, which resulted in noiseless playing.

I always wore a turtleneck for recording so that no buttons

would buzz on the back of the instrument. Also, I used a piano bench to sit on, and since several of Capitol's piano benches squeaked if I moved, we always made sure to use a particular bench that was quiet.

When I was recording Bach's difficult Prelude and Allegro we ran into another problem: My guitar kept sliding on my jeans. A few weeks earlier, I had found a piece of paraffin wax on the beach, rounded into shape—I assume—from a surfer using it to wax his surfboard. I discovered that if I rubbed the wax on my jeans wherever the guitar made contact, I could "cement" the instrument in place. That trick stabilized the guitar and improved the accuracy of my playing.

Not everything that went wrong in the studio was predictable. At Capitol Records, several recording studios were always in use at any given moment. Once I recorded right next door to a rock band that had cranked up their amps so loud that a low bass rumble came right through the sixteen-inch wall. The classical guitar is by nature a soft instrument, and if we were recording a particularly quiet passage, our mikes easily picked up that rumble. One of my sound engineers told me, in fact, that whenever he did a rock session, he used earplugs because the decibel level inside the studio could be as loud as a 747 airplane taking off, and he couldn't afford ear damage. A few times, Patti had to walk next door and politely ask the other recording producer to lower the volume a little since it was bleeding into our track.

Another time, I was in the middle of a good take during a soft passage when, to my surprise, I felt the suction and heard the *whoosh* of the outer door being opened. Then came a second and louder whooshing sound, and when I looked up, a janitor was backing into the studio, mopping the floor as he went. I don't know how he missed the large, red "recording" light outside, but when he raised his head and looked up, he was obviously horrified. Up in the booth, Patti and Bob stood and craned their necks to see what was going on. The only thing we could do was stop the tape and start again.

❦ ❦ ❦

Though my parents had settled in Idaho, my sister, Terry, was still in the LA area, working hard to build a career in modeling and acting. I saw her from time to time, but I wished for her sake that Mom lived a little closer since I was gone so often.

In 1969, when I was playing in Chicago, I gave Jim Sherry a call. At the time, I was playing a 1964 spruce-top José Ramírez guitar that I had picked out of twelve at a store in Los Angeles. Andrés Segovia played a Ramírez guitar on his concert tours, and Jim was now the exclusive distributor of these instruments in the United States. Jim invited me to come see his warehouse.

I felt like a kid in a candy store. There were guitars up and down the aisles, guitars piled so high and so close I could barely walk between them, stacks and stacks of beautiful Ramírez guitars. Jim said I could play as many as I wanted and select my favorite.

I must have played three hundred instruments over the course of three days. Jim would set one in front of me, I'd tune it quickly and then play it. I knew what sound I was looking for, so sometimes it took less than twenty seconds to decide whether an instrument was concert quality.

I picked up each guitar with a sense of excited anticipation. Nearly all these instruments had a nice-sounding bass, but the highest string usually carries the melody, so it was the treble that interested me. Jim told me that Segovia tested guitars the same way, playing down the first string fret by fret to see if each note "sang." There could be no dead notes. The first string also revealed the quality or character of the instrument's sound. Sometimes the sound was on the nasal side, or too bright or tinny. I immediately rejected those. I was looking for a warm, beautiful, rich tone. If I found something that sounded particularly nice, I set it aside to look at it again.

When I'd narrowed three hundred instruments down to about fifteen "gems," I started to play them longer. I used five pieces, playing the same passage on two or more guitars back to back. One of the passages was the beautiful middle section of Prelude no. 3 by Villa-Lobos, which has a high melody and is a great test for the first and second strings. I then reduced the group to four or five instruments. As I played them, they started to warm up and sound richer.

Finally, on the last day, I settled on one particular instrument. At that point, Jim said, "Okay. Now, I'm going to show you the ten guitars that I have set aside to show Andrés Segovia when he comes into town to play Orchestra Hall next week."

After three days, I was now going to see the good stash?

Jim explained. He'd had me do all that work in case he'd missed a great instrument—and he did, by the way, carefully label those instruments I liked. Each one got a little "Parkening" tag on it. That way he could find them again.

The "Segovia group" of instruments all had black velvet ribbons tied around their heads, near the tuning pegs. Two guitars from this group were phenomenal, even to look at. The dark cedar tops had a rich, tight grain, with cross grain visible everywhere, and the Brazilian rosewood on their backs and sides was stunning. Although Jim had a very good ear, he probably picked them as much for the way they looked as the fact that they sounded fabulous. I had picked only one out of three hundred guitars in the other group as outstanding. From Segovia's group, I chose two out of ten.

"I can't sell any of these three best to you yet," Jim said. "I promised Maestro Segovia first pick, and he'll be in Chicago next week."

Though I was disappointed, I said, "Of course." I did rate them—best, second, and third. Two had been built in 1966, and one was labeled 1967.

Back at home, I waited nervously to see which one Segovia would select. When Jim called the next week, he said, "Well . . . I have some good news and some bad news. The bad news is that he picked your favorites, in exactly that order."

Andrés Segovia had evaluated the guitars the same way I had, which meant that he probably would end up buying the one I liked the best.

"The good news," Jim said, "is that he also said all the instruments were too much like the guitar he's already playing on tour. It wasn't necessary for him to get another one." While I was still thinking that over, Jim added, "And I have some more good news. I'm going to *give* you your choice of one of these instruments."

I thanked him profusely and asked him if—since I had gone through so much effort to find the other instruments—I could purchase the other two. He agreed, and I ended up with three wonderful instruments.

In the 1960s, each Ramírez guitar was initialed on the inside by the luthier who had crafted the instrument. Two of these instruments were initialed "MT," which—I learned years later— indicated that they were made by Mariano Tezanos Castro, the legendary luthier who built most of the Ramírez guitars that Segovia played. My 1967 MT was the instrument that I had selected out of the three hundred. I used that one to record *Parkening Plays Bach*, and even today I call it the "Bach Guitar." My "Recording Guitar" is the 1966 MT, and the "Tap Plate" is also a 1967, but it has no initials inside. When I took it on tour, I put a tap plate—a thin, protective plastic shield—on its face to protect it from scratches, then took it off again for recording.

I consider the "Recording Guitar" to be my best instrument, and I never tour with it. One risk is airline damage, and another is overuse. Years ago, Segovia told me that unlike a violin or a cello, a guitar has a life of about fifty years. I determined that it isn't the age of the instrument but the use—the mileage—that causes it to degenerate. So even today, unless I'm in a recording studio, the strings on this guitar get tuned down until they're loose, and the guitar is stored in a safe place. When I flew to London to record with the Royal Philharmonic, the recording company purchased a ticket for my guitar, and it traveled beside me as "Guitar Parkening," with its own seat.

I have other instruments that I use for touring, also beautiful guitars, which are particularly loud and perfect for the concert hall, and a couple of inexpensive instruments that I can take on vacation or use for teaching.

I continued to teach at USC between tours, conducting master classes about once a month in a large rehearsal room where music students who weren't guitar majors could come to watch as auditors. When I was on the road, my teaching assistants gave weekly lessons.

At that time, to my knowledge, there was no modern guitar method book available by a concert guitarist, so Jim Sherry suggested that I write one. "Include some of the techniques you learned from Segovia," he recommended.

I contacted Jack Marshall, who was still playing, composing, and recording in LA, and asked if he would help me. Specifically, I wanted him to compose and arrange some short pieces that would take guitarists through a progression of techniques, instead of having them repeat the effective—but musically dull—exercises that had taken up so many hours of my childhood. I had always been far more motivated to learn a new technique whenever that meant playing a piece of music rather than an exercise or study. Even today I often use a challenging section from performance repertoire to practice a certain technique.

That was the premise of *The Christopher Parkening Guitar Method, Volume I*. Jack was living in Newport Beach, California, and I drove down from LA on weekends to work on the book. We would spread manuscripts all over the table and floor. One thing I particularly tried to communicate in the book was how to get a beautiful sound, using both the shaped fingernail and the flesh of the fingertip. When properly played, the guitar is one of the most beautiful, sensitive, and poetic instruments. Our publisher asked for pictures and illustrations wherever it was easier to communicate an idea with a drawing, so we hired illustrators to draw some pictures and a Capitol Records photographer to take model shots of the sitting positions—showing the right angle to hold the guitar. My sister, Terry, and my cousin Melanie sat for some of the pictures.

When I wasn't touring, recording, or putting in extra hours on the method book, I could usually be found in a small room at my grandmother's old house, writing out fingerings for a guitar arrangement or practicing a new piece.

Whenever Segovia played in Los Angeles, I attended his concerts, and occasionally I had the opportunity to spend some time with him afterward. Once when we were having lunch, I was caught off guard when he reprimanded me for continuing to play a few flamenco pieces in concert. "You must not do this," he said. "I have spent my lifetime redeeming the guitar! Classical and flamenco are two different sides of a mountain, and they do not look at one another." As a result, I stopped playing flamenco music. (See page 241.)

Another time, I asked him, "Maestro, may I ask you how many hours a day you practice?"

"Five hours," he said, which amazed me. *If Segovia needs to practice five hours a day, how many more should I?* I wondered. Some nights the light in my studio burned past midnight. Now I was on a quest, struggling alone to achieve the finest tone and interpretation I could. At twenty-three, I had only seven years to reach my goal of retiring at thirty.

Until then, I couldn't rest. Another tour took me to the Northeast. Because I was preparing material for my Bach album, I had included Bach's "Jesu, Joy of Man's Desiring," transcribed for the guitar by Rick Foster, on the program. Rick was living in Connecticut at the time and teaching at a neighborhood guitar shop, where he had a student by the name of Hunter Mallory. Hunter had offered to drive the three of us on a sweep of four or five concerts in the Northeast, and I gladly accepted. It is always more enjoyable to travel with friends.

At each concert, I made it a practice to introduce Rick prior to playing his transcription of "Jesu." He always stood up, acknowledged the introduction with a mannerly wave, and sat down.

At one concert, however, Hunter and Rick switched places as a practical joke. I knew where they were supposed to be sitting, and when I made my standard speech, ending with, "Would Rick Foster please stand up," I got a shock. Hunter Mallory shot up and spun around, waving both hands, then he clasped his hands together and pumped the air over his head. The audience applauded, and I sat back down on my bench, trying not to laugh. I looked down at the guitar, set my hands in place to start playing the piece, and almost broke out in laughter. It was all I could do to finish the piece. I kept getting flashbacks of Hunter acting as if he'd won the world heavyweight championship, and all through the piece I would smile and then get serious again, almost laugh and then struggle to get my concentration back.

Hunter and I became longtime friends. Whenever I played in the Northeast, Hunter volunteered to drive me on part of my tour, which was always a great relief.

FISH TALE

Trial and Error

My family attended a fly-fishing exhibition one year at the Pasadena Casting Club, and we were able to watch John Tarantino in action. He had set all the fly-casting world records for distance, and his casts were amazing to watch.

After the exhibition was over, a crowd gathered beside the casting pool. I walked up to him and asked, "Mr. Tarantino, how did you break the world record?"

He looked down at me, and I got the impression that he was tired of answering questions—especially from kids—but he said, "I tried two thousand combinations of rods and lines, and only two of them worked."

I was shocked. That meant 1,998 combinations weren't good enough. He hadn't been able to set his records until he found the perfect combination. What perseverance!

He may not have realized it, but John Tarantino gave me a great piece of advice that day: Whether it's fishing or playing the guitar, if you want to improve, you have to keep experimenting until you get it exactly right.

Touring Machine

1971–73

Segovia used to say that he could sense the round-
ness of the globe when he traveled high above the
earth, and I began to understand what he meant. By
this point in my career, I felt like a touring machine.
My life was a series of nonstop performances, with
only the occasional fishing trip to break up the
relentless pace. Each year my number of bookings
increased, and at nearly ninety concerts a year, I felt
that I was being pushed to my absolute maximum.
But I was willing to persevere if it meant that I could
retire early.

In 1971, conductor Zubin Mehta and the Los
Angeles Philharmonic were asked to do an unusual
TV program called *The Switched On Symphony*,
which would include psychedelic light shows,

dancers, rock musicians, and classical soloists with the Los Angeles Philharmonic. The program featured Ray Charles, Carlos Santana, Jethro Tull, and other bands and soloists. I was invited to play the beautiful second movement of Joaquín Rodrigo's *Concierto de Aranjuez*, probably the most famous piece written for classical guitar and orchestra.

The program was taped at NBC studios, and my segment was to begin at 9 p.m. I went into the studio early with my dad, who was in from Idaho to finish up some real estate business. Because the show was so complicated, filming was running well behind schedule. The director told me I would now be rescheduled to perform at 3 a.m. We went home and tried to sleep a little, which didn't work, since I knew I was going to have to get up in two hours and play on national TV.

We returned to the studio bleary eyed at about two o'clock in the morning, and I warmed up again. Right before my piece, they filmed a wild medley that featured Carlos Santana with full orchestra.

At 3 a.m. they set me up to perform. I felt drained, even though I hadn't played yet. "We only have time for one take," I was told, and that's what we did. I was seated so far away from the conductor—a good seventy or eighty feet—that they stuck an earpiece in my ear so there would be no time delay between the orchestra and the guitar. A group of Spanish-costumed dancers performed while we played, dancing between the orchestra and me. The whole thing felt bizarre, playing with whirling dancers behind me, and I was grateful to get home and go to sleep. I couldn't imagine what the orchestra musicians must have felt like.

It's amusing to watch that film now. The program was sponsored by Bell Telephone, and during one commercial, the claim is made that "one day, we will make a telephone you can put in your pocket." At the time, that sounded like science fiction.

At one concert at Ambassador Auditorium in Pasadena, after recently having seen the movie *Butch Cassidy and the Sundance Kid*, I was backstage, waiting to perform. A stagehand stood by, ready to open the stage door for the concert. He turned to me and said, "Mr. Parkening, I just wanted you to know that Paul Newman and Joanne Woodward are in the second row." As I walked out onto the stage, I amused myself by thinking, *I'm about to play for Butch Cassidy!*

Touring kept me away from home for much of the year. In 1972, my fall itinerary listed twenty-three concerts in twelve states, including El Dorado, Kansas, my mother's hometown. She flew to El Dorado to watch me in concert there, and afterward she took me on an enjoyable tour of the places she used to live.

But before I had time to blink, I was off to six more states. Any travel agency that sent tourists on an itinerary like that would go out of business. For me, though, it was simply another step toward my goal. That year I played my solo debut recital at Lincoln Center in New York City. By this time, I had learned a lot about touring. After playing a program three or four times, I started to get into a groove and play it confidently.

Columbia Artists Management had created a wonderful series for audiences in smaller towns. Each city's presenter booked several performers to create a "Community Concerts" series, which they could sell at a price families could afford. People who came to a Community Concert sometimes hadn't had much exposure to classical concerts. Other performers in the series included a tenor, a dance troupe, and a string quartet. I enjoyed the opportunity to introduce people to the classical guitar, and I was able to get a perspective on the country that I never would have gained otherwise.

Because I grew up in Los Angeles, I wasn't as intimidated by Chicago, Philadelphia, or New York as I might have been had I been born in a small town. I also came to appreciate Southern California weather. For the first time, I experienced the changing of the seasons—and true winter.

In Minneapolis, it snowed hard throughout the day of my concert, and the presenter telephoned me several times at my hotel. Canceling concerts is a tough call, and we kept in touch all morning, agreeing he would have to make a decision by 2 p.m. I sat in my room, waiting for his call, constantly checking the weather and the airport's status, and coming to the realization that this storm was becoming hazardous. The presenter called at 2 p.m. and said, "We have to cancel. I've already started getting the word out on radio and local TV." He promised me that he would reschedule the concert, and since the airport hadn't closed yet, I decided to try to fly back to Los Angeles.

Mine was one of the last flights out. The snow was piling up deep as snowplows ran back and forth, clearing the tarmac. Unfortunately, I couldn't convince the airline people at the check-in desk to let me carry my valuable guitar with me on board. I had to check it as baggage.

Takeoff was delayed nearly two hours, and when I finally deplaned in Los Angeles about five hours later, I hurried to the baggage claim area to search for my guitar in the jumble of bags descending the baggage ramp. I lifted the guitar off the carousel, and it felt much too cold—even damp with condensation. It instantly occurred to me that perhaps the instrument had been put in a luggage compartment that wasn't heated or pressurized. It was obvious from the condensation that it had been very cold. When I spotted a big black mark on the case, my stomach rose into my throat. There in the busy LA terminal, late at night, with people milling around, I anxiously carried the case over to a quiet corner, set it down on the floor, and opened it up.

I started fishing even before I picked up the guitar. This photograph is of me at age six, learning to cast at the Santa Monica casting pool, with a "bird's nest" tangle in the line. (page 80)

Practicing on the porch of our cabin during a family vacation at Hot Creek Ranch, age eleven (page 12)

First Guitar Piece
Learned by Christopher at his first lesson (age 11) with Celedonio Romero

Composer Unknown

I learned this piece at my first guitar lesson. (page 16)

Nail braces I wore as a boy to try to reshape my nails so I could play faster (page 28)

After my appearance on *The Tonight Show* in 1964 at age sixteen, with Elmer Bernstein, Steve Allen, and Johnny Green (page 44)

Performing at Andrés Segovia's master class, Winston-Salem, North Carolina, age seventeen (page 58)

A pat on the cheek from Andrés Segovia after my first concert during the Segovia Competition in Santiago de Compostela, Spain, 1968 (page 72)

My father's daily
instructions for
practicing my guitar
(page 19)

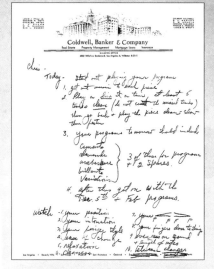

Dad and I display a big
steelhead caught on the
Clearwater River in Idaho.

A more recent picture of
my parents, Betty and Duke
Parkening, on their ranch in
Idaho (page 75)

My pet mountain lion,
Miss Montana
(page 142)

My dad, Ken Peterson, and I ran for
our lives during a close encounter
with a train on this railroad bridge
over the Deschutes River in Oregon.
(page 120)

Photo courtesy Oregon State Archives, State Marine
Board, OMB0040.

A 136 ½ pound tarpon I caught
during the Gold Cup Tarpon
Tournament, Islamorada, Florida,
June 1987. I went on to win the Cup.
(page 229)

A six-pound brown trout, caught
and released, High Sierras,
California, 1988

With renowned American composer Aaron Copland, as he played some of his compositions for possible adaptation for classical guitar, 1971 (page 188)

Recording *The Sounds of Christmas* with Julie Andrews, 1990 (page 195)

Benny Goodman visited my Montana home in 1980, where I took him fly-fishing. He practiced his clarinet every morning in the living room.

Working with legendary film composer John Williams on guitar solos for the *Stepmom* soundtrack (page 186)

With President Reagan after a concert on the South Lawn of the White House in June 1988 (page 190)

Recording in Hollywood at Capitol Records, Studio A, early in my career (page 64)

With composer Joaquín Rodrigo after performing two of his concertos with the Royal Philharmonic Orchestra, Andrew Litton conducting, Royal Festival Hall, London, 1991 (page 201)

Recording Elmer Bernstein's Concerto for Guitar and Orchestra with the London Symphony Orchestra at the historic Abbey Road Studios, Bernstein conducting, 1999
(page 221)

With recording producer David Thomas, composer Elmer Bernstein, and arranger Patrick Russ at Abbey Road Studios, London, 1999
(page 221)

With Andrés Segovia
and my sister, Terry, after
Segovia's Los Angeles
Music Center concert, 1971
(page 105)

At the CBS Grammy telecast performance in 1986. I accepted a
Lifetime Achievement Award on behalf of Andrés Segovia. (page 184)

At the 1987 Grammy telecast
performance with Kathleen Battle.
Our EMI recording, *Pleasures of
Their Company*, was nominated for
Best Classical Album. (page 184)

Performing the *Capriol Suite* with the
Academy of St. Martin in the Fields,
Los Angeles, California, 1993

I took this photo after I had played one of Theresa's favorite pieces as a surprise on the beach at sunset. I handed her my guitar and asked her to play something for me! (page 216)

On my first date with Theresa in 1997, we caught and released this big tarpon in Florida. (page 214)

With Theresa on our wedding day (page 217)

Teaching my son, Luke, the basics (page 238)

Wearing his green boots, Luke, age sixteen months, learns to fly cast at our cabin in the High Sierras. (page 238)

Carefully I pulled the instrument out of its snug case. It was freezing cold. The top looked fine, so I flipped it over, looked at the back, and ran my hands around the lower side. When I felt a damaged, pushed-in area—a definite split in the wood—along the lower side of the beautiful 1967 MT José Ramírez guitar, I felt sick. The damage was precisely at the location of a latch on the case's exterior, which made it easy to figure out what had happened. My guitar had been dropped from a pretty substantial height, maybe the top of the baggage conveyor, and had landed perfectly on the latch.

It's the only time I've ever had an instrument damaged. I found someone who could repair it, but I've never forgotten the horrible feeling I had that night. Later I showed the case maker what had happened. He agreed that the latch had absorbed all the force of the blow, pushing the case in and cracking the bottom side of the instrument. He made a permanent change to his cases after my sad experience, adding bumpers on each side of that latch.

I was still renting my grandmother's house in North Hollywood from my parents, and whenever recording or playing a concert took me back to LA, I stayed there. I had also purchased some property next to my father's ranch in Idaho.

❧ ❧ ❧

My dad had heard that there was great fly-fishing in southwest Montana, so one summer when I was young, instead of spending our vacation at Hot Creek Ranch, we drove from Los Angeles all the way to Hebgen Lake in Montana. Dad booked a ten-day reservation at a ranch where he'd heard the owner was an avid fly fisherman. We towed a boat behind us. Back then, it was a three-day drive.

It turned out this wasn't just a fly-fishing ranch. It was a dude ranch—all about horseback riding, hiking, and swimming, with a little bit of fishing on the side. Everyone sat down for meals together at a table, did "cowboy" activities, and sang camp songs. Unfortunately, there just wasn't enough fishing.

We left after three days and went out on our own. At a tackle shop in West Yellowstone, the nearest town, some fly fishermen directed us to the Madison River. It was there that Dad caught the biggest trout we'd ever seen, a five-pound brown trout that he had mounted. We also drove to Yellowstone Park and saw Old Faithful. The geysers intrigued me, and so did the bears, but the thing that struck me the most was the fishing. Embedded in my mind was the idea that Montana had "the greatest trout fishing in the United States." *Someday,* I thought, *I must come back.*

ॐ ॐ ॐ

From my parents' home base in Idaho, whenever I could take an extended break, we went searching for the perfect, Hot Creek–type ranch and trout stream in Montana. We started out by driving over from Idaho and contacting a few real estate brokers. Most of them didn't know much about fly-fishing. They'd hear "fishing" and show us a piece of land on a big river where anyone could fish or on a rushing, rocky mountain creek. I wanted solitude and privacy—a placid stream meandering through a meadow, mostly fed by springs, but maybe also by some snow water, where there were trout everywhere, rising to feed on the surface.

We consulted some knowledgeable fly fishermen, and a friend of my dad's knew the designer of Winston Rods, a wonderful fly fisherman who lived in Montana. "Tom can find the perfect ranch for you," he said.

Tom, a fly-fishing guide, knew every stream and river in the southwest part of the state. When I described the kind of stream I wanted, he knew exactly what I meant. We started a systematic search that took me back to Montana a number of times.

Among the places we looked was a spot near Livingston that included two great spring creeks. They were on opposite sides of the Yellowstone River, and they had phenomenal fishing. The water was so pure and clean that it was almost like a trout hatchery. My dad casually asked the owner's wife if they had ever been offered a quarter of a million dollars in cash for this place.

"No, we haven't," she answered. "But we've been offered a million." So we figured the place was not for sale.

Six months later, Tom told us about a 150-acre ranch, nestled among larger ranches, about twenty miles west of Bozeman, on two spring-type creeks. He said, "I have caught many large trout in that stream. This may be the perfect ranch for you." He gave us directions and said he would meet us there.

I couldn't wait to head back to Montana. Full of anticipation and excitement, Dad and I drove down a dirt road and pulled across a narrow bridge, where the ranch spread out below us, nestled in a little valley. It was full of tall cottonwood trees, with a stream that meandered through the meadow—exactly what I was looking for. We didn't even bother to walk into the small, yellow house on the property until we were almost ready to leave. The real estate agent explained that the home didn't have indoor plumbing, just an outhouse in the back and a spring at the edge of the bluff that the owners used for drinking water. He apologized for the condition of the yellow house and the run-down barn with wood darkened by age.

The house and barn didn't matter. I had found my Montana Hot Creek! I made an offer and bought the property immediately.

Just knowing I owned that place helped me maintain my pace over the next six years. While I was on the road, my dad drove over from Idaho several times to start fixing up the yellow house. As a special gift to me, he re-covered the seat of an old, solid rocking chair that had been in the house. My mom bought more furniture in the nearby town of Belgrade. We built a screened-in front porch, dug a well, and added indoor plumbing. It was going to be my "summer getaway" between touring seasons.

ఒఫ్ ఒఫ్ ఒఫ్

On a trip to Nashville, where I was to play with the Nashville Symphony, four or five local guitarists picked me up at the airport and threw my bag in the back. As I watched the city passing outside the car windows on the way to the hotel, I said, "Someday I'd love to meet Chet Atkins."

The driver slammed on his brakes in front of a pay phone booth and said, "I know Chet. I'm going to call him and see if we can come over."

"Oh, don't bother him," I said. But he insisted.

When he walked back to the car, he had a big smile on his face. "Guess what. He wants to see us right now." I hadn't even checked into my hotel yet!

We drove straight to Chet's home, where he welcomed us warmly and took us down into the basement to see his state-of-the-art recording studio. He was then the head of RCA in Nashville, and he made his recordings at home.

Chet said to us, "If you'd like to hear the sound in the studio, I'll record you. Each of you can play something." There weren't enough chairs for all of us in the recording area, so some of us sat on the carpeted floor, cross-legged, and we took turns getting up to sit in front of the microphone. Chet called each take from inside his control room. I was about the fourth one to play, and I remember feeling the pressure not only of playing for Chet Atkins for the first time, but also of having it recorded!

Everyone called Chet Atkins a gentleman, and I will vouch for that description. He was cordial and kind to all of us that evening. As we walked back upstairs, I said, "Chet, I'd like to tell you a story that happened to me a few years ago at Fort Benning, Georgia, when I was in basic training."

I told Chet and his wife and all the guitarists my story about getting ready for the base's talent show, concluding with the sergeant's flat statement that Chet Atkins, *not* Segovia, was the greatest "picker" in the world. Chet laughed and took me over to a framed picture that hung on his wall. In it, he and Segovia stood side by side, and the maestro had his arm around Chet's shoulders. Chet chuckled and said, "This was before he knew I played electric guitar!"

For the 1972–73 season, I received so many requests for bookings that although I wanted to play as much as possible, I simply couldn't do them all. We had to turn down more than fifty concert dates. Still trying to emulate Segovia, I continued to transcribe music and ask other gifted musicians to transcribe classical pieces that would fit well on the guitar. I relied heavily on Jack Marshall during those years. When I heard a piece that sounded like it would be beautiful on the guitar, he was the first person I called.

In 1972 I was scheduled to tour Japan; since Jim Sherry had import business there, he came with me. It was a long flight—close to twelve hours—with a horrendous, sixteen-hour time change. As we came through the clouds, I saw for the first time Tokyo's skyscrapers with their neon-lit Japanese characters. I suddenly had the lonely realization that I was on the other side of the world, about to enter a culture totally unfamiliar to me.

Because of the time change, I was awake at about 3 a.m. the first night in Tokyo, so I got out my guitar and started playing softly.

There was pounding on the wall.

Oh, no. I had awakened or disturbed a hotel guest. I played softer, thinking, *This is no louder than a very soft TV.*

The telephone rang. I picked it up. A voice on the other end was shouting in what sounded like broken Japanese/English, presumably berating me for waking him up and playing my guitar too loudly.

"I'm very sorry," I said, and I put the guitar in the case.

Then the phone rang again. It was Jim Sherry, who couldn't sleep either, and confessed that he had pretended to be the irate neighbor. Jim's prank actually relaxed me by reminding me that someone I knew was in this strange city with me.

Performing almost every day for two weeks, I found the Japanese people to be friendly and appreciative of classical music. During concerts, they were quiet, reserved, and very respectful. There wasn't the coughing or other extraneous noise of typical American audiences. At the end, if they wanted to show special appreciation, they stamped their feet in unison.

Jim and I went to some nice restaurants, often eating with only chopsticks and removing our shoes to eat sitting on the floor. Between concerts, we visited guitar makers. One famous Japanese maker, Kohno, let me test-play some of his better instruments so Jim could hear them. We also went to the Yamaha guitar factory to play some of their higher-end guitars.

Touring in Japan gave me a new perspective on what a Spanish-born guitarist, such as Segovia, must have experienced as he traveled around the world. I thought back to one of his concerts I had attended in the early 1970s. The Los Angeles Music Center had just been built, so it was considered the premier place in LA to give a solo recital. Naturally, Segovia played there. I remembered how the audience had seemed especially restless that night, coughing, fidgeting, and moving in their seats. Apparently some people were more interested in seeing the new Music Center than in hearing Segovia play.

I was sitting close to the front, and I knew his mannerisms well enough to realize that he was being disturbed. Segovia always refused to use a microphone, even in a large hall. Sound systems weren't nearly as good then as they are today, and Segovia didn't trust them to reproduce the beauty of the guitar's natural sound. Consequently, he demanded silence when he played. In New York they called this the "Segovia hush," a silence so deep and attentive that three thousand people could hear him clearly. One cough could literally obliterate a phrase.

That night at the Music Center, Segovia would play a few phrases, and there'd be a cough. He would look out into the audience, as if to let everyone know it was disturbing him. Sadly, it didn't have any effect on the audience. The coughing continued.

Finally, he stamped his foot on the stage and stopped in the middle of a piece. He reached into his left pocket and pulled out a handkerchief, and in his thick Spanish accent, he said, "Eet is disturbing to me, and eet is disturbing to the listener. When you have a cough, you do thees." He brought the handkerchief in front of his mouth and coughed into it. The audience applauded and cheered, and then he continued to play. This time there was total silence.

Coughing is just one of the things that can distract a performer. Sometimes a door slams. Another stage door might be left wide open so that a gale of wind blows across the stage. I've had someone yell out a political statement in the middle of a concert. Sometimes the light isn't what I'd expected, and it's hard to see the fingerboard in the near darkness. I've experienced electrical failures and fire alarms during concerts, but as every performer knows, "the show must go on."

FISH TALE

Sink or swim

One summer afternoon I was fishing on the Middle Fork of Idaho's Clearwater River. I decided to cross the river and move upstream where I thought I might be able to catch some cutthroat trout on a dry fly.

Whenever I fished this river with my dad, we wore buoyant wet suits and flotation jackets. I had my certificate in scuba diving, and my dad and I had discovered that in heavy-duty wet suits we didn't have to limit our fishing to only the places we could get to with waders. The wet suits kept us warm, and we could wade rapids or swim to spots where nobody had ever cast a fly on the Clearwater. This greatly improved our chances for catching steelhead, because we were fishing virgin territory—uncharted waters where the fish weren't wary. The excitement with each cast made all the extra effort of getting there worthwhile.

On this warm summer day, however, I went without the wet suit. I simply put on some heavy wading shoes, stuck some dry flies and leader material in the snap-flap pocket of a short-sleeved cowboy shirt, and waded wet.

I spotted a beautiful, wide pool, so deep it was a dark blue-green. It looked to me as though it would be great fishing if I could swim to the other side. Far downstream, a big beaver dam jutted out into the water. I calculated that I could reach the other side about halfway between where I was standing and the beaver dam.

The pool was about two hundred feet across, and it deepened very quickly. Just fifteen feet from the bank, the water was over my head, and I started to sidestroke, holding my fly rod up with my left hand, dunking the reel with each stroke.

I soon realized that I wasn't making much progress. Although I was in good shape and I should have had the stamina to swim across the river, my legs and arms were starting to cramp as I neared the center of the pool. *This is ridiculous!* I thought. *My arms are getting tired, and I'm only halfway! What's going on here?*

Then I realized I had never swum across such a big river without the added buoyancy of a wet suit.

The current was slowly taking me downstream, and I was fighting against it. Finally, I didn't have any more strength, and I wasn't sure if I could make it. I felt as if I couldn't keep going.

Instantly, fear started to well up inside me. I thought about dropping my expensive fly rod and the Hardy Perfect steelhead fly reel that my father had given me, imported from England, and about what he would say if I came back without them. So I held on, and in retrospect, I think that actually might have helped me because protecting the rod and reel kept me from panicking—and then flailing and wasting valuable energy.

Five strokes, I told myself. I knew I could take just five strokes. I stroked and then let myself sink about three feet, which gave my arms and body a chance to rest. I watched the surface of the water go up and up. I remember thinking, *This is how people drown.* The greenish blue water was almost perfectly clear, and my bubbles floated up and away to the shimmering, reflective surface. Four or five more times, I struggled to the surface, stroked a little, quit in total exhaustion, and watched the surface of the water drift up again. Little by little, the other shore came closer.

Ahead, on the far side of the river, I saw the huge beaver dam jutting partway out into the current, with jagged, gnawed-off sticks and pieces of small logs poking out everywhere. In a wet suit, I would have avoided it. Now, I realized that if I was going to make it at all, I would have to crawl out on the sticks and rubble. I wondered if beavers bite.

The current was moving so quickly I almost swept past it, but I grabbed hold of part of the dam, still gripping the rod in my left hand, and then just hung there for a moment, relishing the fact that I could keep my head above water and that my sore muscles and aching, tired body could finally stop and rest. I grabbed whatever I could hold on to, with the current still trying to pull me off, until I gathered enough strength to climb up onto the pile of sticks.

They kept breaking off as I struggled to hold on and put my knee against them, and the jagged sticks hurt through my jeans. It felt as if I were crawling up onto a pincushion. I was exhausted, shaky, and wobbly.

Finally, I made it to the riverbank. I tried to fish for about five minutes, but I was too preoccupied by my return trip. This time I walked downstream to shallower water, where I managed to make my way back across. Grateful to be alive, I thought about what had just happened, and I had a new respect for the Clearwater River, which I never attempted to swim again without a wet suit.

9

On the Road Again

1973–75

I went back to Japan in November 1973 for a festival honoring Joaquín Rodrigo. The great Spanish composer would be attending each concert with his wife, and I was honored to be asked to perform two of his famous guitar concertos, the *Concierto de Aranjuez* and the *Fantasía para un Gentilhombre*, with a major Japanese orchestra.

Besides those well-known concertos, he had recently written a new piece for the occasion, which I would premiere in Japan, titled "Pájaros de Primavera" or "The Birds of Spring." Again, I had the opportunity to study a piece with its composer for several days before the first performance. Throughout the Japanese tour, I was able to ask Rodrigo questions, which his wife translated. As we worked on his guitar concertos, he would play the orchestral part on the piano. Segovia had recorded the *Fantasía para un Gentilhombre* and made a number of changes to the guitar part, which I felt improved the piece. I asked Rodrigo what he thought about Segovia's changes, and with only one exception, he liked them all.

In the 1973–74 season, after Japan, my route sheet showed me playing several concerts in California and Washington state, making a stop in Wyoming, then traveling to Tennessee, upstate New York, Massachusetts, and Connecticut. Then I was to return to Lincoln Center in New York City, where I had debuted the previous year. I would turn thirty in three years, and dreams of retirement were still driving me, though the pressures of the road were taking their toll. My entire life revolved around the guitar.

After a nonstop flight from Los Angeles to Montreal, I checked into a large hotel. Tired, somewhat dazed from the trip, and wanting nothing more than to collapse onto the bed in exhaustion, I took my room key from the desk clerk, carried my bags and guitar to the elevator, and rode up to my room.

I'd gotten into the habit of rapidly unlocking and shoving the door wide open so I could slide my suitcase and guitar inside before it slammed shut. This time, as the door flew open, the door chain—which had been used to lock it from the inside—flew off. "My" room was already occupied! A shocked and embarrassed gentleman stood just inside, holding only a towel over himself. Apparently he had just gotten out of the shower. I hurriedly apologized, took all my bags and guitar back down to the front desk, and requested a room on another floor to avoid the embarrassment of another encounter with the same guest.

A few months later, when I was playing a three-concert series with the Toronto Symphony, I stayed on the twenty-seventh floor of a hotel, with a wonderful view of downtown Toronto. Generally, a soloist is scheduled to perform the first half of the concert before intermission. Since I was tired, I decided the second night not to stay backstage and listen to the entire concert again. I went back to the hotel at intermission, took off my uncomfortable white tie and tails, put on a jogging outfit and tennis shoes, and settled in to relax.

At about 9:30 p.m., I had just ordered some dinner and sat down when the hotel's fire alarm went off—a loud buzzer and a flashing light. I wasn't really worried, since this had happened more than once when I was touring. Always a false alarm, the buzzing usually stopped within a minute or so. So I figured this time it would do the same. I waited for a few minutes, but the alarm didn't stop. I opened my door, looked out, and saw some people from my floor making their way toward the stairs. Still, I wasn't concerned. *Ah, it's a false alarm.* I went back in and sat down.

After a few more minutes, with the alarm still sounding, I began to get slightly concerned. I opened the door once again. This time, I saw a light haze of smoke in the hallway.

My stomach turned, and I hurried back into my room. Far below, I heard sirens outside the hotel. I looked out the window and into the street. A number of fire engines were pulling up and surrounding the block.

I couldn't leave my valuable guitar in the room to be burned! I knew I'd have to take it with me. I quickly thought about the next night's concert. *I'll need my tails, my music—oh well, I'll throw it all in a mess in my suitcase.* I didn't want to have to buy all new necessities in the middle of a tour. The more I thought about leaving anything behind, the more I decided there wasn't anything I could spare. I figured I was strong enough to carry it all down twenty-seven flights of stairs. I flung open the closet, snatched my tails, and threw them into my suitcase, along with my heavy briefcase, music, and shaving kit. I grabbed the guitar with one hand and the overloaded suitcase in the other and ran to the stairs.

To my horror, I saw no one in the hall on this floor. Now I regretted those minutes I had spent packing. Would it cost me my life?

I moved into high gear, found the emergency stairwell, and jumped down three steps at a time, berating myself as I went, *How stupid to wait until the last minute to leave! Why did I have a room on the twenty-seventh floor?*

I ran down floor after floor, seeing absolutely no one, which cranked up my adrenaline to semipanic mode. At the seventh floor, the smoke was so thick I could not see the stairwell below me. I hit the brakes. Wondering if I was about to run down into open flames, I simply stood there, panting and heaving. I looked up and prayed, *Lord, I don't know what to do! Please give me wisdom. Should I go down through the smoke or retreat back up the stairs and risk being trapped?*

I suddenly heard two voices up above me. It sounded like a man and a woman, maybe two floors up. I yelled, "Are you guys headed down?"

They shouted, "Yes!" and I waited until they caught up. We didn't know whether we were the last ones out of the hotel, but we decided we had no choice but to go down.

I took a deep breath so I wouldn't have to inhale, and we ran down right into the smoke. Suddenly it cleared completely, and we met a group of firefighters in full gear running up the steps. As they passed us, we quickly asked, "What's going on?"

One of them said in a commanding voice, "Fire on the fifth floor. Go down to the lobby!"

We made it to the ground floor. The lobby was packed shoulder to shoulder, and through the lobby windows we saw fire engine lights flashing. There I stood in my jogging outfit and tennis shoes, holding my guitar and suitcase. Many of the other hotel guests were wearing even less formal clothes—terry cloth robes and sandals or a hodgepodge of whatever they had thrown on before rushing downstairs.

We weren't allowed to return to our rooms until midnight. When I arrived back in my room, my hands ached from carrying everything downstairs. So much for a relaxing evening!

๑๑ ๑๑ ๑๑

After one concert that season, a woman asked me an interesting question, one that I've been asked only once in nearly forty years of touring. "Mr. Parkening," she said, "have you played 'Jesu, Joy of Man's Desiring' as many as a hundred times?"

It took me a moment to think that through. I told her, "I think I would have to say yes. Even if I had only played it this season, one time in each performance, that would be nearly ninety times, to say nothing of the countless times I practiced it. Really, it would be more like in the thousands." Even though I have played that exquisite piece so many times, I still find it beautiful. Looking back over the years, I have thought about some other pieces I've played many times, and I calculated that I had played the famous *Concierto de Aranjuez* more than a thousand times in concert— again, to say nothing of countless repetitions while practicing. Thinking about that brings to mind a story I once heard, in which a woman told the famous pianist Arthur Rubinstein that "to play like you, I would give my life." To which Rubinstein replied, "Madam, I have."

As my 1973–74 concert season led up to the all-important Lincoln Center return (the subject of chapter one of this book), I felt a little like an athlete preparing for the Olympic Games. New York audiences are musically demanding, and Lincoln Center—though not the end of the tour—was my "finish line." New York is one of the most critical places in the world to play well, with its cultural and media spotlight, and the pressure of trying to equal or surpass my New York debut was almost overwhelming.

Lincoln Center is an impressive place that lives up to all expectations. A friend I was staying with in Connecticut drove me into the city and found a parking spot. I headed for my dressing room, pulled out my guitar, and—as I had previously requested—rehearsed onstage until the house doors were opened. I wanted to get used to the lights and the sounds of the hall. When I returned to my dressing room, I saw that I still had about forty-five minutes before start time. Due to the sold-out house, the stage manager had warned me that we would probably start the concert a few minutes late.

I practiced a little more, isolating some of the difficult passages, and tried to relax.

Eventually, the knock came on my door. "It's time, Mr. Parkening."

I followed the manager to the backstage area, where he turned to me and said, "Are you ready?"

The houselights grew dim and the stage lights brightened. After waiting a few seconds for the audience to settle down, the stage manager opened the thick door and I walked out. Lights glared in my face. I sat down, did a short tuning check, and started to play.

Several of my friends were there, but so were the critics and record executives, as well as the presenter for Lincoln Center, CAMI's management and booking staff for future concerts, and of course, other guitarists. I knew this had to be my best concert of the year. My reputation, my livelihood, and—to some extent—my sense of self-worth depended on my ability to live up to everyone's expectations.

Afterward, though it was one of the best concerts I had yet played, I felt no satisfaction; I was totally drained. I thought I had earned a rest. After all the emotional buildup to that concert, it would have been a perfect time to take a short vacation, but I had no time off scheduled into that season. After playing Lincoln Center, I discovered I was more burned out than I had realized. By the time I ended up in New York's international air terminal, I felt I should cancel the European leg of my tour. But of course, I couldn't. Halls were booked, tickets had been sold, transportation had been arranged.

Though I boarded the plane and flew to Amsterdam, the growing sense of despair I felt was overwhelming. My frustration found an unfortunate outlet the night I filed off all my fingernails in that lonely hotel room. My "success" at Lincoln Center no longer mattered.

Three concerts later, I reached London. At my Queen Elizabeth Hall debut, even before the doors opened, I knew it was going to be terrible. I sat in my dressing room, desperately filing the edges of what remained of my nails, trying to create some kind of shape that would grab the strings. As I watched the clock tick down to that dreadful "start time," a stagehand knocked on the door. "Five minutes, Mr. Parkening."

I grabbed my guitar and tried again, hoping desperately for a miracle. It didn't happen. I still had nothing to pluck the strings with. It was a new feel, sliding past the strings almost as if they weren't there.

There was no backing down, nowhere to hide. The stagehand summoned me. I followed numbly into the wings, holding my guitar in one hand, and then I walked out onstage, resigned to the fact that I was going to play one of the worst concerts of my career. I was able to see a few rows out into the audience, and there—as if things couldn't possibly get any worse—sat one of the most distinguished classical guitarists in England. He had probably come out of curiosity, to hear "the new young American guitarist." I can say without a doubt that he could not have seen me play worse than I did that night.

I struggled through the first few pieces, so distracted by the insecurity of trying to find each string with my fingertips that my mind simply stopped tracking. I started into the Bach Courante, which I had played thousands of times, and my right hand distracted me so badly that I forgot my place in the music. I came to a dead stop. I couldn't even think of a spot to skip ahead to.

I had no choice but to go back to the very beginning and start over. Suddenly it seemed as if everything were moving in slow motion. I felt my face heat up. I thought, *This cannot be happening at Queen Elizabeth Hall. What a nightmare.*

It was one of the most miserable experiences of my career, if not my life. Completely humbled, it was all I could do to finish the concert.

I played another poor concert in Germany. I was due to play in Barcelona, but on the day before the concert, I called the presenter in Spain and said, "I'm sorry. I can't play. Please cancel the concert tomorrow night."

After a mediocre concert in Paris, I flew back to the United States feeling defeated and depressed. Sam would not even allow me to see the Queen Elizabeth Hall review. The tour was a total failure.

Only days before, I had given one of the finest concerts in my life. Oh, how quickly things had changed. It was not a question of my not having been in shape or not knowing the pieces. My playing was at an absolute peak—but I was mentally and emotionally exhausted.

In Europe, I'd had no one to talk to, and I felt completely and utterly alone. I had not yet realized that God is *always* there—that even my failures were bringing me closer to the place where I would finally start looking for Him.

Back in the United States, the tour went on. At least my nails were growing back, and soon I was scheduled to play in Bozeman, Montana.

A trout stream was waiting for me there.

FISH TALE

Running for My Life

My dad, his friend Ken Peterson, and I drove up north to fish for steelhead (a big, oceangoing trout) on the Deschutes River near Maupin, Oregon. The best spot, we were told, was somewhat inaccessible, which only reinforced our fancy to go there.

In order to get to this special spot, we had to cross a high train trestle over the canyon of the Deschutes River. It was about a hundred yards long. There we were, three explorers wearing bulky waders and brand-new, heavy, spiked "logger's boots" for the slippery rocks of the river bottom. Before crossing, we looked down over this vast canyon for a long time, mildly concerned about the possibility of a train coming through, but the chance seemed so remote that we decided it would be safe to cross. We started out across the high trestle.

It was scary because it was so high above the river, and the trestle had no railings. I looked between the slats of the railroad ties, way down to the river below, and suddenly realized just how precarious our situation was. It was summer, and the water was low. I stayed right in the middle of the train track, stepping over the gaps and planting my feet exactly on the railroad ties.

We crossed without a problem, reached the "famous" spot, fished for an hour with absolutely no results, and then it was time to head back. My dad took the lead. I came second, and Ken was third.

Just as we reached the middle of the trestle, the dreadful sound of a train whistle turned us all around, horrified. A locomotive was headed straight for us at full speed! I had never seen a train head-on before. It was like looking down a gun barrel. We were only half-way across, with what seemed like a 300-foot drop below us. If we jumped down onto the shale rock of the Deschutes River, which was only about two feet deep at that point, it would be sure death.

My dad started a flat-out run, skipping ties like a leaping deer. I sprinted after him like I had never run before as we headed for a narrow platform that jutted out over the Deschutes. He reached it, and with terror in his eyes, commanded, "Stand next to me." Ken reached it last.

We huddled together on the platform, holding on to each other's arms, while the train passed at fifty miles an hour, violently shaking the rickety, weather-beaten platform until I thought it was going to break off with the weight of the three of us and plunge into the Deschutes.

I was terrified, thinking I could lose my balance and fall. The train seemed to take forever to pass, only a few feet away. I stared straight toward the train and caught a glimpse of some hoboes sitting in one of the open cars.

I didn't think I had ever seen such a long train, but the end finally rattled past. Literally shaking in our shoes and in a state of shock, we staggered off the platform and back onto the center of the trestle, reeling from what had just happened. Ken joked weakly that although he had been in pain from the many blisters under his brand-new boots, when he heard the whistle and turned around to see the train approaching, he had a "miracle healing."

We laughed uncontrollably until we cried, then laughed some more. I guess it was the aftereffect of the adrenaline of a near-death experience. That narrow platform literally saved our lives, because—we calculated later—the fastest human in the world couldn't have made it to the end of the bridge.

The locals told us later that if they ever crossed that trestle, they always put their ear to the rail first, because they could feel the rumble of the train approaching long before they could see it emerging from that vast, turn-filled canyon.

10

Toward the "Good Life"

1976–77

In 1972, on my tour of the Midwest, I had made a friend who played guitar and whose mother raised beautiful Arabian horses. I had not forgotten the fun of being a "cowboy" at Hot Creek Ranch, so— while in Indiana on tour—I decided that I wanted to buy a handsome young chestnut-colored stallion with a white star on his forehead. Rather than taking money for the horse, my friend asked me to pick him out a Ramírez guitar. We arranged to make the trade on my Montana ranch, near Bozeman.

Shortly afterward, in Southern California, I met a young woman, Barbara Colyear, in a shop that sold riding supplies. Her brown hair was in pigtails, and she wore riding boots and jeans. Matter-of-factly, she asked to see a picture of my horse. She was attractive, with a cute smile, and seemed very outdoorsy. When we walked out of the tack shop, she jumped into her pickup truck and I thought, *Wow, that's unusual for a California girl.*

We soon started dating, and a year later, we were married.

We spent the summer of 1974 at my ranch in Bozeman, Montana. Bozeman is home to Montana State University, and at the invitation of Creech Reynolds, then the head of the music department, I gave a four-day master class there. We returned from Montana to a 1974–75 season that was as busy as ever. I couldn't slow down, couldn't stop practicing. Barbara was very independent, and because she was occupied with her horses, she didn't seem to mind the amount of time I spent touring.

Late in 1974, my cousin, friend, confidant, and mentor Jack Marshall died suddenly. For years, I had turned to Jack whenever I needed an arrangement or a transcription. He knew everything about the music business and had helped me over the hurdles that go with becoming a professional guitarist. Over the years, he had become a close friend and ally. Suddenly, where Jack Marshall had been, there was only a painful void.

Adding to the tension of getting ready to retire, I experienced such a frightening series of airplane mishaps that I asked my manager to arrange my concerts in geographical order so I could drive the tour. I didn't start out worrying about airplanes. I had made hundreds of flights up to this point. But back then, I lacked any kind of trust in God, and I fell prey to fears of my mortality.

The trouble had started on a flight back to New York City from Madrid. I was allowed to bring my guitar on the plane for this flight, and since there was an empty seat in my row, I kept it next to me. We were flying over the Atlantic by daylight in a four-engine passenger jet, about two hours into the flight, when the captain announced, "Ladies and gentlemen, we've had a fire warning in our number four outboard engine, so we've had to shut it down. We are turning the airplane around and heading for the nearest airport." His voice sounded nervous. As we turned around, it became obvious that the flight attendants were frightened as well. One of them came by and snapped at me, "Get the guitar out of that seat. We may have to run out of this plane." I found a place for it in the overhead compartment.

We were now headed for Lisbon, Portugal. After a while, the captain came on the intercom again. "Just so you know, you're going to be seeing a white stream coming out of the airplane. That's fuel we will be dumping to lighten the load for our landing." I actually heard the nervousness in his voice, and I wondered if we would make it to Lisbon—and whether my life would count for anything if it ended at this point.

We came in on three engines, with the plane yawing to the right. I counted fifteen red emergency vehicles lined up on the runway. When we touched down, the airplane lurched sharply to one side, and so did everything inside the cabin. As we headed toward a plowed field, I was sure we were going to slide right off the runway. Fortunately, the pilot was able to stop the plane on the edge of the tarmac. As we deplaned safely, I was never so glad to be on the ground.

Not long after that, I was flying into LaGuardia Airport with my manager, Sam Niefeld, when suddenly the airplane's nose tilted down and the pilot applied full thrust. There was an incredible downward force, and I thought, *We're crashing!* Out the window, I saw the wing of another aircraft swoop past ours. We'd almost had a midair collision!

Next, I'd taken an extremely early flight from the East Coast, and we were the first airplane to land in Kansas City, at about six-thirty in the morning. As we descended from twenty thousand feet, it suddenly felt as if the airplane were dropping out of the sky. All the coffee cups and everything else that was loose flew up into the air. My heart went into my throat. I felt sure the wings were going to snap off. Finally, the pilot stabilized the plane, and then he said over the intercom, "I'm extremely sorry for that. We encountered an air pocket that was associated with some severe clear-air turbulence, and we dropped a thousand feet. Since we were the first flight in this morning, there was no warning."

This was the third difficult flight I'd had in just a few weeks' time, and I hoped it was the last. Little did I know that my midair mishaps were just beginning! Flying late at night into Florida through a terrible storm, lightning was flashing through the clouds all around us. The cabin lights were dimmed so people could sleep, but outside my window, lightning was everywhere. The plane was pitching and rolling. Suddenly, a bolt struck the plane! It sounded like an explosion; all the lights went out, and I could feel the electricity actually flowing through me. *If the lights are out,* I thought, *what if something in the cockpit isn't working?* The pilot quickly assured us everything was okay, that they would switch over to their backup system. "Sit back, relax, and enjoy the rest of the flight," he added.

Oh, sure!

On the next flight, my plane was about to land in Pittsburgh, Pennsylvania. The wheels on the aircraft were just about to touch the ground when the front end of the airplane tilted up, the pilot applied full throttle, and we were taking off instead of touching down. I looked at the guy sitting next to me and said, "I guess we're not landing." A few seconds later, the pilot said, "I'm sorry for that, ladies and gentlemen, but we have just had a missed approach. There was a plane starting to taxi across the runway in front of us, and I had to make the decision to take off instead of land. We're going to go around and try it again."

Finally, on a flight out of Los Angeles, the fog was so thick I couldn't believe the flight hadn't been cancelled. Taking off from LAX, a pilot usually heads west, flies over the ocean, and then makes the turn. This time we taxied onto the runway, and the pilot applied the throttle. We were going faster and faster, and about the time I expected the nose to tip up and the wheels to lift off the runway, the pilot hit the brakes and aborted the takeoff. The brakes released, and we surged forward—then braked again. I started praying. *Please, Lord, help us to stop before the ocean!* We did stop before the end of the runway. When the pilot came on over the intercom, he explained that he had received a mechanical warning, causing him to abort the takeoff. We taxied into maintenance so they could find and fix the problem. I was glad they had discovered the problem while we were on the ground rather than in the air. After my recent string of scares, I wasn't ready for another fearful flight.

These incidents all happened within just a few months, and I was praying like I never had before. Each time, my prayer lasted only until the crisis ended. I flew in some awesome storms, in which the plane was tossed around and it was hard to believe that the aircraft could stand such abuse. These things can be pretty scary when you're not sure where you're going after you die, when you don't know and understand that God is sovereign, that He is in control of all things, and that your times are in His hand, as it says in Psalm 31:15.

During this period, I was beginning to understand that there was something missing in my life. Whenever I finished a tour or put the last touches on a recording, the happiness and satisfaction lasted only a short time.

I was an occasional churchgoer, with a Methodist and Presbyterian background, and since my parents had me baptized when I was twelve, I believed I was a Christian. Obviously I knew enough to pray when I was afraid, and I read the Bible occasionally. I had heard the gospel, and I believed that Jesus Christ was the Son of God, that He died on the cross for our sins, and that he rose again the third day, but I was searching for something more than this knowledge. I just didn't know what it was.

Retirement plus true happiness—if I could find it—sounded perfect! With every successful concert, every scare on an airplane, every step closer to age thirty, I felt a strange pull, something deep inside, that yearned for more. Somehow I knew that "more" was God. I looked through the yellow pages for churches to visit.

One fall afternoon, when I was at our home in California between concert dates, I got to talking with one of my neighbors over the backyard fence. I told him I had been trying different churches, and he said, "I hear there's a really good church down on Roscoe Boulevard, about twenty minutes away." He said he had visited a few times, and he told me how to get there.

Barbara wasn't interested, so I drove myself to Grace Community Church and took a seat in the back. The pastor's name was John MacArthur, and his preaching quickly caught my attention.

I don't remember the name of the sermon or much about it, but I do know it was different from what I had been hearing at other churches. It wasn't about social issues or philosophy—instead, it was straight from the Bible. As I sat in the back of the church that day, I had the unmistakable feeling of God's presence. I had never felt that before.

Still, I knew "the good life" was getting closer, and I decided to put off my spiritual search for a while longer. Between tours, I drove to Montana and continued fixing up the ranch. Barbara and I also bought a house and property closer to Bozeman, where we could be more comfortable than out at the cabin in the winter. We built a large horse barn and indoor riding arena on the property with our new home.

ᵒᵗᵒ ᵒᵗᵒ ᵒᵗᵒ

My 1977 tour was set for January through March. In December, I would be thirty . . . and retired from performance. I had just one album left on the Capitol Records contract.

My old USC mentor, Gregor Piatigorsky, had encouraged me to be conservative with my interpretations when recording—not to bend the phrases too much, lest it sound exaggerated when I heard the record a few years later. It was one thing to try something over-the-top or even a little extreme at a concert. I might like it one night and not the next, but a concert lasted only a couple of hours and then was just a memory. It was another thing to set an interpretation in stone, on a recording that people would hear for many years. Segovia had said, "Burnish a piece at least one year on tour before recording it," explaining that as the interpretation of a piece evolved, any phrasing that wasn't musically good would start to wear on him.

I remembered learning the Prelude no. 7 by Prokofiev, which Jerrold Hyman had transcribed for solo guitar. I hadn't heard the original—but this, I thought, was beautiful on the guitar, and I said to my producer, "Patti, let's put it on the next recording."

"Come up and play it for me," she said.

I brought my guitar to Capitol Records and played it in her office.

Her reaction was immediate. "It's not going to work."

I was a little stunned. "Why?"

"Chris, give me five minutes." She picked up the phone, called the Capitol Records library, and asked for a recording of the piece as it was originally written for piano. It was delivered to her office, and she played it for me.

The original piece was about twice the speed I had been playing it. "Unless you can get it to the speed of the piano," she said, "it's not going to work musically."

She was right. Whenever I recorded a transcription of a piece originally written for another instrument, it had to have the musical integrity to stand up to the composition as played on the original instrument. One transcription, Jerrold Hyman's arrangement of "Empress of the Pagodas" from Maurice Ravel's *Mother Goose Suite*, absolutely flies. Working it up to tempo required days of intense practice, and it did make it onto my "retirement" album.

We had assembled nearly enough material to fill the album and had only one session left, including the difficult Preámbulo and Allegro Vivo by Scarlatti/Ponce. Since the recording was on schedule and I had practiced well that morning, I decided to take the afternoon off.

Barbara and I went out to the Flintridge Riding Club. At the time we owned a spirited, young Arabian stallion. It was suggested that I hand-walk the horse once around the riding club to try to calm him down before he was ridden. I used my gloved right hand to hold the rope as I walked him down the trail. He was jogging in place and rearing up. Every time he saw another horse he acted up—one time he just about jerked my right arm out of the socket—but I finally got him back to the stable and put him in his stall.

That's when I felt something strange inside my right glove. When I pulled it off, I was horrified to see that my right thumbnail was three-quarters broken off right at the quick, connected just on the far left side, flexing back and forth as if it were on a hinge.

Suddenly, all that I had worked for flashed before my eyes.

I can't complete my last recording! I thought. *It won't come out on time! All the work I did to get ready to record tomorrow will be lost!* Spring was coming, and we were moving to Montana for good. I knew from experience that it would take at least two months to grow out the nail again. I had tried to fix broken nails before, and the resulting sound was always inferior.

Reeling from the shock, I sat down on a bench in front of the stable. I felt sick to my stomach and probably looked it. Just then, my sister-in-law, Diane, happened to drive up. She said, "Hi, Chris. What's wrong?"

"I broke my thumbnail. I can't do my recording session tomorrow."

Diane knew this was a guitarist's nightmare. Sounding positive, she said, "I know the perfect place you can go. It's over in Hollywood. If you want, I'll drive you there. I know someone who can fix your nail."

I didn't think that was possible. Guitarists try patching broken nails with slices of Ping-Pong balls, acrylic, precut plastic nails, or superglue. The sound is always twangy and unnatural.

"She can do a silk wrap," Diane said. "That's a natural material. Maybe it will sound like a natural thumbnail."

At this point, I knew I had nothing to lose. It certainly couldn't hurt to try. Barbara had gone back to the stable and was taking care of the horses, so Diane hurried over to the pay phone and called the nail technician. We walked into a salon filled with women getting their hair done, and they peered out at me from under their hair dryers. Diane said, "They do nails upstairs."

I felt embarrassed and out of place but desperate enough to try anything. Upstairs, the technician was doing a woman's nails. I showed her my thumb, and she said, "I can fix that. As soon as I'm done here. Have a seat."

I fidgeted for fifteen or twenty minutes, with assorted ladies sneaking glances at me over their magazines. Finally, the technician called me over. The woman worked incredibly fast as I tried to explain exactly what I needed. She seemed a bit impatient, probably both because she had done thousands of nails and was an expert, and because she had worked me in to her busy schedule. To me, it was my livelihood, my sound, my tone quality, my technical accuracy for tomorrow—the last session for the last recording on my contract! Absolutely everything was riding on what she was doing. To her, I was just another customer.

She slapped a layer of silk onto my nail. I tried, in as few words and as fast as I could, to explain that this thumbnail had to be extremely strong. It was going to undergo a tremendous amount of abuse tomorrow. I didn't care how it looked.

"Okay," she said. "I'll put on three layers."

It took about an hour for the nail to dry, before we could leave the place. I gave her a *big* tip. That repair job was priceless to me.

When I got back to the house, I immediately pulled out my guitar to see if the repair had worked. At first, I found that the sound was a little scratchy from the silk's rough edge. I used some fine sandpaper to smooth the edge of the nail, and my tone started sounding better . . . and then even better . . . until it was just right.

The next day I walked into the recording session as though nothing had happened, and we were able to finish the recording on time.

Parkening and the Guitar was *Stereo Review*'s Record of the Year in 1977, and although it was nominated for a Grammy Award, the recognition was minor compared to finally reaching my goal of the "good life."

FISH TALE

The Knot

I had fished Hot Creek all morning and was walking back to the cabins when I noticed a few small dimples of fish feeding in the S-turn where Hot Creek meandered through the picturesque green meadow, and the creek channel below the bank was undercut, narrow, and deep.

I generally changed my leader whenever it got a "wind knot" from casting, because a knot makes the leader break easily. But this time, I said to myself, *There's a few small fish feeding here. It won't matter.*

I snuck up to the spot on my knees and piled up a cast upstream from the rises. As the sedge fly drifted down, a little dimple formed under it, and it disappeared. I struck. It felt like I had hooked some debris in the stream, so I stood up to look.

About five feet deep in the water, the tail of a brown trout was making a swath two feet wide. I had hooked a thirty-inch, ten-pound brown trout on a number-eighteen dry fly, with pound-and-a-half test leader . . . with a knot in it!

This fish hugged the bottom and the far side of the undercut bank, moving slowly upstream, then abruptly turned around and darted downstream thirty feet, over and over. To land this fish on a dry fly the size of a mosquito would be a monumental achievement. If ever in my life I wished I had taken the time to retie a new leader, without a knot, this was the time.

For the next twenty minutes, as far as this fish was concerned, I was a gnat at the other end of the line, afraid to put the pressure on him that I should have, in order to tire and land him. Finally, he made the downstream turn and about-face and . . . *blink*. The fly came unbuttoned. I could only stand there and imagine what it would have been like to catch and release that ten-pound brown trout, and I promised myself that I would never make that mistake again.

II

Montana!

1977-78

With the last Capitol album finished, I waved good-bye to the performing life, and Barbara and I arrived in Montana "for good" in the summer of 1977. As far as I was concerned, as soon as we officially moved into the house in the Four Corners area, near Bozeman, my career as a touring performer was history. I was euphoric.

I dialed Sam Niefeld, thanked him for all he had done for me, and then told him I was quitting.

Sam said, very seriously, "I want you to remember something, Chris. You will always be known as a guitarist."

I don't think he had an agenda. It was just his way of telling me that as far as the world was concerned, that was my identity. Somehow his words stunned me. To me, the guitar had largely been the means to an end.

I thanked him again and hung up, and then, over the next few days, I called Patti Laursen at Capitol Records and the School of Music at USC and told them as well that I was retiring. I would not be playing the guitar anymore.

It wasn't long before Creech Reynolds at Montana State approached me. "Why don't you head up the guitar department here and teach the fall and spring quarters?"

I decided that a small amount of token teaching wouldn't interfere with my fishing.

For the next three years, I did not practice much, except to get ready for my master classes at Montana State University. Instead, I did everything I had always wanted to do. I fished to my heart's content, almost every day, including all the famous trout streams in southwest Montana: the Madison, the Jefferson, the Missouri, the Yellowstone, the Beaverhead, and especially the spring creek on my trout ranch, about twenty miles from the new house.

Mostly, it was exciting. I enjoyed the chores, driving a tractor, working with the horses, and caring for the trout stream. Since I had no intention of ever playing the guitar professionally again, I was able to do things with my hands that I hadn't dared to do for the last twenty years.

This was horse country too. Barbara was an avid equestrian, and we purchased an Arabian mare that we eventually planned to breed, but in the meantime, we wanted to break her to ride. Unlike some of the other young horses, this mare loved to buck. Nobody had been able to stay on her with a regular saddle.

I wanted to try.

I purchased a bucking rig, like the ones used in rodeos—essentially just a single piece of leather, about six inches wide. It fastens on with a cinch that goes around the horse's girth, like any leather saddle, but it also has a single handle in front that's stitched on at both ends so the rider can hold on with one hand. A bucking rig is very thin, meaning that the rider is basically sitting directly on the horse. There is nothing in back to lean against and no stirrups, so the person's legs are wrapped around the horse. Rodeo cowboys hold on with one hand and keep their feet out in front, spurring the horse and leaning way back. I didn't do any of that. I just hung on.

I had a stable hand help me fasten on the bucking rig, and we cinched it up. He took hold of the halter, and I swung up onto the mare.

Then he let go, and the horse was all over that corral, with her head between her front legs, bucking like crazy, and I barely managed to stay on. After two or three minutes of solid bucking, the mare finally tired, stopped, and sulked. I nudged her with my feet to keep going, and she bucked a couple more times, then stopped again.

Finally, we reached a point where I could swing onto her at any time, and she wouldn't buck.

Eventually the horse was broken for riding, but I had gotten a taste for a new kind of fun. As a kid, I'd always wanted to be a cowboy. As far as I was concerned, that horse had made me one.

Another horse came into our barn for training. Her name was Snow Bird, a rather homely, white and gray mare that nobody could ride. When anyone got on her and asked her to go forward, she just reared up high in the air—high enough to flip over, and she could crush a rider if she fell on him.

I took the first ride on her. I used the bucking rig, not really expecting her to buck, but to rear, and I wanted to be able to slide off quickly and spring away before she hit the ground.

Sure enough, when I asked the mare to go forward, she took

a few steps and then reared up so high that she just kept going backward. As she flipped over, I slid off. She fell partially on my foot and calf, but fortunately I scrambled out from under her. This happened a few times, and each time I climbed back on her I was more reluctant and more than a little nervous. When she flipped it happened so suddenly, even when I was expecting it, that getting a foot caught in a stirrup might have been the last mistake I ever made.

Finally, I broke her of the rearing habit. Though other horses came to us for training, Snow Bird was probably the most dangerous horse I ever rode.

When I look back on the needless chances I took during that time, I can only thank the Lord for preserving me. I guess like many young people, I figured nothing could happen to me. But in a heartbeat, I could have been severely injured. I could have broken my neck or my back or injured a hand or an arm so seriously that I would have been unable to play an instrument again.

I wasn't thinking about any of that at the time. I simply wanted to have fun, to spend the rest of my life fishing, riding, and enjoying the "good life." God knew otherwise, however, and His grace protected me when I was too foolish to value the gifts He had given me.

One winter in Los Angeles, Barbara and I picked up a truly beautiful Thoroughbred stallion at an auction. High Country was a gorgeous bay horse: brown with a black mane and a distinctive, off-center white marking on his forehead; beautiful conformation—a well-proportioned head and body; a long, strong neck; and three white socks. One day we received a call from a horse trainer in the movie business. He had heard about High Country through his horse-buddy grapevine. "We're looking for a beautiful Thoroughbred stallion for a film with Robert Redford and Jane Fonda." They asked if High Country was gentle and easy to ride.

"Yes, he is," I said. "I've ridden him. In general, he has a very docile personality for a stallion."

"May we come look at him?"

The trainer came over, along with director Sydney Pollack. This was going to be a major feature film from Columbia Pictures. The director and the trainer loved the horse's looks and immediately offered us a contract to buy him. Later the trainer called again on short notice, asking to come over and try him out.

High Country hadn't been ridden in several days, which meant he had a lot of pent-up energy, and so he was feeling a little feisty. The trainer wanted to ride him without doing any hand-walking or other warm-up. He just threw a heavy Western saddle on the horse and jumped on. Naturally, High Country started to jog in place, fidget, and even buck a little.

The trainer got off. "This is too much horse for the movie. He's too spirited." Now Columbia Pictures wanted out of the contract. We were fine with that. We liked High Country and were happy to keep him. For the next two weeks Columbia looked all over Southern California for another Thoroughbred stallion, but they just could not find one as majestic as High Country. They came back to us and said, "We'd like to revisit this."

I told them, "Listen, this is a very nice horse. He was a little feisty before because he hadn't been ridden for a couple of days."

They repurchased High Country, who went on to star in the 1979 movie *The Electric Horseman*. Much of the movie was filmed in Utah, and in the process of transporting him from one spot to the next, there was an accident that resulted in a leg injury for High Country. In order to continue filming, the screenwriters had to actually write his injury into the script!

The film included a great scene at the end, in which the supposedly $12 million racehorse is finally turned loose in a Shangri-la meadow—high, grassy, and full of wild horses. The director needed to get a running shot of High Country galloping free, with no bridle or rope on him. In order to get the shot, the horse needed to run in a straight line so the truck-mounted camera could follow along at high speed. Just outside the camera angle, they brought in several mares. When the director gave the cue, High Country took off at a full gallop toward the mares, and the director got his spectacular action shot.

Robert Redford liked High Country so much that after the filming was complete, he purchased the horse and took High Country to his Utah ranch. He sent us a picture of himself on horseback, signed "Thanks for High C—Robert Redford."

In addition to the horses, we had a menagerie that included two very unusual pets: a mountain lion, bred in captivity at an animal rescue organization in Southern California, and a Malaysian small-clawed otter, which was given to Barbara by some people who didn't want him anymore. The mountain lion we named Miss Montana. The otter was called Woodstock.

We'd had a pool at our home in California, and when I went out to swim laps, Woodstock often hung on to the back of my swimming trunks. He enjoyed it so much that he hung on, even during the turns. When we moved to Montana, he *loved* to go fishing with me. I would take him out in a little crate that I'd put in the back of the car, and he always knew when it was a fishing day. He almost jumped into the crate, he was so excited to go fishing. As soon as I let him out, he trailed behind me in the grass, usually about five feet back. Sometimes the grass was so tall that all I could see was its parting as he followed me. I never needed to put him on a leash, though he had a little harness for when we took him to a school or to visit one of our friends.

He played along beside the stream as I fished. He was too slow to catch wild trout, but he could catch little chubs and squawfish below the undercut banks. Whenever I hooked a trout and it splashed or jumped, Woodstock jumped off the bank and swam around looking for the fish. It was an amazing sight.

Woodstock loved people. He would go up to a new person and try to jump into his or her lap to make friends. He only weighed about eight pounds and was very cute. One day I was out fishing on the Gallatin River, and when I looked up, I didn't see Woodstock. About a hundred yards upstream, I spotted a couple and their dog, hiking along the river and sightseeing. I thought, *I bet Woodstock went up to visit them,* so I began walking toward them.

As I drew closer, I noticed that they were huddled against a rock wall near some trees, looking scared and holding their dog. Woodstock was on point like a hunting dog, about fifteen feet away from them.

At that point, I realized they might pick up rocks and throw them at him. I yelled, "That's my otter; don't hurt him!"

"Thank goodness," they shouted back. "We thought it was a wild, rabid otter that came up from the stream to bite us or our dog."

Woodstock's extreme friendliness often got him in trouble. One summer day I was fishing a spring creek with Woodstock following along. Upstream from us, a lady wearing chest-high waders stood in deep water, fishing intently. I was headed in that direction, dry-fly-fishing, and moving upstream faster than she was. I wanted to leave plenty of room when I passed her, so I quit fishing before I got near and made a big arc around her, back toward the stream a hundred yards above.

I assumed Woodstock was following me, but he had seen the woman, and by the time I noticed that he wasn't behind me in the grass, I heard a commotion. Woodstock had taken the stream route, swum up to her, and tried to jump into her arms. She screamed, tossed her rod, and started running out of the water. I raced back downstream and yelled, "Don't worry, that's my pet otter. He won't hurt you—he just likes people!"

ᏬᎡᏬ ᏬᎡᏬ ᏬᎡᏬ

We built Miss Montana, the mountain lion, a quarter-acre cage of eight-foot chain-link fence, with a warm, insulated doghouse for her to sleep in. Miss Montana and I enjoyed playing a little game I called run-go-hide. She would hide in the long grass at the back of her enclosure, and I would walk in through the main gate, pretending I didn't see her. She would hunker down, ears pinned, and stay motionless until I was in range. I'd walk around . . . la-di-da . . . then she'd charge, leaping through the air, and we would wrestle in the grass. She was incredibly powerful, but she never tried to hurt me. I loved that mountain lion, and she trusted me. She often let me carry her, purring as we walked.

We also had a Jack Russell terrier named Scooter, which actually lived in the enclosure with Miss Montana. He was a brave little guy. When he was a puppy, upon meeting her for the first time—she promptly jumped on him and turned him over on his back on the ground—he did what a little boy might do in the middle of a diaper change. Right into her face. She got an amazed, funny expression on her face, her nose went back, and she squinted—*yuck!* And after that decisive moment, Scooter knew the lion wouldn't hurt him, and they were buddies. They lived and played together constantly.

Woodstock eventually died of old age. Miss Montana died at a ripe old age too. She was fourteen. In captivity, mountain lions live about as long as domestic dogs. I understand that's longer than they usually survive in the wild.

The animals were great, and they kept us busy. For a while they even distracted me from coming to grips with where my life was headed. Inside, that sense of emptiness was starting to come back. Even as everything seemed to be going according to my plan, doubts were starting to creep in.

Deep down, I knew I ought to be doing something worthwhile. Life lasts only so long. Riding the lawn mower or staring at the sunset, I often caught myself thinking, *Time is passing. Am I really doing what I'm supposed to be doing in Montana?* I would sometimes lie down at the end of the day thinking, *Is this all there is?*

In a way, I felt like a guilty little kid, doing something other than what he knows he's supposed to be doing. This now makes me think of Psalm 90:12: "Teach us to number our days, that we may apply our hearts unto wisdom." A life of fishing, mending fences, and feeding the animals was fun, but it wasn't balanced with something truly meaningful. My life had no real purpose.

As Creech Reynolds had suggested, I taught year-round the first year at Montana State University. "You can go south for the winter, if you want," he had said, but since I had no mental image of winter in the Bozeman area, I wasn't sure why anyone would ever want to leave.

Winter was a shock.

FISH TALE

Lazy Day on the Spring Creek

My own "Hot Creek Ranch" was on a spring creek near Manhattan, Montana—nothing like Manhattan, New York. It's ironic that we ended up calling it the Manhattan Ranch. It was the total opposite of huge buildings, traffic, honking horns, and crowds of people. It was my Shangri-la. Near the tall, leafy cottonwood trees, the grass in the meadow was filled with wildflowers. As I walked from the little yellow cabin toward the river, I was in heaven. In the distance I could see Saddleback Mountain, shaped like a Western saddle. It was often snowcapped, even into June. On a July morning, it was usually dark green in the distance. The sky was always blue with big white clouds.

I loved to hear the birds singing, particularly the red-winged blackbirds and the meadowlarks, which have a beautiful eight- to ten-note song. And sometimes, as I'd come through thick brush to approach the stream from a different angle, I'd flush out three or four white-tailed deer that had nestled there during the night. I'd see hawks soaring high above the ranch, or even a bald eagle. Often amusing were the little prairie dogs and gophers, which stuck their heads out and warned each other of my approach with a high-pitched whistle. Occasionally I saw a fox or a badger, and sometimes I came upon a pool and nearly jumped out of my skin at the cracking sound of a flat tail slapping the water. A beaver had built his dam in the area, and when he warned his friends of approaching danger, it sounded like a firecracker going off. I'm sure it warned the fish, too—"put them down," as fishermen say.

And oftentimes, near the opposite bank of the creek, I saw a muskrat swimming along, with his thin tail waggling behind him as he swam stealthily upstream, keeping close to the opposite bank.

Occasionally, walking across the ranch, I came upon a clear spring flowing out of the ground or out of the side of the hill, meandering its way to the stream. The water was so pure and clean that it invited you to cup your hands for a little refreshment.

Tranquil. Peaceful. I could put everything out of my mind but the experiences that were ahead for that day, the adventures waiting for me. There were no flights, no telephones to answer, no schedules to worry about, no practicing to be done. It would be another beautiful day in "Big Sky Country," just enjoying nature.

My excitement mounted as the creek came into view. Baker Creek had beautiful, clear water. Sheets of weeds laced through the stream, providing cover for big brown trout. At about 9:30 a.m., the caddis flies started to emerge, floating down the stream. I could see the subtle rise of the trout as they sipped in the floating insects.

I loved to pick out the trout I thought was the largest. Crouching low, I stalked closer. As I stripped out the fly line and prepared to try to place the fly right where I wanted it, I often thought, *There's nothing much better than this—all I ever wanted, heaven on earth.*

12

Examine Yourself

~~~~~~~~~~~~~~~~~~~~~~~~~~~~~~~

1978–80

Having always seen Montana as a land of blue-ribbon trout streams in summer and autumn, with rising fish and with green leaves on all the trees over beautiful green meadows, I was unprepared for the change of seasons.

Then came October. The trees lost most of their leaves and stood stark over the brown meadows. In November, vegetation froze, snow fell, and the stream on our ranch property ran off-color, with ice along the banks.

By late November, the fishing was pretty much nonexistent. There was almost no insect hatch, so no trout were rising. When I did go out to the ranch a few times on the nicer days—twenty degrees or so—my hands were freezing and my ears hurt. The guides on my rod froze solid from water that the line shed when I stripped it in. There came a moment when suddenly I couldn't pull the line through anymore, and when I looked at my rod tip and a couple of guides down, it was a solid sheet of ice. I had to break ice out of my guides to cast again, and I even felt sorry for the fish. All the ones I caught were sluggish and drab, and even though I released them, I felt guilty for taxing them of their strength, because I knew they had a long winter ahead. Why was I adding stress to their lives?

Since I couldn't fish, I went skiing a few times, but I wasn't a hard-core skier. I had heard native Montanans say, "We have nine months of winter and three months of guests." Now it seemed to ring true. I had never experienced so much cold weather.

There's an old proverb: "Be careful what you wish for; you might get it." Perseverance and hard work had gotten me a dream ranch at thirty, but as the next two years passed, something amazing began to happen.

I had accomplished my goals and ended up with everything that I thought would make me happy, but really, my "good life" had begun to unravel some time back. Though I enjoyed the animals and I loved fishing, I was rapidly becoming bored without knowing why. It was like Solomon said in the Bible: "Vanity of vanities; all is vanity" (Ecclesiastes 1:2). I began to ask myself, *If you have everything you ever wanted, but still there's that emptiness, what's left?* I needed something more, something to provide the fulfillment success couldn't seem to give me.

A friend invited Barbara and me to the Rose Bowl game in Pasadena, California, on January 1, 1979, and I certainly did not expect to find answers to life's deepest questions at a football game, but the warm weather sure sounded nice. I told the mechanic who serviced my car for the trip that Barbara and

I were leaving on December 30 and driving through West Yellowstone; over Targhee Pass; through Idaho Falls, Salt Lake City, Las Vegas; and finally to Pasadena. He warned me that it was going to be extremely cold that night, and he suggested I put a newspaper in front of my radiator to keep as much heat in the car as possible. If I didn't do that, the car would get progressively colder and finally stop. He suggested carrying a goose down sleeping bag in the back of the car, in case we broke down.

We started out early in the morning, driving carefully because it was eighteen below zero with solid snowpack on the pavement in Bozeman. By the time we reached West Yellowstone, the bank marquee said it was fifty-one below zero. When a dog ran across the street, I wondered how he could survive.

We continued nonstop and arrived in Pasadena on a beautiful sunny day, in sixty-five-degree weather. For the first time, I wondered if we had made the right decision to move to Montana. After the football game, we decided to stay in California for a while in order to visit friends and family. While we were there, I went back to visiting different churches in the area.

At one, which was close to the place where we were staying, I heard a sermon that stuck in my mind, though not for any reason the pastor would have liked. It was titled "It Shows in Your Face." The pastor kept saying things such as, "It shows in your face! You walk down the street, it should show in your face." The sermon seemed shallow and pointless. *Who cares about my face? What about my life? Why do I feel so empty?* I wondered.

Finally, I returned to Grace Community Church, where I heard a deep, challenging, Scripture-based sermon. Feeling hopeful for the first time in months, I bought a stack of taped sermons to take to Montana. Winter was still hanging on when we returned. Late at night, I sat alone in the dark in my rocking chair, looking at the lights from houses dotting the distant mountainsides and listening to the cassette tapes. It was a peaceful time, a time for reflection and meditation with no distractions, a time just to think about life.

I was intrigued by the idea that this world isn't going to last forever, and like many other people, I wanted to know what would happen to me when I died. Many of John MacArthur's taped sermons covered those topics. One sermon, called "Believers' Rewards," discussed the different judgments predicted in the Bible. In 1 Corinthians 3:11-15 and 2 Corinthians 5:10, Scripture says that believers will stand before Christ at the "Bema" judgment seat. John MacArthur likened this judgment to the Greek Olympic Games, saying that we will ascend that platform to stand face-to-face with Jesus Christ, and then everything we have done in our lives will fall into one of two categories: either wood, hay, and stubble—selfish, and useless in eternity—or gold, silver, and precious stones—done for God's glory. In the final test of fire, only the gold, silver, and precious stones will remain.

I sat in my living room, thinking, *Everything I have done is a washout. It's all wood, hay, and stubble. It's been done so I could retire early. Here I am, just barely into retirement, and I'm seeing nothing but emptiness.*

I had done nothing for the Lord. I tried to envision standing before the King of kings and Lord of lords with nothing to give Him.

Here—at last—was something that was truly worth giving my life to. *This is it. This is what I have been missing! I have to change my life.* Sitting in the rocking chair that night, I prayed, *Lord, forgive me for this wasted life, forgive me for my selfishness.*

All of a sudden, everything was clear-cut in a way that's almost impossible to put into words. I finally could see what real value and worth was, and I knew that I didn't have it yet. Like

Matthew 13:44-46, which talks about finding the pearl of great price or the treasure hidden in the field, once you finally discover it, it's so valuable that you'll sell everything you have to possess it.

I was hungry for more scriptural truth, but although I knew that I needed to do *something*, I wasn't sure yet what that something was. For the next year, I continued to listen to sermon tapes and wonder what I could do that would make my life worthwhile and meaningful.

The next winter in Los Angeles, I heard John MacArthur preach from Matthew 7 and 2 Corinthians 13:5, "Examine yourselves, whether ye be in the faith." In Matthew 7, Jesus says, "Ye shall know [true Christians] by their fruits. . . . Not every one that saith unto me, Lord, Lord, shall enter into the kingdom of heaven; but he that doeth the will of my Father which is in heaven. Many will say to me in that day [the day that they die], Lord, Lord. . . . And then will I profess unto them, I never knew you: depart from me" (verses 16, 21-23). Those words of Scripture cut deep into my heart, and I realized that I wasn't a Christian at all! *That's me,* I thought. I had believed some facts about Christ—I had believed that He was the Son of God, that He died on a cross for the sins of the world, and that He rose again on the third day. I had even wanted a Savior to save me from hell, and I had thought that was saving faith. What I did not want, prior to that moment, was a Lord of my life to trust, follow, and obey. But that day I learned that you can't separate the saviorhood from the lordship of Christ. Jesus is both Savior and Lord!

My whole life flashed before me. I pictured myself standing before Jesus Christ and saying to Him, "Lord, Lord, I believe who You are. I went to Sunday school. My parents even had me baptized!" In my heart I knew that Jesus would answer me, "You never cared about the things of Christ. You never cared about being obedient to My commands. You never cared about glorifying Me with your life or with your music. All you cared about were your ranches and your trout streams. Depart from Me. I never knew you."

It wasn't too late. I needed to get my life right, repent of my sins, embrace Christ as both Savior *and* Lord, and live for Him. That night I lay awake, broken over my sins. My dream had been shattered, and my life was empty. I was spiritually bankrupt, self-centered, and unhappy. Finally understanding that I was a sinner before God, I asked Him to forgive me. I repented of my materialistic, selfish life, and I asked Jesus Christ to be my Savior and my Lord, for real. I told Him in my prayer, *Whatever You want me to do with my life, Lord, I'll do it. I tried it my own way and it failed.* I took a tape of that sermon back to Montana.

A few months later, after joining a small church in Montana, I heard that John MacArthur would be holding a pastors' conference at Grace Church, and I invited two pastors from Montana to drive down with me. I sat in on the sessions, and I was thoroughly enjoying the teaching until someone pulled me aside. It seems one of the pastors had told John MacArthur that I was a former classical guitarist and a new Christian. John had asked if I could play for the pastors. Then he wanted me to give my testimony in the form of an interview with him after one of the sessions.

My first thought was, *I can't do this!* I had not practiced seriously in a long, long time. I hadn't even brought a guitar to LA, and I had never given my testimony before. Yet also I thought, *I have been listening to tape after tape of John's sermons and learning about the Bible, and he's asking me to do one thing. I can't say no.*

Reluctantly I agreed.

I called a friend, Ronald Ravenscroft, who lived in Los

Angeles, and asked if I could borrow his guitar. I practiced three Bach pieces, just enough to fill up the time allotted for music.

The next day John introduced me, and I played in the chapel. Then he asked me a series of questions about my spiritual journey and how I had come to God. I nervously answered them. As the pastors filed out of the chapel, I packed up my footstool and guitar. Walking down the center aisle, I had the guitar slung over my back and I was carrying my other things when I felt an arm over my shoulder.

I looked up, and it was John, walking alongside me. He thanked me for playing and then said, "You know, Chris, you could have a wonderful ministry with the guitar."

This simple comment would become a pivotal moment in my life, although at the time I didn't want to accept it. I kept trying to find a satisfying balance of fishing, teaching a little, reading my Bible, and listening to tapes.

Another year passed. Barbara didn't seem to care that I'd had a spiritual awakening—but gradually, responding to God's call on my life was becoming my priority. Reading 1 Corinthians, I came across verse 10:31, which says, "Whatsoever ye do, do all to the glory of God." I truly wanted to live for God now, and if He had given me any ability or talent, I finally felt convinced that I needed to use it for His glory.

There were two things I knew how to do well. One was fly-fishing for trout, and the other was playing the guitar. When I tried to imagine a career of "fly-fishing for the Lord," it was easy to see that wasn't going to cut it!

That left just one option.

Time had passed—three summers and winters—in my "paradise." I seemed to have it all, but I was starting to be overcome by the combination of boredom and now guilt, feeling as if I'd thrown away a career that I might not get back. I didn't even know if I could still play well enough to record again. Since 1977, I had only picked up the guitar when demonstrating something to a student. Primarily, I had been riding horses and fishing—doing things with my hands that serious classical artists should never do.

As disturbing as it was to think about playing the guitar again professionally, I was willing to obey if the Lord led me to that. I felt that it was my duty to the Savior who had given His life for me. "Know ye not that your body is the temple of the Holy Ghost which is in you, which ye have of God, and ye are not your own? For ye are bought with a price: therefore glorify God in your body, and in your spirit, which are God's" (1 Corinthians 6:19-20).

The day after I made the decision to play again, I made another series of phone calls. I told Sam Niefeld and Patti Laursen that I wanted to play the guitar again, but this time for a different purpose: to honor and glorify the Lord.

Capitol Records immediately offered me another contract, and Sam seemed glad to hear from me. I told him, "I want to play concerts again, and I have two recordings on my heart, one for solo guitar and one for guitar with orchestra."

Sam didn't pull any punches. "Chris, you threw away a career most artists would die for. I don't know that you can get it back." He promised to call me back in a week or two. When he did, he didn't sound very excited. "You know, some people are starting to say, 'Parkening? Who?' Five years ago, we were turning down nearly a hundred dates a year. I have to tell you it will be hard to get your career moving again."

I stood in my living room in Montana, shocked, but knowing he was right. Only by God's grace would I be able to reestablish a major concert career.

FISH TALE

Committed

One day at Hot Creek Ranch, owner Bill Lawrence finished his morning's fishing by telling me—a young teenager at the time—that up above the bridge "there's a goody working in a small channel, between the weeds."

I walked upstream and spotted a fish feeding three feet down in the two-inch-wide channel, creating tiny dimples as it sipped in mayflies. I cast a few inches above the channel, and my fly floated downstream and disappeared in a very subtle sip. I struck—and to my shock, a six-pound rainbow trout jumped straight out of the water in a flying leap. It plunged back in and ran upstream, taking all my loose line, and then my fly reel sang as line sizzled off.

Fifteen seconds of elation ended when I felt the line go suddenly slack, and I knew the fish had broken off. I was sick.

Bill was watching. He asked gruffly, "Why didn't you follow the fish?"

That startled me. For years, I had heard that wading muddied the water for anyone fishing downstream and disturbed insect life in the gravel. "I thought you weren't supposed to wade in a spring creek," I said.

"Listen," Bill said, "If you hook a big trout on a very light leader, the only way you can land him is to stay right with him. If that means jumping into the stream and following him, that's what you need to do. The reason that fish broke off was that he made a right angle in the weeds, and you lost your leverage. When you lost direct contact with the fish, he snapped your leader in the weeds."

I have always remembered that. Whenever I hook a big fish, I know I have to stay with him. Whether that means running down the bank or jumping into a stream and wading to stay close, I do what I have to do. A fisherman has to commit.

13

Light at the End of the Tunnel

1980–83

I once heard Segovia say, "If I go one day without practicing, I know it. The second day I go without practicing, my wife knows it. The third day I go without practicing, the public notices it."

I had gone years without practicing, and Sam Niefeld had said it was going to be difficult, if not impossible, to regain my career. If that was not God's will for me, what would I do? Though I had a willing heart, the idea of going on tour again was very unappealing.

Musicians are quickly forgotten in the music world if they are not out there performing. I didn't make it easy for Sam to find concert bookings when I decided that I would play only sacred music. However, I felt strongly about showing that there had been a change in my life. If God wanted me to return to performing, I believed He would supply the bookings.

By God's grace, I had a supportive group of wise and gifted friends, former guitar students, and fellow musicians who guided me musically and professionally. Several were committed Christians who gave me prayer support and kept in constant touch so that I felt responsible—or *accountable*—for continuing to grow in Christ. They gave me good advice and sometimes even strong exhortation. Because they, too, were accountable to God and other believers, I found I could trust them. They encouraged me as I thought about touring again. Sam informed me that he had booked eighteen concerts, which were to start immediately. This was a far cry from previous seasons, but they were the only bookings he'd been able to find.

I don't know what the Lord wants me to do, I thought more than once. It was humbling to think Columbia Artists Management could book so few concerts, and I did not feel emotionally ready. Eighteen concerts in six weeks—could I do it? Helena and Missoula, Montana; Seattle; Portland; Berkeley, Cupertino, Santa Barbara, and San Diego, California; Tempe, Arizona; College Station and Mesquite, Texas; Salem, Virginia; Towson, Maryland; Newark, Delaware; Storrs, Connecticut; Trenton, New Jersey; Evanston, Illinois; Salt Lake City, Utah; Los Angeles; and then back home to Montana. At least they were arranged in drivable order, so I headed west. Barbara chose not to join me because the Arabian horse nationals were being held at the same time as the tour.

Whether from anxiety, nervous tension, or a fear of performing again, I had a continual migraine on the road. I made it through four concerts, but after Portland, I called Sam. The pain was too intense to go on. I was concerned that I might have a brain tumor.

Sam canceled the rest of my tour, and I ended up at the Mayo Clinic. They diagnosed extreme stress.

I felt like a failure—to myself and to the Lord. Had I thrown away my career a second time? I continued to question whether this was truly what God wanted me to do.

Back in Montana, I decided that I still was committed to making two recordings, and I realized that I felt more ready to do this than to tour. In 1981, I started working on *Sacred Music for the Guitar*, which was later retitled *Simple Gifts*. Recording again was a formidable challenge, but the project moved along fairly well, until I started recording a piece that involved a very difficult passage.

An hour and a half before the recording session, I couldn't play the piece cleanly. I tried altering the top part of my right hand, tilting it various directions. I experimented with a slightly different nail shape, removed a slight amount of fingernail (a dangerous thing to do right before a recording session), and tried different right-hand fingerings, but nothing worked.

Preparing to go into Capitol Records at two o'clock with four sacred pieces, I thought, *I can't do this passage. If I can't do it in my practice room, I sure can't do it when the red light comes on in the recording studio.*

Desperate, I tossed my guitar onto a couch, flopped facedown onto a bed, and cried out to the Lord, *Please help me. I can't play this!*

As if a light had switched on, I instantly thought of a different fingering for that section. I got off the bed, picked up the guitar, sat down, and . . . it worked! Overwhelmed with gratitude, I looked up and said aloud, "Thank you, Lord."

Although that was a difficult time professionally, I was already experiencing joy and peace and a deep-down happiness that I had never known. I was learning how to base my life on Scripture, and I was excited to tell people about my newfound faith. I met a lot of opposition, however, from my friends and even some of my family. First, a neighbor came over with her minister to say I had "too much zeal for the Lord." I thought of John 2:17: "The zeal of thine house hath eaten me up." Then a close friend who was walking with me to a theater said, "You're turning into a religious fanatic. I would downplay it if I were you, stay more in the middle—like me. I'm lukewarm." However, I had recently read the Bible verse that says, "I would thou wert cold or hot. So then because thou art lukewarm, and neither cold nor hot, I will spue thee out of my mouth" (Revelation 3:15-16).

The most devastating criticism came over the telephone, from an intimate family member. "You know, Chris, maybe you have gone a little overboard with your Christianity."

Maybe they're right, I thought.

As it happened, I had just bought a stack of sermon tapes to give away, and I decided to listen to at least one of them first. I chose one on 1 Corinthians 15:58: "Be ye stedfast, unmoveable, always abounding in the work of the Lord, forasmuch as ye know that your labour is not in vain in the Lord."

"Abounding," John expounded, "means *super*abounding. You can never do too much for the Lord."

The Lord brought that tape across my path literally five minutes after that phone conversation. I went instantly from discouraged to supercharged. I said to myself, *Why am I listening to human opinion when the Bible says the opposite?* I even made a secular connection. All my life I had believed in giving 100 percent when I wanted to do something well. Holding back, when it came to the most important thing in my life, just didn't make sense.

In 1979, my sister, Terry, had married Dennis Duggan. Dennis had been a childhood friend whose family went on outings with ours. He, too, was a fly fisherman. One of the joys of that time was that Terry also committed her life to the Lord.

Barbara and I, however, grew further apart. She thought I was taking "this Christian thing" too seriously. We spent more of that year in California than we did in Montana, purchasing a small townhouse in the suburbs of Los Angeles. Barbara seemed happier there, and I liked being closer to Grace Church, recording studios, and the life God seemed to be calling me toward. We spent that winter in LA, and as I became more active with my church and my music, Barbara began to devote more of her time to equestrian shows. We made the decision to permanently relocate to LA a few years later.

I maintained a relationship with Montana State University and pledged that I would return to Bozeman one week during the summer to host a master class, no matter how busy I became throughout the year.

Buying a Montana ranch and trout stream had been my life's goal, and I had lived and breathed and played the guitar around the world in order to acquire my "heaven on earth." Now the fishing ranch became a symbol of my having made something material more important than God. With much prayer over several months, I decided to sell it.

When it sold, I expected to have some regrets, but I found that I was really okay with it. I felt I was doing what the Lord wanted me to do. When Jesus told the rich young ruler to give all he owned to the poor, that wasn't something He asked from everyone. Christ seemed to see that this young man had valued his wealth more than God's Kingdom. I could identify with him, in a way. I had many, many blessings to thank God for. I thought that I would never own anything that wonderful again—but I was at peace.

One of the youth pastors at Grace Church asked me to play and give a message in January 1982. I decided to preach on the theme of "Running the Race with Endurance and Perseverance." I talked about Epaphroditus, who was so lost in serving Christ that he became physically ill, and I used that to illustrate my thoughts when people accused me of overdoing Christianity. I showed how the Bible compares the Christian life to a race. In Philippians 2:16, Paul says, "Holding forth the word of life; that I may rejoice in the day of Christ, that I have not run in vain." Paul writes in 2 Timothy 4:7, "I have fought a good fight, I have finished my course." Hebrews 12:1-2 says, "Let us lay aside every weight, and the sin which doth so easily beset us, and let us run with patience [endurance] the race that is set before us, looking unto Jesus the author and finisher of our faith."

I used the story of my own first experience running the quarter mile. My high school coach had agreed that I could train with the team, even if it was only one day a week because of my guitar-practicing schedule. Up to that point, I'd run only the 100- and 220-yard dash. They were over quickly and didn't take much stamina. At one track meet, our 440 runner got sick, and the coach asked me to run the quarter mile in his place.

When the gun went off, I was out of the block, running as hard and fast as I could. That was the only way I knew how to run. By the first turn, I was nearly ten yards ahead of the next guy. I came into the straightaway feeling great, but halfway down the back stretch, I started to get a strange tingling sensation in my legs. By the time I hit the next curve, I felt nauseous and dizzy, and I was getting a headache. One runner passed me, then another. They had saved something for the end. I saw the finish line ahead, but my legs felt like deadweights, hobbling unsteadily down the track.

I crossed the finish line, thankful for third place, and collapsed.

I learned that running a longer race is different from running a sprint.

During my talk, I likened this to our faith. I think there are plenty of 100-yard-dash Christians, who whisk from here to there and then collapse. But the Christian life is more like running a marathon, in which consistency brings ultimate victory. As Paul said to the Ephesians, "Having done all, to stand" (6:13). That involves hard work, preparation by reading God's Word and praying, and hanging in there through trials and tough times.

ⱺⱻ ⱺⱻ ⱺⱻ

When the *Simple Gifts* album was released, I turned to the second recording project, and I set about trying to create a sacred suite for guitar and orchestra. It didn't happen quickly, and in fact, the first attempt didn't work at all.

It concerned me that some of the Christian music I had heard played on solo guitar sounded simplistic, and for both albums, I wanted to select high-quality music that would both honor God and continue to elevate the instrument musically. My friends Patrick Russ and Ronald Ravenscroft prepared a suite that featured three pieces by Bach—"Jesu, Joy of Man's Desiring," "Sheep May Safely Graze," and "What God Hath Done Is Rightly Done"—combined with "Evening Prayer" by Humperdinck and the traditional Shaker hymn "Simple Gifts." My manager arranged for the Atlanta Symphony to premiere the work, titled *Sacred Suite for Guitar and Orchestra*.

In December 1982, Sam flew to Atlanta for the performance and attended the morning dress rehearsal. This would be my first concert with an orchestra after coming out of retirement. I learned much later that after the rehearsal, Sam took Ronald and Patrick aside and told them, "This will hurt his career. It's a hodgepodge of music that will not be accepted in the classical world. I don't want you to say anything to Christopher until after the performance." It was too late to cancel.

A nice review followed the concert. However, another orchestra had booked the same suite, and when they called Atlanta to see how it had been received, for some reason the concert presenters in Atlanta said, "Don't book the date," and the other orchestra backed out. It was devastating, but when I told Patti Laursen about my desire to do a sacred album for guitar and orchestra, she had an idea. "Chris, why don't you do an all-Bach program instead? Transcribe movements from Bach's sacred cantatas, and instead of calling it a 'sacred suite,' call it a 'Bach suite.' That would give it unity, clarity, and distinction. Besides, Bach's tricentennial is coming up, and we could release the recording in celebration of that year."

I loved the idea. I appreciated Bach's genius, coupled with his commitment to Christ. He once said, "The aim and final reason of all music should be none else but the glory of God," and at the end of many of his compositions, he wrote "S.D.G." for *Soli Deo Gloria*, or "to God alone the glory." Bach's devotion to God and his drive to express that devotion musically gave the world a musical legacy that the great composer Wagner would one day appraise as "the most stupendous miracle in all music."

Running with the Bach suite idea, Patrick and I spent hours at the university library. We listened to movement after movement of nearly three hundred cantatas, nine of which were sparkling gems with excellent potential for transcription. We divided the music between Patrick and Ronald Ravenscroft to orchestrate.

We premiered the Bach suite with the Cincinnati Pops, conducted by Erich Kunzel. The concert was a success, and from that performance, I received bookings for the Bach suite with other orchestras, culminating in a recording with the Los Angeles Chamber Orchestra.

ᚨᚾ ᚨᚾ ᚨᚾ

I returned to Spain in 1983 on another concert tour, and while there, I stopped in Madrid at the famous José Ramírez guitar shop on Concepción Jerónima Street. In a display case that was their "museum," they had some of Segovia's concert guitars. The label inside one striking instrument identified it as a 1967 MT.

I asked if I might be allowed to try the instrument. It was one of the greatest guitars I ever touched, with singing, beautiful high notes and excellent basses. I reluctantly handed it back to the store manager, who locked it back in the display case.

The highlight of that trip, however, was visiting Andrés Segovia in his Madrid apartment. The maestro was now ninety years old and quite frail, but more than gracious. Above the flat where he lived, he had a complete floor where he practiced and did his work. It was filled with memorabilia, and I stood overwhelmed, seeing Andrés Segovia's practice area, pictures of him with kings and queens, and most of all, the maestro himself in this inner sanctum. The Ramírez shop had sent over four guitars for him to look at, and he generously let me play them. Although they were all lovely instruments, I knew that the best one was in the display case.

I told him how much I had loved playing that instrument, and since it had been displayed as one of his guitars, I was not sure who actually owned it. I asked, "Do you think it would be possible for me to purchase that guitar?"

To my shock, he said, "Let me see if they will give it to you."

My emotions went wild with hope and gratitude as he picked up his cane, walked over to his telephone, put on his thick glasses, and leafed through his personal, leather-bound telephone book. I could not believe his kindness. I listened to half of a conversation in Spanish, some of which I didn't understand.

José Ramírez III called back a few minutes later, and Segovia spoke very quickly for about five minutes. When he sat back down, he said that the Ramírez family wouldn't take a million dollars for the guitar. After I returned to Los Angeles, he tried again to get that guitar for me, but I was not surprised that the Ramírez family would not part with it.

☙ ☙ ☙

Once I returned home, I received a surprising phone call. The neighbor boy who years ago had heard me share the gospel during Vacation Bible School had contacted my parents in Idaho and gotten my phone number. Though we hadn't spoken in twenty years, Richard wanted me to know he had received Christ—for real. I was overjoyed to be able to reminisce with him now as a true brother in Christ.

God knew how much I needed that encouragement, especially now. I wished that Barbara shared my zeal for the Lord, but over time, God gave me the grace to be content in our marriage. Since she continued to work full-time with horses, I had great freedom to fully devote my time to God.

I started to ask the Lord how to best use my career to glorify Him. Almost immediately, opportunities began to open up. I decided to give my Christian testimony at the end of my next master class at Montana State University. First I told the students what I was going to do and dismissed those who chose not to stay. I didn't want to have a forced audience. That year, National Public Radio happened to be recording the entire four-day class. The sound engineer left his tape recorder running while I gave my Christian testimony, simply speaking from my heart to the students who chose to stay and listen.

I took that tape to Grace to You ministry for duplication, and it became a valuable tool for telling others about Christ. For years, I gave copies to people when we didn't have the opportunity to sit down and talk.

As I focused my life and career on honoring the Lord, I knew I had finally found a purpose worth living for. God had given me some talent and the discipline to pursue excellence and, therefore, the opportunity to honor Him. However, that didn't make returning to a performing career easy.

FISH TALE

Hammerhead

One day in the early 1980s, I was twenty miles out of Key West, Florida, with fishing guide Rick Ruoff. We were looking for tarpon on the outside of the Marquesas Islands, once a notorious place for pirates. The islands formed a loose circle, and pirate ships would launch their attacks from this hidden area. Ours was the only boat out there that day, and we were fishing in five to twelve feet of water. A light wind was blowing, and the sea was relatively tranquil.

Since there were no other boats around, we fully expected to see some tarpon that afternoon, acting unafraid and lazy, swimming undisturbed near the surface. After about half an hour, Rick said, "Look! Here comes a string of tarpon, but they're flying by, close to the bottom. What scared these fish?" These frantic tarpon were big fish, over a hundred pounds. Rick scratched his head.

Moments later, we understood. Standing on the wobbly ice chest at the bow of the boat, hoping to sight tarpon, I had a perfect view of a rooster-tail wake, about a hundred feet away from us, making it appear as if an invisible water-skier were following the school of fish. Water rained down out of the air, and as we stared in disbelief, we saw a three-foot dorsal fin coming closer. In front of this spray fled a second school of terrified tarpon. They looked like dolphins, frantically breaking the surface in torpedo-like jumps.

The fin belonged to a gigantic hammerhead shark—Rick guessed it was perhaps eighteen feet long—and it completely dwarfed our tarpon boat as it swam by. The shark chased the school of silver king tarpon into shallower water until it caught one that looked as if it weighed about eighty pounds. As the shark rolled aside, the six-foot tarpon in his mouth looked like a trout by comparison. We could see the tarpon's whole side, with its silver scales glistening in the sunlight.

Rick said, "Chris, you need to step down off the ice chest and stand in the center of the boat. This would not be a good time to fall into the water."

We moved the boat and continued fishing elsewhere.

14

Through the Fire

~~~~~~

1984–86

As I started concertizing again, I asked Ron
Ravenscroft, one of the arrangers who worked on
the *Simple Gifts* album, if he would tour with me
and perform some of the guitar duets I had
recorded. He agreed, and for the first time, I toured
with another guitarist. Audiences seemed to like the
variety when we added duets to the second half of
my concert programs, and I enjoyed the company.

In 1984, Ron decided to pursue other musical
endeavors, so I asked one of my gifted young students from Montana State University, David
Brandon, to fill in. David, who had also studied
with Segovia, did a magnificent job. David and I
would tour together for nearly fifteen years.

I quickly developed a deep admiration for and

a wonderful friendship with David, as well as a great respect for his commitment to Christ. He was helpful, courteous, and humble, consistent in his playing, and technically accurate, and he had such an even temperament that it was always a pleasure to be around him.

Another of my good friends at the time was David Thomas. Dave was likable and loved sports. We quickly hit it off. I soon had a great respect for his ability to judge sound, especially when selecting instruments. We enjoyed playing through hundreds of guitars together, and almost invariably, we came up with the same favorite.

Because I respected Dave's ability to hear subtle differences, I invited him to a recording session for the *Bach Celebration* album. Dave was invaluable when we placed the microphones, as was my friend and arranger Patrick Russ. Patti Laursen was in charge, but oftentimes I also asked Dave's opinion on the quality of a take. Patti retired several years later, and after recording *A Tribute to Segovia*, I worked with Dave and Pat as my producers.

Just before Sam Niefeld retired in 1985, he said to me, "Chris, I have never suggested that you do a recording with anyone before, but I am managing a brilliant young soprano named Kathleen Battle. Her voice is high, pure, and beautiful, and I believe it would be a perfect match for the classical guitar. She's performing in San Francisco. If you want to hear her sing, we'll get you tickets."

Pat Russ and I drove up and attended Kathleen's performance, and just as Sam expected, the beauty of her voice greatly impressed me. Sam immediately put together two concerts for Kathleen and me, one in New York at Lincoln Center and one at the Ravinia Festival in Chicago.

In New York—the first time we performed together—the pressure was great. The house was sold out, and the audience included recording executives, our manager, and a *New York Times* reviewer.

The first half went well. After intermission, we were called from our dressing rooms five minutes before the start of the second half. As we sat just offstage, waiting for the lights to dim, Kathy asked me, rather hurriedly, if I could play a few bars of the piece we were scheduled to play after intermission.

My sheet music was out on the stage. Trying to remember a relatively new piece, I thought, *This is not something you want to do right before you perform. You may be practicing wrong notes.* We were only about twenty seconds into it when she said, "Oh, I can't remember the words."

I thought, *What are we going to do?* Believing we had a couple more minutes to figure this out, I was startled when the stage manager opened the stage door wide and said, "Miss Battle, Mr. Parkening, the stage is yours."

Kathy looked at me and coyly said, "Oh, well." Confidently, beautifully, she strolled out onstage as if nothing were wrong. We bowed to the audience, I sat down, and the piece went perfectly.

Generally, performers plan their encores. Not only did Kathy and I plan three encores, but we also planned their order. For the second encore, as she had done for the first, Kathy introduced the piece and explained the Portuguese translation.

I was tuning, thinking about the guitar part I was about to play, not really listening carefully, so I didn't realize that she had skipped the second encore and was introducing the third one. When she finished speaking, I resolutely started the second encore, which opens with a twenty-second solo guitar introduction. I got to the end, and—no Kathy.

I looked up at her, horrified, thinking, *What's wrong?*

She said, "Oh, I'm so sorry, Chris." Then, speaking to the audience, she said, "We had planned to do a second encore, and I skipped it. It's all my fault. Chris, do you mind if we just go straight to the one I introduced?"

I don't think I said anything. Kathy was so gracious and funny about the whole incident that the audience chuckled warmly, delighted by her candid explanation.

After the Chicago concert, we recorded the album *Pleasures of Their Company* for EMI—Capitol's parent company. Because this was an album that included sacred and secular music, I wanted to make a statement on it that I was a Christian, so I asked John MacArthur for some advice. He asked me what was going on the album.

"Some Dowland songs, Brazilian songs, spirituals, Spanish songs."

He wrote a few lines and handed them to me. They read, "Performance has true integrity when the heart of the artist is conveyed in the music. Such is the case with Kathleen and Christopher, for whom the spirituals, in particular, reflect their faith."

He asked, "Is that okay?"

Delighted, I said, "I could have spent a month on that and it wouldn't have been as good."

Concert by concert, recording by recording, my career appeared to be getting back on track. However, I still had things to learn.

To a reviewer and sometimes to an audience, you may be only as good as your last concert, and some reviewers were not very kind. In 1986, I received a blistering review from a Southwestern newspaper. Before the concert, I had done an interview for the religious section of the paper and given my Christian testimony. After the concert, the reviewer quoted from my previous interview and ripped me apart, saying, "Bach would have thrown him out of the choir loft."

During another concert series, I played the Rodrigo *Fantasía para un Gentilhombre*, which has a lengthy guitar solo in the last movement that ends in a long, fast, and difficult run. To my frustration, I dropped several notes in the first performance. After the concert, I was invited to a restaurant for dessert with a Christian couple. I don't often get asked this question, but they asked, "How do you think you played?"

I said, "I generally assess my performance of that concerto based on one passage, the difficult run in the last movement. So tonight, I honestly don't feel that I played very well."

They asked, "You told us that you practiced hard and dedicated the concert to the Lord, didn't you?"

"Yes."

Then the woman said something profound, which has stayed with me ever since. "God is sovereign, and He can have the people hear exactly what He wants them to hear."

I agreed, theoretically, but I also knew I had dropped notes in the run. The next day, though, my review in the local newspaper appeared under a headline that read, "Parkening Plays Flawless Concert." She was right. God can have people hear exactly what He wants them to hear. I don't like to presume on God's grace, so I practice hard for every concert, and after committing it to the Lord, I try to leave it to Him to take charge of the rest.

�k꘏ ꘏k꘏ ꘏k꘏

I always feel more pressure when I'm getting ready to play in the Los Angeles area, and on the night before I was to play a concert at Ambassador Auditorium in Pasadena—I had practiced hard and felt ready—the telephone rang. It was on the floor, so I had to lean over to answer it, and as I did, I felt a sharp pain on the left side of my lower back. I finished the conversation massaging my back with one hand, trying to alleviate the muscle cramp. It got worse, so I tried some exercises. Nothing helped. The pain became unbearable, and suddenly I felt as if I was going to throw up.

My sister, Terry, is always good for a quick diagnosis, and when I called her to describe my incredible pain, she didn't hesitate. "Oh, Chris, you have a kidney stone. You need to get to the hospital."

Barbara drove me to the emergency room around midnight. I was in great pain. After about an hour, a doctor did an X-ray and confirmed a stone in my left kidney.

A nurse walked in and told me, "I need to find your vein. The doctor has ordered morphine for you. In about twenty seconds, you're going to feel some relief."

He was right. I literally felt the pain melt away. Within thirty seconds, it was gone. I slept a couple of hours at the hospital and then went home. The following morning, I told my personal physician what had happened.

She said, "If it happens again, I can prescribe a very strong pain medication. If you get another attack, you can either take two of these pills or else go back to the hospital."

As the concert day began, my entire body ached, and the last thing I felt like doing was practicing, much less performing that night. I called the presenter late that morning and told him I'd had a kidney stone. He said, "Oh, Chris, I've had one too. My wife says it's worse than childbirth. We can cancel the concert. In fact, I think you should. Those we can't notify by radio we can stop in the parking lot."

I said, "No, Wayne, I'd like to play the concert."

"Then I'll make an announcement just before the concert that you've had a kidney stone—"

"No," I insisted, "that will make the audience uneasy. I'll just play." I prayed all day, asking for the Lord's grace to get me through.

At about four o'clock that afternoon, I had another attack. I remembered that my doctor had said to either go to the hospital or take two of the pills she had prescribed. I tried the medication and kept praying.

I walked out onstage that night at 8:05. I played as well as I could, under the circumstances—the fingerboard looked fuzzy, and I felt as if I were in a haze, like a dream sequence. Very unnerving. Though I had practiced hard, I certainly didn't play my best first half of a concert.

I walked offstage at intermission and took the elevator downstairs. During the second half of the concert, I was going to play some duets with David Brandon. As I walked by his open dressing room door, I said, "Did you hear the first half?"

"Yes. The monitor was on in my dressing room."

"I didn't play very well, did I?"

"Chris, you were trying your best and playing for the Lord. So He is well pleased. Go out in the second half and give it everything you've got."

The second half of the concert went as well as I have ever played. God's grace was poured out upon me, I know, that night at Ambassador Auditorium.

❧ ❧ ❧

In 1986, Barbara and I found a buyer for our horse property near Bozeman, which included the home and a large barn with an indoor riding arena. We had put an enormous amount of planning, physical labor, and expense into building that arena, where we could raise and train horses. The barn was nearly as big as a football field and could be seen for miles.

Three days after the sale went through, at about two o'clock in the morning, the telephone woke me up out of a dead sleep.

I picked it up and heard frantic yelling. I could tell it was a woman, but I couldn't make out who it was or what she was saying.

Finally, I recognized the voice as a friend from Montana, a woman who had kept her horses at our barn. She had an absolutely tragic tone in her voice. "Your barn is burning down! Your beautiful barn is burning to the ground! You can see the fire from ten miles away."

When I finally calmed her down, she told me that our horse barn with the riding arena was in flames. There was no way of saving it.

I hung up and then stood in the dark room in a state of shock and bewilderment. It wasn't my barn anymore. We had sold it three days before. Still, how could that have happened?

Slowly, we learned more news, although not much. Arson was suspected, but fortunately there were no animals inside.

That was all we heard.

A few months later, when I next returned to Bozeman, I drove out there and walked through the rubble and the scarred landscape, seeing things I vaguely recognized. I remembered how much work had gone into that building. It was all gone. Burned up, along with that part of my life.

As I walked through the charred, smelly debris, I felt as if I'd been handed a final statement regarding the value of all the labor I'd put into acquiring and improving my "heaven on earth." A chapter of my life had ended. I thought again of 1 Corinthians chapter 3, which says that the believer's deeds will be judged by fire, and only those done for Christ's Kingdom will remain. Martin Luther once said, "I have held many things in my hands, and I have lost them all; but whatever I have placed in God's hands, that I still possess."

I got into my car and drove away without looking back.

FISH TALE

Running from the Storm

In the late 1970s, having fished for tarpon for five or six years, I thought it would be smart to buy my own tarpon boat. I could spot the fish nearly as well as the fishing guides could, and it would save an enormous amount in guide fees. I purchased an eighteen-foot tarpon boat with an outboard motor that could cruise at forty miles an hour.

A tarpon boat has a platform over the outboard motor that allows the guide to stand up and pole the boat around with a twenty-foot-long fiberglass pole. In the Florida Keys, this kind of fishing is generally done in five to ten feet of water. The angler stands in the front of the boat, often on an ice chest, to help "sight" the fish. The cast isn't made until the school of fish has actually been spotted in the water.

To get out to the fishing spots, which can be as far as twenty miles from the dock, the fisherman often navigates between flats, sandy bars with narrow channels winding through them. Some of the channels are marked with stakes.

On this particular trip, I invited my friend Ernie along. I told him that I would teach him how to pole the boat and that we would alternate casting for the tarpon, or "poons," as fishermen call them.

We flew to the Florida Keys, checked into a motel, and without asking about the weather, went to the marina where they kept my boat. I took Ernie out to Sandy Key Basin, where there had been reports of tarpon on a certain tide.

A number of other tarpon boats were scattered here and there, and tarpon seemed to be rolling everywhere. A few clouds were blowing in, and the overcast sky made it difficult to see the fish and line up a cast. At that time, the guides often used CB radios, which I did not have, to communicate. No other fishermen were within shouting distance, and I noticed that one by one, the other boats started to leave our area. But the tarpon were still rolling, so Ernie and I kept fishing.

We could see a black line on the horizon, but it was far away, and we didn't pay any attention to it. Out in the Keys, you generally have at least a light wind, but that day, it became totally calm. Even when the last boat I could see left our area, Ernie and I kept fishing.

Poling the boat along, Ernie said, "Chris, listen to this." He stuck his pole into the air. It went *bzzzzz*. He lowered it. Nothing. He raised it again. *Bzzzzz*.

I raised my fly rod. *Bzzzzz!*

At that moment, Ernie and I looked at each other with the sudden realization of the electrically charged atmosphere and the fast approaching blackness on the horizon and said, "Let's get out of here!"

There were no other boats in sight. It dawned on me that my inexperience might have gotten us into big trouble, and a deep fear began to well up inside me. I put the rod away, fastened the pole to the side of the boat, raised the outboard motor, and shouted, "Ernie, we're going in at full speed." I got the boat up on plane and cranked the motor up to full rpm. It was still dead calm and now completely overcast, so the water looked silvery, making it difficult to find the stakes that marked the channels through the flats. I stood up, looking with all my might. If we missed a channel, we would run our boat up on a sandbar, dry-dock it, and be stranded miles from the dock.

My heart was in my throat. I couldn't find the stakes, and suddenly—there they were! After about forty minutes of running the boat flat out, we pulled into the marina to find two dockhands waiting for us, like parents waiting for their children to get home from a late date. One guy was already seated on the forklift. He hoisted my boat out of the water and drove it into the secure barn. They told us a tremendous storm was approaching, with hurricane-force winds over eighty miles an hour.

The storm was just starting to sweep over us with its powerful wind and heavy rain. Ernie and I looked at one another and shook our heads. We could easily have been caught in that storm. If we'd stayed out five minutes longer, we might not have made it in. Looking back, I see that this was another thread of God's amazing grace running through my life. I learned that it was worth paying for the vast amount of experience that the guides possessed. This wasn't about trout fishing on a stream bank. This was the dangerous ocean.

I sold the boat.

15

Mr. President

1986–90

When Sam Niefeld retired, he passed the management baton to Andrew Grossman. I told Andrew
about my retirement, my conversion, and my desire
to play again for the glory of God. Andrew had
enormous respect for Sam, and because he believed
in the beauty of the classical guitar as a concert
instrument, he pursued some ambitious goals on
my behalf. Early on, he said, "I want you to appear
on a televised *Live from Lincoln Center with
Placido Domingo*. You should do some duets with
the legendary tenor, play a solo, and perform with
the orchestra." I thought, *I'd love to, but I don't
think it will happen.*

It did. Moments before I walked out onstage—

after all the rehearsals and backstage interviews, even as Placido Domingo was introducing me—the presenter told me, "This is the biggest thing you've ever done, Christopher, the most important concert you've ever played. If you do well tonight, your career is made." Then he opened the stage door.

As I walked out in front of a live national audience, I couldn't help but think of the reverse: *And if you play terribly, your career is ruined.* But this time, I didn't let the pressure get to me. I drew strength by reminding myself, *God is in control, and I'm playing for Him.* To my relief—and I hope, to God's glory—I was able to relax and still play well.

Kathleen Battle and I performed for the Grammy Award show that same year. Our *Pleasures* recording had just received a nomination for Best Classical Recording. I had played at the Grammys the year before, accepting Segovia's Lifetime Achievement Award on his behalf, and I remembered how nerve-racking it was. Backstage, people frantically rushed around making last-second preparations. CBS cameras were everywhere, and the first few rows of the Shrine Auditorium in Los Angeles were packed with musical celebrities.

Kathy and I prayed together backstage, asking for God to be glorified. During the commercial break, backstage staff escorted us to center stage, where the camera was set up and our mikes were placed. I looked out over eight thousand people sitting in the audience, and one of the stage directors said to me, "Mr. Parkening, we have twenty seconds till air."

I tried to keep my focus.

He went on. "In twenty seconds, you'll be performing live for more than 200 million people."

I couldn't believe he said that. It was the last thing I wanted to hear just before the performance. I looked up at Kathy and said, "The only important thing is for us to play and sing for the Lord."

She agreed.

ⲟᎷⲟ ⲟᎷⲟ ⲟᎷⲟ

Sharing my faith on the road was not without problems. Once, I played several rehearsals and performances with a major symphony, and one driver was assigned to take me to and from the hotel, so we naturally got to know each other. It turned out he was a Beatles fan, and he brought up John Lennon's famous statement that the Beatles were "more popular than Jesus."

It seemed a perfect segue for me to share my brief, personal Christian testimony. "It's interesting that you mention Jesus," I said, and then proceeded to tell my story. About two weeks after those concerts, I received a call from my manager. The artistic director of the symphony said that the limo driver had been offended by our conversation. Andrew said, "Chris, you can't push your faith on people."

I thought of Mark 8:38, in which Jesus says, "Whosoever therefore shall be ashamed of me and of my words in this adulterous and sinful generation . . . of him also shall the Son of man be ashamed, when he cometh in the glory of his Father with the holy angels," and Matthew 10:32-33: "Whosoever therefore shall confess me before men, him will I confess also before my Father which is in heaven. But whosoever shall deny me before men, him will I also deny before my Father which is in heaven."

I said, "Andrew, it was just a friendly conversation. I only told him about my experience when he brought up the subject. I am sorry that he was offended, but I believe that I was gracious in my conversation."

❧❧ ❧❧ ❧❧

We never know when death will touch us or someone we love. I was vacationing with friends several months after that conversation when Andrew called with sad, shocking news. Maestro Segovia had passed away in Madrid, at the age of ninety-four.

I suppose one might have expected it since Segovia was in his nineties, but the news saddened me greatly. My musical inspiration, mentor, and friend was gone.

I felt a great sense of loss, as though a father figure had passed away. The words of Jack Marshall from so many years before rang in my ears: "Get the records of Andrés Segovia. He's the greatest guitarist in the world." I felt an even deeper sense of commitment to help carry on his legacy. In my opinion, no guitarist ever had played as beautifully and musically as Andrés Segovia. To me, that wasn't simply admiration. It was fact.

I wanted to honor him with a recording, *A Tribute to Segovia*, which was an all-Spanish CD that included many of the compositions he loved most. At my request, the U.S. distributor of Ramírez guitars asked Amalia Ramírez and her brother José Ramírez IV if I might use that beautiful instrument Segovia had wanted me to have from the Ramírez museum, to record the tribute album.

They kindly sent it to me, and I was able to perform on that phenomenal guitar for almost two years, while I toured to promote the recording. I also used it to record composer John Williams's music for the movie *Stepmom*. When John announced to the orchestra at Sony/MGM studios that I was playing a very special instrument that once belonged to Andrés Segovia, they gave the instrument—and therefore Maestro Segovia—an ovation.

On a return trip to Europe, I learned another tough lesson.

I had a concert in Queen Elizabeth Hall in London in the fall of 1986. When I walked out onstage, I happened to glance into the audience and was startled to see the same famous English guitarist who had attended my horrible Queen Elizabeth Hall debut. Throughout the entire concert, I kept thinking things such as, *He would have done it better than that* or *That part went pretty well.* The only thing on my mind through the whole evening was how well he might think I was doing, and consequently, I didn't play my best.

After the concert, as I sat in the greenroom signing programs, I happened to look up and see the man as he walked into the room. He was the spitting image of that English guitarist . . . but it wasn't him! I had played the entire concert for a person who wasn't even there. I promised myself never to do that again.

Also in the autograph line was a young Israeli classical guitarist who was vacationing in London. As we spoke, he asked fervently if we might have lunch together the following day. Normally the day after a concert is a travel day, but this time I had a layover, so I agreed.

We met at a restaurant around noon the next day. I learned that he lived in Tel Aviv and that during his London vacation, he happened to see the advertisement for my concert. I told him of my great love for the Jewish people, and I started to share with him some of the prophecies relating to the Messiah, the Anointed One of Israel, the promised Savior of the nation.

"Oh! *Mashiach*!" he said, using the Hebrew term for "Messiah." He seemed interested in what I had to say.

I asked, "Have you ever read Isaiah 53?" That chapter is one of the most explicit prophecies of the Messiah in the Old Testament.

He said he had not, so I found a telephone book and located a Christian bookstore close by. We went there from the restaurant.

I got him a Hebrew Old and New Testament, then sat down with him and read him Isaiah 53 from my English Bible as he followed along in the Hebrew version. He said, "That is an excellent translation. That has to be talking about Jesus Christ."

We have not kept in touch, but I hope a seed was planted that day.

On the same tour, in Vienna, I happened to encounter Leonard Bernstein, who was finishing a rehearsal with the Vienna Philharmonic. I was getting ready to perform at the Musikverein, and he was finishing a rehearsal. I introduced myself and asked if he would ever consider writing a concerto for the guitar, as I had suggested to Aaron Copland years before.

He thanked me for asking but declined, saying, "You have the beautiful Rodrigo concerto. You're much better off than some of the other instruments."

A year or two later, when I was preparing to play a guitar-and-orchestra arrangement of "America" from *West Side Story* with the Philadelphia Orchestra (as part of Bernstein's seventieth birthday celebration), I asked him to look at Pat Russ's arrangement, which he approved, and we performed "America" as an encore after the Rodrigo concerto. As always, it was important to me that the arrangement remain as faithful to the original composition as possible.

I was in New York, playing at the Mostly Mozart Festival, when a call from my sister, Terry, brightened my day. She and her husband, Dennis, had just visited a place that she called "the most wonderful trout stream I have ever fished in my life." I wasn't surprised to hear that it was close to Hot Creek Ranch. The ranch was privately owned, and Terry and Dennis had been invited by a member to spend some time there.

Just knowing there was another such place encouraged my

heart in the middle of a long tour. To my delight, Terry added that the ranch member who hosted them, Bud Hartman, loved the classical guitar. Since we had guitar and fishing in common, I invited him to my upcoming Hollywood Bowl concert, and I was excited when he invited me to come and fish at the ranch.

The fishing was spectacular. I asked him, "If a membership ever comes up for sale, would you let me know?"

He shook his head and said, "Don't hold your breath. Memberships are kept in the family. It's very rare that one becomes available—only every ten years or so."

I put it out of my mind and focused instead on my upcoming concert, a very important performance. I had been invited to perform at the White House for President Reagan. Two days before I was scheduled to fly to Washington DC, Bud telephoned me and said, "A membership has just come up for sale. It's going to go fast; it comes with a cabin. I'll fly you up after you get back if you want to see the ranch again." The idea thrilled me.

The White House concert was to be held in July 1988 on the South Lawn, with the Washington Monument in the background. If the weather turned inclement, they would move everyone into the East Room. I was also invited to have dinner with the president and his guests in the Rose Garden before I performed. The attire was "tux, black tie," but the social secretary suggested that for the performance I wear a white tie and tails, so it involved a change for the performance.

I was able to bring Barbara, Terry, and Dennis to the event. When we arrived, we went through security screening, were assigned protocol escorts, and then were ushered to a room, where we waited to meet the president. It was amazing to see original paintings of presidents and realize that we were actually standing *inside* the White House. Everything—furniture, carpets, chandeliers—was exquisite. There were many distinguished guests, news anchors, and others I recognized from television.

We talked for a little while, and when the military band played "Hail to the Chief," we formed a greeting line. President and Mrs. Reagan and their special guests, Turkish president Kenan Evren and his wife, came in one by one. We met each of them, shook hands, and chatted briefly. The whole occasion was extremely formal and dignified.

We were then escorted to a table in the Rose Garden. Sitting at my table was George Herbert Walker Bush, who was then the vice president. We talked about a number of things, including a mutual love of fishing.

The formal dinner was impeccably laid out and had several courses, and I asked to be excused from dessert because I needed to warm up and change into my white tie and tails.

Actually, I felt less pressure about playing my guitar than I felt about the introduction I'd been asked to make onstage. The social secretary had said, "They would like some brief comments about the program. But you must start your opening remarks exactly according to protocol: 'President Reagan, Mrs. Reagan, President Evren, Mrs. Evren, and distinguished guests.'" I was very concerned that I do it properly and pronounce the Turkish president's name correctly.

After dinner and dessert, all the guests moved to the South Lawn, and after I was introduced, I walked up the long carpet runway onto the stage. It was a beautiful, clear evening, with the brightly lit Washington Monument standing out in stark relief against the night sky.

For an encore, I had learned a traditional Turkish folk song to honor President Reagan's special guests. Everyone stood at the end, and President Reagan came up onstage and thanked me, followed by Mrs. Reagan and President Evren and his wife. Pictures were taken, and we chatted briefly—a chance to relax together after the evening's formal program.

Just before the Reagans retired for the evening, I had a chance to speak briefly with the president. I told him that I prayed for him often. He thanked me, and I'll never forget what he said next. "This job has dropped me to my knees many, many times. I thank you so very much for your prayers."

After I put my guitar away and most of the guests had left, an aide asked if I would like a private tour of the White House. With the pressure off, the tour was a magical end to a very special evening.

As soon as we got home, I hurried to Bud's fishing ranch and fished with a dry fly for about three hours, catching and releasing over fifty trout.

The next time I stood in that stream, I was a member of the fishing ranch, and I thought, *Isn't this just like the Lord? When you give up something, He sometimes gives you something better.*[2]

FISH TALE

The Frog Fly

Hot Creek is a "dry-fly-fishing only" stream. A dry fly floats on the water. With wet-fly-fishing, the imitation insect goes down under the surface. Typically, you fish a wet fly by casting downstream and stripping the line in through the index finger of the right hand, moving the fly underwater toward you. You cast a dry fly upstream and let the current carry it down toward you, as though it were an insect floating freely on the stream. The typical "hatch" insect at Hot Creek was a caddis fly, which was a small, mothlike insect that floated on the surface. I had learned to tie flies when I was six years old, because they always worked better than the ones you could buy, and I always came to Hot Creek with a box full of caddis flies—"sedges"—specially tied for our vacation.

One day while I was out fishing with one of these flies, I started hearing explosions in the water. When a big trout feeds on a live caddis fly, it is typically very quiet. It rises up to the surface slowly and rolls on the fly—its head sticks out of the water momentarily and then sinks again. A smaller trout might jump, but Hot Creek had some very large trout that generally fed quietly.

I continued casting, quietly working along . . . then *boom*— *splash*—there was that noise again. It happened sporadically, and generally close to the bank.

I reeled in my line, put my fly in the rod clip to hold it, and walked over to where I had heard the explosion. To my astonishment, I saw about a dozen one-inch frogs working their way from a little rainwater pond toward the creek bank.

One by one, they would leap into the stream and swim away. This was like a floating banquet for a big trout, something that he couldn't feed on quietly. It made an implosion in the stream, almost as if you'd flushed a toilet.

Really intrigued now, I walked back up the bank, caught a few of these little frogs, and headed over to the edge of the stream. Trying not to move my hand much, so as not to be seen by the trout, I tossed one out, watched it float along the surface for a few seconds, and then—POW!

I dashed back to the cabin and started to tie a "frog fly" out of deer hair. It had to float, or it wouldn't be legal on this dry-fly-only stream. I made some little legs, and a body about the same size as the frogs I'd seen. I tied up three of them and then asked my mom to drive into town (Mammoth Lakes) and buy some green and brown markers, so I could paint this deer hair frog the color of real frogs. She bought me the colors that I wanted, I applied the finishing touches, and then I headed out to try them.

I tied one "frog fly" on the end of a rather long leader, and with my dad standing beside me, I threw the fly across a deep pool and started stripping the frog back toward me. Nothing happened. I made another cast. Still nothing happened. Third cast. About that time, my dad said, "You can't do this! You look like you're wet-fly-fishing, stripping the fly back like that."

Dejectedly, I cut the frog fly off, put it in my fly box, and went back to using the standard caddis-fly pattern. My dad went off to fish somewhere else.

I had learned to cast with a very long leader, which enabled me to fish downstream with a dry fly. I was fishing a deep spot along the bank with a caddis fly when I heard it again. The implosion—

in the same channel where I was fishing! There was a huge trout there, feeding and waiting for another frog to jump off the bank.

It was just too much of a temptation.

Without changing my leader, I tied on the frog fly. On my first cast, I threw it out and piled up the line, so the frog fly floated completely free downstream, to the point where that big trout was. *Boom!* He sucked down the frog fly, making a commotion that spread ripples across the entire stream—but I struck so hard that I broke him off.

I sprinted back to the cabin and said, "Dad, look at this! If I cast this frog fly upstream, it can drift perfectly free. Can I show you?"

He agreed to come watch. When he saw that it worked, he went to the ranch manager, told him about our discovery, and asked if my frog fly could be fished legally as a dry fly. The owner gave me the okay.

It was wonderful! I started fishing it upstream in the big, deep channels, where I would cast a frog fly up at the end of a pool and then wait for a monster trout to hit it. One after another, I was hooking huge trout that would fight hard and jump, and give me an exciting time before I released them. I was catching bigger trout than I'd ever caught in my life, because these frogs were irresistible to them.

It was phenomenal fishing.

16

Recording Rodrigo

1990–97

The early 1990s were busy years for recording and performing. I played about fifty concerts each year, and David Brandon and I released an album titled *Virtuoso Duets* in 1990. That same year, my manager, Andrew, received a call from the Hallmark card company, asking me to play "Silent Night" with Julie Andrews and "Jesu, Joy of Man's Desiring" with the London Symphony Orchestra on that year's Hallmark Christmas album, *The Sounds of Christmas*. I met with Julie several times and found her delightfully warm and kind. *A Tribute to Segovia* was released in 1991.

During the early 1990s, I was scheduled to play a concert in San Francisco. After arriving in Oakland, I caught a taxi in front of the airport and settled in for the long ride into the city. In the course of travel, I could tell by our conversation that this taxi driver was a Christian, so we spent the last half of the ride talking about the Lord. His parting remark stuck in my mind: "Remember, we're all slaves for Christ. Right?"

I said, "You're right." He had been paraphrasing 1 Corinthians 4:1: "Let a man regard us in this manner, as servants of Christ and stewards of the mysteries of God" (NASB), and I found it interesting that he didn't use the word *servant*. That might have been considered more politically correct, especially considering he was African-American, but he used a stronger word, quoting the apostle Paul, who said he was a *bondslave* of Christ.

I was so impressed by that man. He had reminded me that the greatest in the Kingdom of God is the servant of all. He had communicated a real servant's heart for the Lord, something I wanted to emulate.

During Carnegie Hall's hundred-year celebration season, in 1991, I was invited to perform Joaquín Rodrigo's *Concierto de Aranjuez*. I had just toured with *Aranjuez*, arguably the best-known work for the guitar; nevertheless, it's an artistically demanding, virtuosic composition. The first movement gives the soloist no chance to warm up. It opens with a *rasgueado*, an extremely fast, flamenco-like strumming technique, then the orchestra restates the theme, and when the guitar comes back in, it's like running a 100-meter dash over and over again. I felt honored and humbled to finally perform at the landmark Carnegie Hall during that important season.

ᐧᐧᐧ ᐧᐧᐧ ᐧᐧᐧ

The following summer, six days before I was to play the *Concierto de Aranjuez* again—this time at the Hollywood Bowl with the Los

Angeles Philharmonic—I was in the High Sierras with Terry, her husband, Dennis, and their three children, Christi, John, and David. Barbara had stayed in Los Angeles to care for her horses. Terry's two boys slept on a couch bed in the living room of the cabin. In the morning, after everyone was up, I started to close up the heavy couch bed.

As I started to fold the bed, Terry—trying to be helpful—ran over to the other side of the bed and gave it a shove. Neither of us noticed that the ring finger of my left hand was between two hinged metal struts.

The bed's metal scissors crunched down. Blood streamed from my lacerated ring finger. It looked so horrible that Terry got sick to her stomach. We found bandages, towels, and ice, and my brother-in-law went to fetch a doctor, who fortunately was staying in a cabin about a mile away. We all sat down in a circle and prayed for healing, wisdom, and direction.

The doctor concluded that the bone wasn't broken. "You'll just have to be careful about infection. If I were you, I would head back home where your doctor is and ice your hand on the trip back."

I agreed we should go home, but I was determined to play my concert in six days. We packed up immediately and made the six-hour drive home, stopping at fast-food restaurants to get cups of ice for my finger.

The next day, with five days to go before the Hollywood Bowl concert, I should have been practicing the difficult concerto. My stiff left hand ached, and my finger turned black and blue. I didn't even try to practice. The day after that, my hand still ached, but I knew I had to practice a little. I pressed down gently on the fingerboard, careful not to reopen the laceration. The third day before the concert, I went through the piece very slowly, but I cut my practicing short because my hand hurt so badly.

Two days before the concert, I was able to practice a little more but still not enough to adequately prepare me to perform. The night before the concert, I listened to a tape entitled "The Sufficiency of God's Grace." John MacArthur quoted 2 Corinthians 12:9: "My grace is sufficient for you, for power is perfected in weakness" (NASB). It hit me that the suffering that humbles us, that forces us to God in prayer, and that makes us cry out for grace to endure, is the very source of power in our lives. I had lost all human ability to deal with this difficulty and was left to trust totally in God's power to sustain me.

I prayed for God's strength and went to bed that night in perfect peace. The next day I practiced for a short time and then drove to the Bowl. I couldn't put a bandage around my ring finger because I needed full mobility, and when I walked out onstage in front of the immense audience and the hot stage lights, I told no one what had happened—and I played the Rodrigo concerto as well as I had ever played it. Afterward, the manager of the Los Angeles Philharmonic said something like, "Christopher, great concert."

I said, "Ernest, look at my left hand."

He gasped. "When did that happen?"

"Six days ago."

"How could you possibly play?"

"It was the grace of God—completely."

For years, I had been asked when I was going to record the Rodrigo concerto. I had played it many times on tour, but the only time it was recorded—in Japan, with the composer present—the recording we made was not intended for release.

In 1993 I played the Tokyo recording for my producer, David Thomas, who made an interesting comment: "As well as you were playing then technically, your waiting twenty years to record this was musically important. You have matured with the piece. Had you recorded it then, it would have been a fine technical recording but not as good musically."

Now EMI asked me to record both Rodrigo concertos in London with the Royal Philharmonic, Andrew Litton conducting. I had a concert booked at Royal Festival Hall several days before the recording, which would give us extra rehearsal time, plus the performance experience.

I asked Dave Thomas and Pat Russ to produce the recording, which would include Pat's adaptation of William Walton's Five Bagatelles for Guitar and Orchestra. My mom and sister flew over from Los Angeles for the concert.

I arrived in London before the others, feeling jet-lagged and a little lonely. While in London, I received a phone call in my hotel room that cheered me up dramatically. The manager of the Royal Philharmonic Orchestra told me that Joaquín Rodrigo and his daughter had flown to London from Madrid as part of his ninetieth birthday celebration, and he was going to attend the concert! "They would like to know if you want to meet with them before the first rehearsal."

I said, "Absolutely! Anytime they want!"

We set a time, I hung up, and then I said, "Thank you, Lord, that you arranged—without my even knowing it—for Joaquín Rodrigo to be here."

Over the years, many small changes had been made to both the *Concierto de Aranjuez* and the *Fantasía para un Gentilhombre.* Now we could get his corrections and, we hoped, his stamp of approval. Both would be priceless. What a blessing and a tremendous privilege.

The next day everyone else arrived in town. I met with Maestro Rodrigo at Abbey Road Studios before the first recording session. EMI had arranged for a pianist to play the orchestral parts, which enabled Andrew Litton's questions about the orchestration to be answered by the composer himself.

I was ready to go through the guitar part of both concertos. I had made red Xs in my music at every place I had a question so I would not waste his time. Rodrigo had been blind from the age of three and did not speak English. His daughter, Cecelia, translated as we started with the *Fantasía* concerto, including Andrés Segovia's many small changes to the guitar part. I would play the change and sometimes the original music too. As it turned out, he liked all of Segovia's changes better than his original version—except for one.

A change had been made to the guitar part, but in the following passage, the orchestra still "echoed" that theme as originally written. Rodrigo wanted the two parts to match, so he asked me to play that guitar part as it was originally written.

Also, Pat had heard a chord in Segovia's recording, during the cadenza of the final movement before the long and difficult run, that was different from the printed music. We had played the Segovia recording many times, and Pat felt sure that he heard a D-sharp against a D-natural, but that chord wasn't written in the printed music. I played the chord for Rodrigo and asked him which one was correct.

He said that Pat had heard correctly: Segovia played it right, and the printed music was wrong. It had been recorded incorrectly by many artists, but the D-sharp against the D-natural was, he said, "more Rodrigo," and he wanted that chord. We guessed that when the publisher's copyist saw the dissonance, he made the "correction."

The most memorable moment came when we asked the composer if he would play the opening of the second movement—that beautiful adagio theme—so that we could capture his phrasing for the recording. Cecelia led him over to the piano. The ninety-year-old composer felt his hands on the keyboard, started that beautiful theme, and played so exquisitely that everyone present was moved to tears. For the recording, and every time since then, I have tried to remember that phrasing.

After we performed the concertos, the composer was introduced. The orchestra and an audience of over five thousand people stood up as Rodrigo's daughter led him down the aisle to the stairs of the stage. Andrew Litton and I escorted him to center stage, where he was presented with a bouquet. My sister, Terry, captured the moment on film, and EMI used it for the CD cover.

Some have complained that there is too much yellow in that shot, that it's grainy, and that maybe I should have had a studio picture taken for the cover, as with most of my other recordings. But what would that be, compared to having the composer of the world's most magnificent concerto for guitar and orchestra standing with me on a concert stage? For me, having that photograph is comparable to a concert pianist having a photograph of Liszt or Rachmaninoff onstage next to him after he performed their composition.

We started recording the following day. During all those rehearsals, extra sessions with the composer, and the performance, I had worn down my nails. The first movement includes a number of fast, difficult runs, and after a couple of takes, I confessed privately to Dave that my middle fingernail was too short to play accurately and at tempo.

Dave called a break. Everybody else headed out while Dave and I walked over to a corner of the studio and prayed.

During that twenty-minute break, I experimented with the possibility of playing the runs with I-A (index finger, ring finger) of the right hand, not using the middle (M) finger at all. I thought, *How can this be? I haven't practiced the piece like this!* Yet I remembered, many years ago at the LA Music Center, watching Segovia play the Gigue by Weiss/Ponce, which has several difficult runs. When he started the first run, I noticed that he struggled a bit. Then when the section repeated, he switched from I-M to I-A right in the middle of the concert. The second time, it sounded perfectly clean.

So on the brink of an extremely important recording session, there I sat—experimenting with playing the runs I-A! As a young guitarist, I'd played exercises for the right and left hand, some of which included scales with alternate fingerings. I hadn't done those exercises in years. It was slow going at first, and it felt awkward, but as I kept at it, I was able to play faster and cleaner. When Dave came back from his break and walked over to where I was practicing, he said, "That's an answer to prayer. Those runs sound perfect!"

In just twenty minutes, the Lord had given me the ability to play all those difficult runs with completely new right-hand fingerings.

༺ ༺ ༺

Recording is an extremely important part of a musician's career. Recently I was talking with some of my guitar students about the big picture of making recordings, and I gave them several suggestions.

First, it's important to be very prepared with your music, including interpretation. You don't want to experiment in the recording studio. Record yourself before you ever get to a professional studio so you can hear musicianship, tempos, and timing, and decide where you want to use certain tone colors. As I have mentioned, Segovia told me years ago, "Burnish a piece at least one year on tour before recording it," although of course, recording companies want you to do it the other way around: first record and then tour to sell the recording. I believe that if you play the music first, you'll subtly change things and mature with the piece, and you'll have a much better record.

You also want beautiful sound reproduction. At the outset of each recording project, we devote a three-hour recording session strictly to getting the sound right. We experiment with different microphones, as well as their distance and placement, and with whether or not to use carpeting on the floor. All these change with every recording.

Sometimes we check the sound in several different recording studios. Most studios allow us to come in for a sound check. Dave, Pat, and I once scheduled studio tests all around Los Angeles to determine where we could get the finest sound quality.

At Capitol Records, their building had several different echo chambers, and one was Patti's and the engineer's favorite. It was underground beneath the parking lot, and it had to be reserved in advance of the recording sessions. We could get some ambience from the studio itself, plus a bit of enhancement from the echo chamber.

Although it's important to have a piece technically clean, there's also a certain amount of abandon needed for spontaneous musicality. If you get preoccupied with the piece's technical aspects, you can forget the fact that you need to play it expressively. We're looking for the truly exceptional take. Sometimes it comes at the beginning of the recording session, and sometimes on the last take.

I remember an example of each. I was recording the Arioso with the Los Angeles Chamber Orchestra, and the second take was something special. We did several takes after that, but it became too "careful"—controlled and uninspired. Another time, when I was recording Prelude no. 6 from the *Well-Tempered Clavier* by Bach, Patti Laursen said, "We have five minutes left. One last take, and then we've got to get out of the studio. There's a rock band coming in, and they need to set up." Something about the pressure that day and knowing that we had one take left helped me to try all that much harder, and that was the take that we used for the recording.

Sometimes at the end of a session Dave will say, "Okay, you've played the piece cleanly, but we have time for one more. Now put everything you've got musically into this final take." It is wonderful to have a recording producer who's an encourager, like a football coach who says, "Okay, these are the final seconds of the game. You have one shot at this. Give it everything you've got."

For recordings I practice about five hours a day, except on the day of the recording session. On those days, I just warm up, to conserve my strength. A lot of things have to be right. The bottom line is creating something that's beautiful and that hopefully will stand the test of time.

෨෩෨෩෨෩

As busy as I was with performing and recording, other changes were brewing in my life in the early 1990s. The opportunity to move to another of the most respected management companies, IMG Artists (International Management Group), arose through one of my friends. It would be difficult to move from Columbia Artists Management, but after much prayer and consideration, I made the change to IMG. This happened during a period of other major, difficult changes.

Since I had become a Christian, Barbara and I had drifted in different directions. We never had children, and we were both focused on our professions. Still, I had been content during our twenty-year relationship. When we moved back to California in the early 1980s and I returned to touring, she was increasingly involved with her horses and equestrian touring. Eventually, on an extended horse tour, she met someone, which led to our divorce. After several years, during which I remained committed to what I saw as God's standard for marriage, I made one last try at reconciliation. Having done that gave me the peace of knowing that I had done what I could to try to save the marriage.

I tried to keep my heart on the Lord and my mind on music. I memorized Philippians 4, about being content in all circumstances, even the painful ones. I found a Christian roommate, a seminary student, who had a great sense of humor. We often prayed, and Todd also helped me see the lighter side of life. The will of God, I have discovered, will never take me where the grace of God cannot keep me, protect me, sustain me, calm my fears, and teach me. The Bible says everything happens for a purpose, so I tried to believe, day by day and moment by moment, that everything that happened to me was covered by Romans 8:28: "We know that all things work together for good to them that love God, to them who are the called according to his purpose."

During that time, part of the healing process was being able to pray for Barbara. God protected me from becoming bitter, and I knew that forgiveness is the foundation of any relationship. Paul says that we are to forgive as we have been forgiven: "Be ye kind one to another, tenderhearted, forgiving one another, even as God for Christ's sake hath forgiven you" (Ephesians 4:32).

๑๖ ๑๖ ๑๖

In early 1997, Kathy Battle and I made our Christmas CD, *Angels' Glory*. We assembled a group of wonderful arrangers and, as with every album, spent many hours going through sheet music and recordings, gleaning what we believed were beautiful Christmas pieces that glorify the birth of the Lord Jesus Christ.

Some were not well known. The first time I played Kathy a recording of "Mary, Did You Know?" she had tears in her eyes from the beauty of the music and the power of the lyrics.

Deciding where to record the CD, we did sound checks at many top studios in New York. Yet, it was the Abyssinian Baptist Church in Harlem where the sound of her voice was most glorious.

The only drawback to working in this church was the traffic noise during the day, so we had to record between midnight and 3 a.m. One night Kathy and I wrapped up a session at 3 a.m., and then I started to record a guitar solo, "Jubilation" by Andrew York, at about four. Exhausted, I prayed for God's grace and the energy to play this difficult piece well, both musically and technically. He answered my prayer. When I returned to Los Angeles, I invited the composer to my home to hear the recording before it was released. He seemed genuinely pleased.

FISH TALE

Miss Montana and the Poachers

Miss Montana, the mountain lion, was about two years old when we brought her to Montana. Like Woodstock the otter, she enjoyed fishing with me.

Typically, she would walk about twenty yards behind me. Part of our ranch was full of cottonwood trees, bushes, and tall grasses that kept her hidden as she followed me. Once, as I got close to the place where I wanted to fish, I saw two poachers—gruff-looking guys sitting in portable chairs, resting bait-fishing rods in V-cut sticks. They were bait-fishing in one of the best holes, not as catch-and-release sport fishermen who would have been welcome to fish the ranch.

I tried to speak kindly. "Excuse me, but this is a private ranch, and it's fly-fishing only, by permission. If you want to come back and do some catch-and-release fly-fishing, just call me. That'll be fine."

They answered with a streak of four-letter words. Just about that time, Miss Montana came into sight, stealthily and determinedly walking toward me through the brush—eyes straight ahead and intent on me.

Their eyes got big, and I never saw two people move so quickly. They grabbed their gear and ran toward the highway where their car was parked, never to be seen again.

Of course, the truth was that Miss Montana wouldn't have bitten a warm biscuit, but they didn't know that.

17

Theresa

~~~~~~

1997–98

During the years following my divorce, I worked
hard to focus solely on my commitment to the Lord
and to my music. Many friends tried to "fix me
up" with this girl or that one, but I was so hurt by
the divorce that I was uninterested in further relationships.

In the midnineties, I was blessed with the
encouragement and support of some wonderful
Christian friends, Ken and Joni Eareckson Tada.
Ken loves to fish, so I invited him to join me at
the ranch where I now had a membership. On a
beautiful summer evening after a great day of fishing, Ken and I were sitting on the cabin porch when
his cell phone rang. It was Joni, back home. After

they talked for a while, she asked to speak to me. "Chris, describe the stars for me. What does it look like up there?"

Joni is wonderfully articulate, and I fumbled for words to describe the magnificence of that night, the sky, and how at seven thousand feet, the stars made a canopy of bright, sparkling lights. I said, "Joni, I can see the Milky Way in tremendous contrast to the vastness of the heavens."

She said, "You know, Chris, I have a picture in my mind of your future wife. I picture a girl who is as comfortable wearing blue jeans while out fishing with you on a stream as she is in a gorgeous long black dress, at your concerts."

That sounded good to me! Ken encouraged me to pray for a godly wife, as one of his other friends had done. I started to pray that she would love music, especially the guitar, but first and foremost that she would love the Lord . . . and, if it was okay with Him, that she would at least *like* fly-fishing.

Like so many other times in my life, I would have to wait on the Lord's timing. Two busy years passed, and during the 1996–97 season, I played more than forty concerts. One of those dates was Spivey Hall in Atlanta.

After the concert, I stood behind a table in the lobby, signing programs and CDs. When I looked up, I saw about three places back in the line two lovely women—obviously mother and daughter—who both seemed to have an inner glow about them. When they reached the front of the line, the younger woman asked me to sign the back of the CD booklet. I asked her name.

"My name is Theresa."

Teresa. Theresa? I put the pen to the paper. "How do you spell that?"

"My name is spelled with an *h*."

"I have a sister named Teresa, who spells her name without an *h*," I said, making small talk. I wrote on her booklet, "To Theresa, with best wishes, Christopher Parkening. John 3:16."

"I recently heard a radio broadcast where Joni Eareckson Tada was speaking about you," Theresa's mother commented.

They must be Christians!

"Theresa plays the guitar," her mother volunteered.

"You do? That's wonderful." I wished I could talk with them longer, but the line was long and people were waiting. I pointed to the stack of postcards on my right and said, "If you'd like to order my free Christian testimony tape, just take this postcard." The postcard had a toll-free number that people could call to request a tape.

Theresa said, "I'm going to do that. I'd love to know how you became a Christian."

I watched as they walked off, wishing I could have spoken with them longer.

Back in my hotel room, I called my secretary, Sharon. "If a Theresa from Atlanta calls, let me know." I had never done this before, but I couldn't think of any other way to follow up with or talk to her again.

When I finally got home, I asked Sharon if "Theresa from Atlanta" had phoned.

She had—and Sharon had saved her address!

I wrote Theresa a letter, saying something like, "It was a pleasure to meet you and your mother after my Atlanta concert. I remember hearing that you play the guitar, and I wanted to let you know that I give a master class every summer at Montana State University. I'm enclosing a brochure for you. Perhaps you can attend." I also wrote, "I'm leaving shortly on a long tour, and I'll be back May 21."

After that May tour, the first thing I did was check my stack of mail. There it was—a letter from Theresa! I immediately opened it, and it was one of the most gracious, lovely letters I'd ever received, responding to my testimony. I wrote again, thanking her for her beautiful letter, and I said that if she wouldn't mind giving me her telephone number, I would like to call her and tell her a little about the master class at Montana State.

When I finally worked up the nerve to call, she was home. It was early evening, but I knew there was a three-hour time difference between Los Angeles and Atlanta.

We had a wonderful talk about the Lord and the guitar, and I did end up telling her a little about the class, but not much. I hung up thinking, *WOW, what a special person!*

I tried hard to let at least two or three days go by before I called her again. During the week following our first conversation, Theresa and I struck up a cross-country relationship over the phone. We often talked long into the night, sometimes until one-thirty in the morning, her time. After the pain and the trials I had been through, Theresa was a breath of fresh air, inspiring and encouraging every time I spoke to her. Her voice was warm and gracious, and so were her words. The Bible says, "Out of the abundance of the heart the mouth speaketh" (Matthew 12:34), and it was easy to tell what was in Theresa's heart.

She was thirty-seven and had never been married, yet she trusted the Lord's timing. She used to say to her family and friends, "The Lord will have to conk me over the head when He finds the right man for me."

May was almost over. I told her I had reservations to go fly-fishing for tarpon on the west coast of Florida, about a hundred miles north of Tampa.

She said, "My grandparents have a place in St. Augustine, and for my vacation, I was thinking about visiting them."

"Would you, by any chance, be up for meeting me in Tampa

and going out on the tarpon boat for one day?" I asked, then quickly added, "I would book you your own hotel room." I wanted her to know that my intentions were honorable.

She agreed, and I was thrilled. I said, "You'll need a good pair of polarized sunglasses and a baseball cap, and I would definitely bring sunscreen. Why don't we meet there on my last day of tarpon fishing? I'm going down with my old friend Frank. He's sharing a tarpon boat with me and our guide. I'm sure he'll let us have the boat for the afternoon."

I was about to have a "first date," and if ever there was a great first date for a fly fisherman, it would be on a tarpon boat!

After several days of fishing, I nervously drove to the airport. Hers was a morning flight, and I arrived in plenty of time. The flight arrived, and I stood and watched people deplane.

Almost last off the plane came this absolute vision, blonde with glistening blue-green eyes, walking down the Jetway with a big smile on her face. She told me later that she was nervous, too, but I certainly couldn't tell. She appeared confident and happy. We got her bag, walked to the rental car, and started up the West Coast. I felt absolutely relaxed with her.

At the hotel I said, "After you check in, we'll get some lunch, then head to the dock where Al's going to meet us."

I proudly introduced her to Al and Frank, and to Frank's parents, who happened to be there fly-fishing as well. Frank had taken the morning shift, and Al and I would take the afternoon shift with Theresa. We jumped in the boat and were off.

In order to catch a tarpon on a fly rod, the general consensus is that it takes an average of fifty casts. Still, I really wanted Theresa to see a tarpon. Al said, "There's some weather coming in, so our visibility's not going to be very good. This morning, Frank got a couple of casts at some fish going by, with no success. Don't expect much."

After an hour and a half, we were facing the coast, looking into the wind, when Al said, "Here comes a string of fish." He had an "emergency" sound in his voice. Swimming head to tail, from right to left—up the coastline—they came, about eighty feet from the boat. Al said, "Chris, this may be your only cast." I knew that the accuracy of my cast was all-important, because I was casting to a moving target in the wind, and even if I did make the right cast, the fish might not bite.

I said a quick prayer and cast just ahead of the lead fish, giving the fly enough time to sink down to his level. The fly was just about at the right depth, so I stripped it once, and the big tarpon opened his jaw and peeled to the left on the fly. I struck . . . and *boom*, he was on.

It felt as if I were attached to a freight train. This was almost unbelievable, hooking a tarpon on one cast. However, I knew that when the fish jumped, he could still throw the hook and come loose.

Forty minutes later, I pulled the fish up alongside the boat, and Al grabbed the tarpon by the jaw, holding it by the side of the boat. "Chris, grab the other pair of gloves, and I'll help you pull him into the boat and hold him up. Give Theresa the fly rod—I'll snap a picture, and then we'll release him."

I grabbed the jaw of that hundred-pound tarpon, lifted him as high as I could, and stood there with Theresa for the picture. Then Al helped me slide him back into the water, and he swam away. I thanked the Lord for letting me catch a tarpon in front of this special woman.

We returned to the dock later that afternoon, and Frank asked, "How did you do?"

"We got one."

"Great! How many casts did you have?"

"One."

"Chris! This relationship is meant to be! You can hook twenty fish sometimes before you land one."

We had a great dinner with everybody that night, and the next day at the airport, when Theresa's flight was called, I gave her a hug good-bye. "I'd like to get to know you better," I said.

"I'd really like that," she responded. I watched her walk down the Jetway, feeling a mixture of sadness and joy. Sadness at having to say good-bye, but joy because my heart was filled with new hope for the future.

Back in Los Angeles, I continued to call Theresa regularly. She agreed to come to Los Angeles and visit me there. In the course of our conversations about the guitar, she mentioned that one of her favorite pieces was "Andecy" by Andrew York.

I told her that I knew Andrew York. "When you come out to LA, maybe I can get him to play you that piece," I said.

"That would be wonderful," she replied. "But the only thing that would be better than that would be if *you* played it for me."

As soon as we hung up, I called Andy and told him about Theresa. "I just spoke with her, and she absolutely loves 'Andecy.' Would you be willing to play it for her?"

"Sure."

Then I asked him to fax the music to me.

A few minutes later, I picked up the music, sat down at my music stand, and started to learn it.

I performed in some pretty exotic places that year, including Istanbul, where David Brandon found me practicing "Andecy" backstage before the concert. Normally, I only practiced whatever I was about to perform, but now I had a new goal: to play "Andecy" for Theresa.

A week or so later, Theresa arrived in Los Angeles. We went to one of my favorite restaurants in Malibu, and after dinner, I drove her to a place with a rock jetty sticking out into the ocean.

It was getting close to sunset when we arrived, and I said, "Theresa, let's walk down to the beach. I'd like to get a few pictures." I popped the trunk and grabbed a guitar.

Looking kind of surprised, she said, "Are you going to play something for me?"

I walked her down and sat her on a rock; then, sitting across from her on another rock, as the waves were coming in, I played "Andecy."

There was joy all over her face.

I took a picture of her holding my guitar. I still carry that picture in my wallet.

The next day she flew back to Atlanta. When we spoke later on the phone, I said, "I don't know if we're on the same page or not, but I'm getting rather serious about you." She confirmed that she shared my feelings.

I've heard my pastor say, "Have a spiritual relationship and a short engagement." The Montana master class was planned for the last week of July, and at that point I was planning to ask Theresa to marry me. I invited her to the class, explaining that it would be a very special trip, and it would mean a lot to me if she would come.

Several days before she was due to arrive, I decided that I had to pick the perfect spot to propose. I asked a dear friend, Mark Tyers, to help pick out a place where I could take Theresa—a picturesque place to take some pictures and talk. I wanted her to see a beautiful part of Montana.

Every winter Mark and his wife, Kathy, performed ballad-style folk music with flute and guitar at the Lone Mountain Ranch. Mark said, "I know a nice, private spot from which you can see Lone Mountain."

The day finally arrived. I asked Kathy to pick Theresa up at the airport, because her flight came in while I was teaching my master class. Kathy drove her to a bed-and-breakfast in the Bozeman area, and that afternoon Mark and Kathy gave us a wonderful private concert.

It was a great afternoon, and as the moment I had been waiting for drew closer, we drove up the Gallatin Canyon to Big Sky. Seeing that Lone Mountain was sunny and bright, I drove out to the point Mark had suggested before the weather could change.

I grabbed the camera, and we walked out to a rock. I asked Theresa to sit down and, with my heart in my throat, said, "Before I take any pictures, I have something to say to you. A few years ago, Ken Tada told me that I should pray for my future wife. And I believe you are the answer to that prayer. I would like to marry you."

There was a long, gigantic moment of silence. Theresa didn't say anything. My heart sank. I thought, *It's a no.* Quickly, I added, "If you would like to think and pray about this, I certainly understand."

Then she looked up at me, and she said with a big smile on her face, "Yes, I'll marry you, and every morning you wake up, you will know that you are the most loved and cherished husband in the entire world." She put her arms around me, and we kissed for the first time.

The following March, Theresa and I were married in Atlanta, with a beautiful evening ceremony that was as much a celebration of God's love and faithfulness in orchestrating our relationship as it was rejoicing in beginning our lives together as husband and wife. John MacArthur performed the ceremony.

When I married Theresa, I married my best friend and the love of my life—and yes, she even loves fly-fishing.

FISH TALE

What, No Fishing Story?

Chapter 17 is, for me, the ultimate fishing story.

Pepperdine

~~~~~~~~~~~~~~~~~~~~~~~~~~~

1998–2002

Back in the early 1990s, I had tried to convince my
longtime friend Elmer Bernstein to write a guitar
concerto. He felt unsure about whether he could
write properly for the classical guitar, and I assured
him that he could. Finally, in 1998, he agreed to
meet me at his Santa Monica office, and we discussed the guitar concerto. I played some of my repertoire for him and showed him some scores for
guitar and orchestra.

   We also enlisted Pat Russ's help. Pat had started
his film orchestration career with Elmer and knew
the classical guitar well, so he would help coordinate
the project.

   After spending a great deal of time thinking
about how he would begin the piece, Elmer decided

to start with the open strings of the guitar, almost as though I were tuning the instrument. In fact, he asked me to tune offstage so the audience would be in suspense as to whether or not the concerto had started. We worked together, week by week, as Elmer wrote the music. If I was on tour, he would call Pat and say, "Patrick, is this chord possible?"

One day Elmer and I were talking, and he said, "For the second movement, I am thinking of going in a 'bluesy' direction. What do you think?"

I had a different idea. "Elmer, what made the *Concierto de Aranjuez* such a wonderful piece was the beautiful theme of the second movement," I said. "I love the themes you have come up with for films like *To Kill a Mockingbird*, and I would prefer something with a beautiful melody."

He chuckled and said, "You're a tune man, huh?"

About a week later, I was practicing when the phone rang. "Christopher, it's Elmer. I've come up with an idea for the second movement. I'd like you to hear it and see what you think." Over the phone, he played a brief introduction on his piano, then the melody he had composed for the second movement.

It was all that I could have hoped it would be.

During the time I was working with Elmer at his Santa Monica studio, we often discussed spiritual issues. I told him the story of my spiritual journey and about the Old Testament prophecies of the Messiah. I asked him to read Isaiah 53 and tell me what he thought.

The following week when I walked into his studio, the first words out of his mouth were, "I read Isaiah 53. That has to be talking about Jesus Christ!" Then he told me this story. "When I was a young composer, Cecil B. DeMille asked me to write the music for his movie *The Ten Commandments*. He looked at me sternly and said, 'I want a theme for Moses and a theme for Aaron, and I want a theme for God.'

"Needless to say, I was intimidated. A theme for God? What immense pressure, to come up with a majestic theme for the God of the universe! I felt discouraged. But Cecil B. DeMille's assistant was still in the room, and he said, 'Elmer, I am going to be praying for you, that you come up with a wonderful theme for Moses and Aaron, but a magnificent theme for God.'"

Elmer said, "Christopher, I was able to do that, and I know that it came from . . . above." He pointed to the ceiling. Elmer was sincerely interested in spiritual things.

The third movement came into existence quickly, and by then we had a premiere date with the Honolulu Symphony. That September, the premiere was recorded by National Public Radio for broadcast, and we recorded it with the London Symphony at Abbey Road Studios a few months later.

Elmer and I talked about God many times. Elmer had been my friend and a musical mentor ever since I was fourteen years old and associated with the Young Musicians Foundation. When he passed away in 2004, it was a great loss to the musical world—and a great loss to me.

ॐ ॐ ॐ

Every musician starts the journey as a student. It seems appropriate to finish as a teacher and share what one has learned. For some time I had felt that it would be good to once again be associated with a major university and pass along to the younger generation what I had gleaned from a concert career of more than thirty-five years. I was approached by UCLA regarding the possibility of chairing their guitar department. I had several meetings with the dean and some of the music faculty, and they prepared a proposal regarding the creation of a position called the Christopher Parkening Chair of Classical Guitar, University of California at Los Angeles.

Through another series of "chance" meetings over the next few months, Theresa and I were invited to meet Dorothy Stotsenberg, who with her husband founded Pepperdine University's Stotsenberg International Classical Guitar Competition. We joined her for a lunch in Malibu, along with the managing director of Pepperdine's Center for the Arts, Marnie Duke Mitze. Carol Weller and Janice Barker, who had set up the meeting, were also there. During lunch, Marnie said, "Why don't you come to Pepperdine instead?"

That spark ignited a future dinner at the home of the provost, Darryl Tippens, where we first heard the mission statement of Pepperdine University: "Pepperdine is a Christian university committed to the highest standards of academic excellence and Christian values, where students are strengthened for lives of purpose, service, and leadership." To have the opportunity to openly speak of the gospel and what motivates me whenever I play the guitar was the deciding factor.

I met with Pepperdine's president, Andy Benton, David Baird, the dean of Seaver College, and the other fine arts professors, and was very impressed by them all. Their integrity and their commitment to Christ, to the school, and to academic excellence made me feel sure I had made the right decision.

In training future generations of guitarists at Pepperdine University, it is my goal to emphasize the importance of playing with beauty, warmth, and lyricism. Most students are taught solid technical skills, but I feel that at many universities, learning the skill and discipline necessary to perfect an *art*—the legacy of learning to play an instrument beautifully—is undervalued. I'm grateful to the leadership at Pepperdine University, who recognize this as an essential element in the educational process. A principle that has held true in my life is that someone who never does anything except what can be done easily will never do anything of lasting value.

I have shared with my students that every artist, whether beginner or professional, has strengths and weaknesses. For example, left-hand technique always came fairly easily for me, but the right hand was more difficult. The complications of having a particularly curved nail shape initially required more concentration on my right hand, but that shape also lends itself to playing expressively with a nice sound. Each guitarist faces his or her own difficulties, and excellence always comes at a high price.

Segovia used to say, "Artistic instinct is natural born. You can educate it, but it's there or it isn't." With music, there's a balance between technique and passion. Some guitar teachers teach their students to keep their right hand absolutely still, turning out technically accurate players, but minimizing the students' ability to vary the sound greatly for expression. It's much like asking a painter to render a landscape using only two or three colors.

I once heard a fine guitarist say, as a joke, "I try not to let the music get in the way of my technique." That was funny, but playing musically, with a beautiful tone, is something I strive for. Of all the things my father taught me, I'm especially grateful to him for always saying, "Play it beautiful, play it beautiful. If it's not beautiful, it's not music." As Segovia said, "Without a beautiful sound, the charm of the guitar disappears."

In recent years, I have seen a growing trend away from Segovia's romantic musical spirit in favor of colder, mechanistic, purely intellectual playing. One of my friends recently said, "The guitar is being taught in the vast majority of universities today as though it were an inferior miniature keyboard instrument, not the beautiful, poetic, lyrical instrument that it is." My recording producer has even said that it is difficult to distinguish between the playing styles of many of the new generation of classical guitarists. "You could always tell Segovia from John Williams or Julian Bream. Their styles were distinctive and convincing." Segovia utilized a full palette of expressive abilities and elicited the full range of emotional responses from audiences. I have heard an entire audience sigh when he finished a piece.

The legendary Russian pianist Vladimir Horowitz once said the following:

> All music is the expression of feelings, and feelings do not change over the centuries. Style and form change, but not the basic human emotions. Purists would have us believe that music from the so-called Classical period should be performed with emotional restraint, while so-called Romantic music should be played with emotional freedom. Such advice has often resulted in exaggeration: overindulgent, uncontrolled performances of Romantic music and dry, sterile, dull performances of Classical music.
>
> As far as Mozart is concerned, we know from his letters that he showed great concern for musical expression: he continually criticized performers whose playing lacked freedom for their "mechanical execution" and the absence of "taste and feeling." As for Beethoven, historical accounts describe his playing as very free and emotional—the trademark of a Romantic.
>
> All my life, ever since I was a young man, I have considered music of *all* periods romantic. . . .
>
> The notation of a composer is a mere skeleton that the performer must endow with flesh and blood, so that the

music comes to life and speaks to an audience. . . . An audience does not respond to intellectual concepts, only to the communication of feelings.[3]

ᘒᕲ ᘒᕲ ᘒᕲ

Many people have asked me how to become an excellent guitarist. I generally answer, "Be a hardworking perfectionist." Our goal as performers should be to overcome whatever we lack in talent or ability with what we can develop through dedication and commitment. This requires self-discipline.

One overarching principle that has been evident throughout my life is that progress with the guitar is a little like climbing a mountain. You start up one trail and hit a dead end. Then you have to backtrack and be willing to go downhill a bit until you find another trail that leads to a higher point. In the same way, progress with the guitar is not linear. It's more like a graph that goes up, down a little, up higher, down a little, and so forth. One must be willing to experiment—to change positions, for example—and regress for a brief time in order to improve.

At the end of my first year at Pepperdine, I assembled my guitar students and told them what a pleasure it had been to teach them throughout the year, how much I appreciated their hard work, how much they had improved, and that I was looking forward to seeing them in the fall. I turned around and was about to leave when one of the students said, "Mr. Parkening, we have a gift for you."

He reached behind his chair, pulled out a rectangular box wrapped in orange and blue Pepperdine paper, and handed it to me. It was quite heavy, and I assumed it was a box of candy. I was about to take it home when they insisted that I open it.

When I unwrapped the paper, I found a Bible. They had inscribed my name on the cover, and inside each one had written a paragraph about what it had meant for them to study with me that year. I was deeply moved.

Theresa later commented, "This is what teaching is all about."

FISH TALE

Gold Cup

Early in June 1987, I participated in the "Wimbledon" of fly-fishing competitions, the Gold Cup Tarpon Tournament held off Islamorada, Florida, a five-day invitational event for twenty-five fishermen. I was invited to compete when another competitor dropped out at the last moment. The competition included then-world-record-holder Billy Pate and many other fishing legends, so Harry Spear, my tournament guide and friend, assured me that I had little chance of winning. "Let's just have some fun," he said.

I was glad just to be there! Fishing ended each afternoon at three o'clock; then all contestants had two hours to return to the weigh-in dock. You could keep "playing" any tarpon you hooked before three, as long as you weighed in by 5 p.m.

On the first day, the boats left the docks at exactly 7 a.m., released in groups of five. About half an hour later, Harry spotted a tarpon just under the surface of the water. These are enormous fish, sometimes more than six feet long and over two hundred pounds. I made a decent cast, and the fish struck immediately. After a long fight of about an hour, we landed our first fish, a 131-pound tarpon—a big one, for the Keys. To our surprise, when we arrived at the dock at the end of that day, we were in the lead. Harry said, "We were just lucky, so don't get excited."

The next day didn't go as well. I caught only two fish, both under seventy pounds and too small to keep, so we released them.

Nevertheless, my first day's catch—plus a few points that were added to my score for the release fish—kept me in first place.

At two-thirty on the third day, after seeing nothing all day, Harry spotted a big, laid-up tarpon facing away from us. Casting ahead of him and against the wind, I got the fish to turn around, quickly made another cast, and he struck.

Ninety minutes later, he was still on my line. When I got him close enough to the boat, Harry used his gaff but missed, and the fish took off. I played him for another ten minutes. Harry's second try caught only a scale. On his third try, he got a thin layer of skin. Almost simultaneously, my shock tippet (the short, thick leader connected to the fly) broke. "Oh, no—he's off!"

Harry immediately leaped overboard into waist-deep water and followed the fish away from the boat, holding on to the gaff. If he pulled on that gaff at all, the fish would come loose. He had to hold on as if we were attached to the fish by a two-pound test line. "Get him!" he yelled.

I, too, jumped into the water and grabbed for the tarpon's tail, but it was too slippery to hold.

"Get the hand gaff," Harry shouted. "The boat's drifting away!"

I waded back to the boat, sinking a good foot into the thick, muddy bottom and losing my tennis shoes in the process, and found the tool. I trudged barefoot back to Harry and the tarpon. I tried once with the hand gaff, to no avail. Then the tarpon opened his mouth and gills, like a huge largemouth bass. You could put a watermelon inside a tarpon's mouth, it's so big. Suddenly inspired, I clenched my left hand and thrust a fist into his gills and out his mouth, seized my left wrist with my right hand, and pinned my fist to the center of my chest.

Then I held on tight. The tarpon thrashed like a giant alligator.

Harry said, "I can't believe you did that!" I'd always found fishing guides to be extreme in their pursuit of the giant tarpon—the silver king—so his comment surprised me.

He trudged back for the boat while I continued to hold on. Harry returned in the boat, jumped overboard again, and helped me hoist the tarpon on board. It was only when I pulled my arm out of the fish that I realized why he made that statement: my forearm was covered with blood, and it looked as though it had been slashed with razor blades. We wrapped it with a towel.

At that point, I had other things to worry about. It was 4:48. We had only twelve minutes to race back to the dock. We barely made it. My tarpon weighed 136½ pounds, which put me way in the lead. What had begun as "let's just have fun" was shaping up to be an entirely different proposition. That afternoon at a local clinic, I got eight stitches in my left hand.

My parents had asked for a "Gold Cup report" by phone each evening, and as the tournament progressed, they became more and more excited. We had only two days left, and now I began to feel some pressure. Without telling Harry, I started thinking, *We could possibly win this.*

On the fourth day, we were humbled. I "jumped" (hooked) ten tarpon without landing any of them. Only at the very end of the day was I able to land two modest-sized fish, which we released. Neither would have helped my score very much.

I had been talking about the Lord with Harry on and off, and toward the end of this day he sat down in frustration and said, "We need to pray about this. I'll start." It was the first time I ever heard him pray. He apologized to God for wanting to win the Gold Cup for his ego's sake and asked for God's will to be done. It was short, humble, and sincere. Astounded, I followed him with a similar prayer.

I was still holding a slight lead when Harry and I set out on the final day of the tournament. We headed toward a spot called Oxfoot Bank, which was—among other things—a notorious haunt of big hammerhead sharks. The weather could hardly have been less cooperative: windy, cloudy, and blustery. We knew we would only get a few chances that day, during breaks in the clouds.

No sooner had we settled in than Harry spotted three tarpon moving in a line from our left to our right. This could be our only chance! I cast to the lead fish but failed to compensate enough for the wind, and my fly landed right on the lead tarpon's back, spooking all three fish. I thought, *There goes the Gold Cup.* I looked back at Harry, and his head dropped in disappointment. There was no need to speak.

Amazingly, twenty minutes later, the sun broke through and four tarpon appeared about ninety feet from the boat, swimming in a line from right to left. The wind had shifted 180 degrees. I prayed, *Please, Lord, help me cast well.* My fly landed one foot in front of the lead tarpon.

It struck. This fight started out as a repeat of the third day, another hour-and-a-half battle with a one-hundred-plus-pound fish. By this time, the fish had pulled us into deep water. As with the third day's tarpon, Harry was unable to gaff this fish on his first two attempts. He succeeded on his third try, when to my amazement and with a big explosion, the fish pulled him overboard and dragged him one hundred feet away and five feet underwater, like Captain Ahab and Moby Dick. It looked like a surrealistic water show, with Harry refusing to let go of the fish. I watched in a daze. I had heard tales of tarpon pulling guides overboard before, but now I was a believer. Harry—still holding onto the gaff—was now being pulled twelve feet under!

He came up kicking frantically, still gripping the gaff with both hands. The red bandanna he wore around his neck was wedged in his mouth, and he couldn't get a gulp of air before the tarpon pulled him back underwater. The boat was drifting with the current, farther away. For several long moments I saw nothing. Then the tarpon jumped perhaps twenty yards farther away, followed by Harry, who was still hanging on. This time he was able to get a good breath, and knowing the danger from big sharks in that area, he screamed for me to bring the boat over.

I started the motor, put the boat on plane, and got there at full speed. I steered alongside him, he handed me the gaff and leaped into the boat, and then we both hoisted the big fish on board. The entire episode, from hook-up to landing, had taken more than two hours.

Harry sat there, dripping wet, beside a huge tarpon lying in the bottom of our boat, and we looked at each other in disbelief at what had just happened. Could this fish be the Gold Cup? Harry prayed once more—that we would not take any more of these beautiful fish than was absolutely necessary, if we still had a chance to win. Harry caught his breath and then said, "Let's head for Nine Mile Bank."

He amazed me! After all that, he still wanted to go on fishing! He moved us to a likely spot, where I hooked and jumped three more fish, but landed none.

At the final weigh-in, my tarpon registered 115 pounds.

I called my parents. Mom says they were both breathless, waiting to hear from me. All I said was, "We won." I heard yells, cheers, and screams of delight. Mom says that both she and my dad were literally jumping up and down.

19

Luke

~~~~~~

2002–04

When I was dating Theresa, we had made a day trip
up the coast to Solvang, a charming town north of
Los Angeles with a Scandinavian influence. Walking
around the different shops, we came upon a quaint
perfume store, where a nice older gentleman showed
Theresa some perfumes, and we ended up purchasing one. As we were about to leave, he announced to
us, "You know, nearly every couple who comes into
this shop ends up getting married."

On the way back to LA, we talked about a lot
of different subjects, including children.

I had always considered myself fairly neutral
about whether I would want children. I loved playing
with my nieces and nephews and with my friends'

children, but when it came to my own life, I felt that I could be happy with or without children.

I asked Theresa how she felt. "I always thought, *If I get married someday, and it's the Lord's will for my husband and me to have a child, that would be wonderful; if not, that's fine, too,*" she said. When we did get married, we discussed whether or not we should try to have a family. We wondered about being older parents and about my tour schedule, and we decided to ask our pastor and his wife to dinner to talk about it.

The four of us had a wonderful conversation, and then I asked, "What would you think about Theresa and me having a child?"

John's wife, Patricia, responded, "That would be fantastic. Oh, you two would make wonderful parents. My children are such a blessing."

I looked at John, and he simply said, "Every day, my children bring me joy."

From that moment on, whenever we prayed together, we would pray that if it was God's will for us to be parents, He would allow that for us. We knew that if we did conceive, it would be by God's grace, considering that by now Theresa was in her early forties and I was in my early fifties. We put our faith and hope in God for a child. We wanted to give God the glory by relying on Him.

Almost immediately, Theresa became pregnant, and we were elated. Sadly, that pregnancy resulted in a heartbreaking miscarriage early the next year. While not expecting such joyous anticipation to end so painfully, we both continued to pray for God's will in all areas of our lives.

A few months later, she became pregnant again. We were so happy, as were our families, but again Theresa miscarried three months into the pregnancy. It grieved us to have this happen a second time. I often heard her pray, "Lord, we hope for a child someday, if it's Your will, but please, Lord, I couldn't bear another miscarriage."

Theresa wrote this letter to our unborn children.

You, our precious ones, are with the Lord.

One day your father and I will hold you both in our arms. Knowing that God answered our prayers so fast and gave us you made us rejoice with happiness. You were and always will be so loved. You gave us a time of both great joy in anticipation of your arrival and great sadness when we found out you were not going to be held in the earthly arms of your parents. At the same time, both your dad and I can rejoice, knowing you are in your heavenly Father's arms— eternally secure in the Savior's presence.

This is the hope and promise we have that helps us through the sadness.

We thank God for the miracle of you, the life of you, and the precious gift of you to us, and we know that someday we will be together again with our Father in heaven.

One autumn night after the second miscarriage, we were in a store where Theresa saw some children's boots. They were dark green, with a little frog face on the top of each foot. She said, "Aren't those adorable? I could just see our little child fishing in these little Wellipet boots."

Not wanting to put a damper on her enthusiasm, I said, "Yes, they are very cute," and I tucked the thought away.

A month or so later, as Christmas approached, I called her mother and said, "Belle, you know those little Wellipet boots that Theresa told you about a while back? What would you think if I bought those for Theresa, for Christmas?"

She said, "Oh, Chris, absolutely. Get those little boots. That would give her such hope." I went back to the store almost immediately, and they were still there. I purchased them and tucked them away in a secret place so I could bring them in my suitcase to Atlanta for Christmas.

On Christmas morning, after everyone had opened up their presents around the tree, I said, "Oh, Theresa, there's one more present that you have left to open."

She pulled out the Wellipet boots and started crying with joy, knowing in her heart the significance of the gift and the hope that it inspired.

Another two years went by, and though Theresa and I continued to pray, I must admit that I was losing heart, figuring that it probably just wasn't God's will for us to have children. Anyway, we had a wonderful ministry and so many other blessings.

Then one day in July, Theresa surprised me in the kitchen by telling me that she was pregnant. I could hardly believe it. Again we thanked the Lord for being so gracious to us. This time the doctor suggested that Theresa take it easy and not do anything strenuous. She was about three months into her pregnancy when we moved into a new house, and we were very careful about her activity level.

In October her father was diagnosed with cancer and went in for surgery. We were told that it had gone successfully, but shortly after the operation her mother called and said that Theresa's father had taken a turn for the worse. His body was shutting down. She said, "He is not getting better."

The next day she called and said, "You'd better come to Atlanta. Your father is dying."

Even knowing the potential risk of travel during this pregnancy, we packed that night and headed for LAX the next morning. We were on the road when my cell phone rang. It was Theresa's mother, who simply said, "He's gone."

Somehow we continued on, praying for the Lord's strength, grace, and comfort. Theresa sobbed in my arms on the street at LAX after we unloaded our baggage. We flew to Atlanta—concerned, all the time, for our baby but knowing that the child was in God's hands.

The difficulty, strain, and sadness of the funeral and its preparations took their toll. Because I was scheduled to play a concert in a few days, we decided that I should return separately, and Theresa would rest a little longer, spend some time with her mother, and fly back a few days later.

I returned to LA, played the concert, and went up north to close my cabin at the fishing ranch for the winter. While I was out in a meadow, my cell phone rang. It was Theresa, saying that her mother was taking her to the emergency room due to some complications.

I dropped to my knees in the meadow, with the sound of the stream running by and the beauty of the big sky and the Sierra mountains around me. I closed my eyes and begged God in His mercy not to take our baby. I prayed, *Lord, I don't know how she can bear the pain of losing another baby right after her father's death.*

A few hours later, my cell phone rang again. It was Theresa. A doctor had performed an ultrasound, and our baby was all right. Still in the meadow—with tears running down my cheeks—I dropped back down to my knees and thanked the Lord over and over again for His goodness.

At the seventeenth week of Theresa's pregnancy, our doctor scheduled an ultrasound. The ultrasound technician checked one by one the vitals of our little baby—heart good, lungs good, brain good. Finally, my curiosity got the best of me. "Can you tell us the sex of this child?"

He said, "Congratulations, you are going to have a little boy."

Theresa and I burst into tears and hugged one another. We just couldn't believe it.

Until now, not knowing the sex of our child, we had been calling our baby "Butter Bean." Now we had to pick a name. Theresa and I had been looking through baby name books but hadn't decided on a name quite yet.

One day I received a letter from a nice older lady I had known in Bozeman, who mentioned her grandson, a young man now in his midtwenties who had impressed me years ago. His parents had named him Luke, after Luke in the Bible.

At dinner that night, I looked at Theresa and said, "What do you think about the name Luke?"

She exclaimed, "That's my favorite name for a boy! That's the only name I had pictured myself being able to call our son." It was decided that moment that his name would be Luke. Theresa had also said that she loved the name Christopher, but I didn't want to saddle our son with my name, as people might presume that he'd be a guitarist. I wanted him to be his own person. But Theresa convinced me to use Christopher for his middle name.

Luke Christopher came into this world on March 18, 2004, a beautiful baby boy with big blue eyes that melted our hearts. Every day Theresa and I praise God for His amazing love and grace poured out to us through the birth and blessing of our son.

Opening Christmas gifts from my sister, Terry, that year, we found she had bought Luke the rest of the little green Wellipet outfit, including an umbrella and raincoat. Each piece is green, with a little frog face.

From Luke's Birth Announcement

For this child I prayed, and the LORD has given me my petition which I asked of him. So I have also dedicated him to the LORD.

1 Samuel 1:27-28 (taken from NASB and KJV)

EPILOGUE:
SOLI DEO GLORIA

I used to work very hard for worldly success. I still work hard for excellence, but there's a constant battle that takes place within me. I want to bring glory to God. *He* is the audience. But there's a side of me that still wants good reviews, strong record sales, critical acceptance. I tell myself, *If I don't succeed, it doesn't glorify God.*

I have come to believe that it is vital to pursue personal excellence based on your own God-given potential, rather than success. Success is external—how you have done in comparison to others. Excellence is internal—seeking satisfaction in having done your best in relation to your potential. It's the pursuit of quality in your work and effort, without regard to worldly recognition. I believe that you will always pay the full price for excellence; it is never discounted. Whenever I finish a concert or complete a recording, I feel a deep sense of satisfaction and gratitude that the guitar has become my platform to glorify God and share the gospel. Still, I continue to learn.

At the Hollywood Bowl in 2002, I played the Bernstein Concerto for Guitar and Orchestra, with the composer and my recording producer, David Thomas, in attendance. I practiced diligently, prayed for the concert, and played a very good rehearsal. During the concert, though, I missed the last note of a difficult descending run. Sometimes I feel that it might be nice to get a "second take," and after the concert I complained to Dave, dissatisfied with the performance. I asked if the missed note was very noticeable.

He exhorted me, "Chris, we prayed that the Lord would be

glorified, and you played for Him. You tried your best, so thank Him and don't dwell on your mistake. Be grateful for the performance God gave you!"

Dave was absolutely right. Many people have asked if performing is easy for me now, after giving so many concerts. Sometimes I still feel as if I am walking out onto a tightrope. The only One I have to hold on to is the Lord. Every concert is difficult. When I walk out onstage, my confidence is in Him.

Over the years since I started playing the classical guitar, I've had many great teachers—Andrés Segovia, Gregor Piatigorsky, and my father, to name a few. Some truths I've learned on the concert stage, some on clear creeks in California and Montana; yet as I look back on my life, I can now see that I have always experienced grace, even before I consciously committed my life to Christ. Some readers may focus on what might have seemed to be successes, but I know the struggles that so often were overcome by divine mercy. I look back in wonder, grateful that God chose me and through His love overcame my shortcomings, personal and professional, to build a career that, more than anything else, I look upon as the foundation of my ministry.

On my music stand at home, I have taped a note that reads, "Chris, what are you here for?" Just as my touring guitar bears the scars of having been used to create music, I pray that my imperfect life will be an instrument in God's hands, for His purposes, and to His glory.

LETTER FROM ANDRÉS SEGOVIA

[Sent in response to *Parkening Plays Bach*]

Madrid 16, June 1, 1971

Dear Christopher:

I have listened to your record and am very pleased with it. The new compositions by Bach you have transcribed and my old ones sound beautifully. The only advice I may give you, for instance in the Prelude in D major, arranged by me, is not to make the retardando so early before the end. More than a retardando seems to be a change of tempo. However, you play it with excellent musicianship and clarity. Concerning "Wachet auf, ruft uns die Stimme" your transcription is skillfully made and the result is very nicely played by dividing yourself. Nevertheless I prefer the last transcription which ends the record. My principle has always been not to put in the guitar anything made for voice, unless for my own satisfaction and never for the public's either on record or in concert programs. Your technique is extremely fluent and sure. Nobody, with the exception of John Williams, could equal it.

· The use of the microphone is against my taste. It is true that we have to employ it for making records and playing for television and Radio but nobody expects the sound of the guitar to be true through those devices but playing directly in front of the public is different. We have to give the exact quality of the beautiful tone of the guitar, without adulterating it. Try to make your pulsation on the strings stronger but not harsh and reduce the body of instruments which will accompany you as well as their sound to the level of the guitar tone. No critics or musicians listening to you will expect that the volume of it may equal the robust and overwhelming sound of the piano. The beauty of the guitar resides in its soft and persuasive voice and its poetry cannot be equaled by any other instrument. I am giving concerts in large halls since the beginning of my carreer and the public that continues to come to hear me never complains in its totality that it was hard to listen.

The flamenco. What you have learned from the best players of it, even if nice, is absolutely untrue. I am an Andalusian. I love the real folklore of my country and I know it very well. Myself, I sometimes used to play it for my own satisfaction or for my most intimate friends but never for the public. As an American you have not been forced to redeem the guitar from the ugly amusements to raise it to the concert stage. You have found already this operation done without struggling against the musicians who did not believe the guitar to be apt for serious music but only for flamenco. Thus you have no scruples for mixing both natures of the guitar. Remember that I always said that the guitar is like a hill with two sides that, naturally, coexist but they do not look at each other. Finally my last advice is that you may omit the flamenco from your concerts in order to give the guitar its true dignity. You don't need, as I have told you, the applauses of the ignorants who like more the noises of the "rasgueados" than the simple, moving and expressive "falsetas".

Enough of preaching to you the artistic morale of your conduct. Anything that you may play will be accepted with enthusiasm by every listener because you are talented and a nice boy who may increase incessantly the success.

I hope to see you next time in Los Angeles. I don't know yet the distribution of my concerts. The list given to me by Mr. Hurok before departing from New York has been lost and I am expecting the new one. But it will very easy for you to know the dates of my appearances in California.

> My best regards to your family
> and affectionately yours,
> A. Segovia

REFLECTIONS

It was my desire to include this chapter that contains many of the principles that have encouraged, guided, and helped me to shape my life. I hope they are a blessing to you as well.

True Christianity

I asked one of my relatives if he was a Christian, and he said that when he was young he had been baptized and confirmed. He thought that made him a Christian. So I asked him another question, "If being a Christian were illegal, would there be enough evidence to convict you now?"

I went through a period of my life when I was coming to the conclusion that I wasn't a true Christian, even though I believed the facts about Christ.

Here is one definition of true Christians: people "which worship God in the spirit, and rejoice in Christ Jesus, and have no confidence in the flesh" (Philippians 3:3).

Saving faith is believing in the person of the Lord Jesus Christ to the degree that you are completely satisfied with Him so as to commit your life to Him in loyalty, faithfulness, allegiance, submission, duty, fidelity, and obligation. It is not mere intellectual assent, though your conception of God will control your worship and your life.

For many American Christians, Jesus is only a part of their lives, instead of being the point of their lives. Matthew 7:20-23, to me, is the scariest passage in all of the New Testament: "Wherefore by their fruits ye shall know them. Not every one that saith unto me, Lord, Lord, shall enter into the kingdom of heaven; but he that doeth the will of my Father which is in heaven. Many will say to me in that day, Lord, Lord, have we not prophesied in thy name? and in thy name have cast out devils? and in thy name done many wonderful works? And then will I profess unto them, I never knew you: depart from me, ye that work iniquity."

The following poem is engraved in a cathedral in Lubeck, Germany:

> *Why do you call me Lord, Lord, and do not the things I say?*
> *You call me the Way and walk me not*
> *You call me the Life and live me not*
> *You call me Master and obey me not*
> *If I condemn thee, blame me not.*
>
> *You call me Bread and eat me not*
> *You call me Truth and believe me not*
> *Ye call me "Lord" and serve me not*
> *If I condemn thee, blame me not.*

If you're a Christian and you're forgiven, is it okay to sin?
I remember hearing a young woman in a Bible study ask, "If you're a Christian and you're saved by God's grace so you'll be forgiven of any sin you commit, does that mean you can pretty much do whatever you want?"

I made a personal study on what happens when a Christian sins, and I came up with six points.

1. Jesus said, "If ye love me, keep my commandments" (John 14:15), so habitually sinning shows that you don't love Him.
2. He disciplines us as children, as Hebrews 12:6 says. "Whom the

Lord loveth he chasteneth." Life is tough enough without God disciplining us.

3. Our prayers are hindered (Psalm 66:18). He doesn't listen to the prayer of the sinful person, apart from repentance. "If I regard iniquity in my heart, the Lord will not hear me."

4. As Paul said in 1 Corinthians 6:15 (NASB), our bodies are members of Christ. "Do you not know that your bodies are members of Christ? Shall I then take away the members of Christ and make them members of a prostitute? May it never be!"

5. There will be a loss of reward in heaven, as the Bible states in 2 John 1:8: "Look to yourselves, that we lose not those things which we have wrought, but that we receive a full reward."

6. This is almost the most devastating one of all, another illustration of God's discipline. In the twentieth chapter of the book of Numbers, when the Israelites had no water, Moses was told to speak to a rock. Instead he lost his temper and struck it twice. Water flowed, but God told Moses he had sinned. After years of leading God's people in the desert, Moses forfeited the tremendous privilege and honor of leading them into the Promised Land, although God graciously showed it to him from a mountain far away just before he died.

Here's the principle: The forgiveness of sin does not always carry with it relief from the consequences of the sin. When I entertain the thought of sin, I think of the consequences—the damage to my testimony, the discipline I would undergo, the disappointment of those who know me, and most of all, the idea of disappointing my Lord. After that, maybe the most devastating thing is the loss of my service to Him. It takes a lifetime to build a reputation but only a moment to destroy it.

THE BIBLE AND DOCTRINE

The Bible's role in our lives

The Word of God is truth. I've heard it said that when you buy a car, you look at the owner's manual because the auto manufacturer knows how it runs best. I believe God is my creator, and I believe God wrote an "owner's manual" in the form of the Bible: a library of sixty-six books, written by more than thirty-five different authors, in a period of approximately 1,500 years. Those authors represent a cross section of humanity—both educated and uneducated—that includes fishermen, kings, public officials, farmers, teachers, and physicians. The Bible covers such subjects as religion, history, law, science, poetry, drama, biography, and prophecy. Its various parts go together as harmoniously as the parts that make up the human body.

For so many authors, with such varied backgrounds, to write on so many subjects over such a long period in absolute harmony seems to me an impossibility. It could not happen, except that—as 2 Peter 1:21 explains—"Holy men of God spake as they were moved by the Holy Ghost."

The Bible reveals the mind of God, the state of man, the way of salvation, the doom of sinners, and the future happiness of believers. It is necessary to read it to be wise, safe, and holy. It is a light to direct my steps, food to sustain me, and comfort when my heart is sad. It's been called a map, a compass, a sword, and the Christian's charter. Christ is the majestic subject, and God's glory is its end. I am learning to memorize it, to let it rule my heart and guide my steps, and to read it frequently and prayerfully. It is, as I've been told, a wealth of treasure and a river of pleasure. I love that. It rewards those who labor with it, and it condemns any who trifle with its sacred contents. It is wisdom for those who trust it, and salvation and power to those who obey it.

The Bible is the Word of God. Believe it, honor it, obey it, love it, study it, proclaim it, and defend it.

Why does God allow suffering?

People who hear me talk about my faith often ask why there is so much suffering. If God is both good and all-powerful, as the Bible says, why does He sometimes permit the best of people to suffer the worst of calamities?

A whole book of Scripture is devoted to that complex problem. It's the story of Job, whom Scripture describes as "blameless and upright, and one who feared God and shunned evil" (Job 1:1, NKJV). God Himself said there was no one else like Job on the earth (v. 8).

Yet, a series of shattering calamities struck Job and his family all at once, leaving him physically wasted, emotionally spent, and crying out to God for answers. The answers Job finally received were not really answers to the "why" questions (although the Bible does give us a peek behind the scenes in heaven, where we get a small glimpse of why Job suffered). But the thrust of the book is primarily a reminder of two important, rock-solid truths about *God* that encourage us to trust Him through hard times.

First, God is *sovereign.* He has not lost control, even if that's how it seems from our perspective.

Second, God is *good,* and His tender mercies are over all His works. Satan, not God, was the evil agent who devised all Job's suffering and personally afflicted him. God gave permission, but He had good reasons for doing so. He set careful boundaries on what the devil could do to Job. And he ultimately used all those trials for Job's eternal good and His own eternal glory.

God promises to use all things for good in the lives of *everyone* who loves Him (Romans 8:28). That means there is always a good purpose in the bad things that happen to us, even if we can't yet see the good. I know this is true from personal experience (and perhaps you do, too). Some of the most difficult things I have ever suffered have reaped the richest rewards in my life, and as I look back on them, I can sometimes see clearly *how* God used them for good, and therefore I can even thank Him for my sufferings.

That was the perspective of Joseph, whose brothers sold him as a slave into Egypt. God brought Joseph through a lifetime of distress in order to raise him to a position of influence in Egypt. In the end, Joseph saved the lives of multitudes, including the brothers who betrayed him. Instead of being bitter and resentful against them, he told them, "You meant evil against me, but God meant it for good" (Genesis 50:20, NASB). That's the perspective we ought to have about all our trials (see James 1:2-4).

Some have asked me, "Why do bad things happen to God's people?" I came up with nine reasons:

1. To test the validity of our faith—to see if it is a lasting (saving) faith (2 Chronicles 32:31)
2. To wean us from the world (John 6:5-6)
3. To call us to heavenly hope (Romans 5:3)
4. To show us what we really love (Genesis 22)
5. To teach us obedience—sin has painful consequences (Hebrews 12:5-6)
6. To reveal God's compassion in our misery (Psalm 63:3)
7. To develop our spiritual strength for greater usefulness (James 1:2-4)
8. To enable us to help others in their trials (2 Corinthians 1:4-6)
9. To display God's astounding power (2 Corinthians 1:8-10)

God the creator

It's hard for me to imagine anything more difficult than the atheistic formula for the explanation of the universe: Nobody times nothing equals everything.

I believe God is creator not only because Scripture says so, but also because I can see the evidence of His handiwork in the design of creation itself. Paul says God's invisible attributes are on display in all that He has made (Romans 1:20). Paul suggests, for example, that the vastness of the universe testifies to His power. I would add that the beauty of creation testifies to God's goodness and His own love of beauty.

I can no more look at the glory of creation and imagine that it evolved from nothing by chance than I can hear a Bach partita and believe it's just a collection of random noises that fell together by accident.

What is true salvation?

Arthur W. Pink wrote this in 1937:

> Salvation is by grace, by grace alone. . . . Nevertheless, divine grace is not exercised at the expense of holiness, for it never compromises with sin. It is also true that salvation is a free gift, but an empty hand must receive it, and not a hand which still tightly grasps the world! . . .
>
> Something more than "believing" is necessary to salvation. A heart that is steeled in rebellion against God cannot savingly believe; it must first be broken. . . .
>
> . . . Only those who are spiritually blind would declare that Christ will save any who despise His authority and refuse His yoke. . . . Those preachers who tell sinners that they may be saved without forsaking their idols, without repenting, without

surrendering to the Lordship of Christ, are as erroneous and dangerous as others who insist that salvation is by works and that heaven must be earned by our own efforts.[4]

Is Jesus God?

I used to wonder how Jesus could be both eternally God and the Son of God. After all, we naturally think of a son as subordinate to his father. If we call Jesus the Son of God, aren't we really saying He is something less than the eternal, self-sufficient, omnipotent God? That question troubled me.

At the same time, it was clear to me that certain texts of Scripture emphatically say that Jesus is God and fully equal to God the Father. For example, He is plainly called the eternal Word *and* "God" in John 1:1.

Then I learned that in Hebrew usage, the expression "son" denotes an absolute equality of essence, privilege, and right. A "son" was different from a "child" in exactly this way: the "son" was regarded as a full heir with all the adult privileges and power— not a subordinate, but an equal in every way (Galatians 4:1-6). That's why when Jesus referred to God as His Father, John 5:18 says His enemies "sought the more to kill him, because he not only had broken the sabbath, but had also said that God was his Father, *making Himself equal with God*" (emphasis added). Thomas said after seeing the resurrected Christ, "My LORD and my God" (John 20:28).

Who matters most to you?

A certain lady used to cut my hair. She was of Jewish heritage, and I remember her telling me that when her mother was sick, she prayed and prayed that God would heal her. He didn't, and she said, "I've resented God from that moment on. I want nothing to do with God at all, because He did not answer my prayer."

I told her the story of Job. God allowed Satan to put Job through some of the most severe trials man has ever encountered. Satan's claim was that if everything was taken away from Job, he would curse God. Then God told Satan that he could take everything from Job but his life. (See Job 1–2.) So that's exactly what Satan did. In the middle of it all, Job's response was, "Though he slay me, yet will I trust in him" (13:15). Job passed the test, proving that a true child of God worships Him regardless of his circumstances.

In a recent discussion with one of my friends, she said, "I will never put God first in my life. My children will always be first."

I told her, "The greatest example in Scripture is Abraham's attitude toward Isaac. He loved Isaac more than anything else, but he understood that even our children are not our own, but God's." I said, "You can't put your children first. God has to be first in your life. Your children belong to God. If God hadn't allowed Jesus Christ to suffer and die for us, we would still be in our sins."

She said, "Well, you wouldn't put your son, Luke, after God."

I said, "I believe I would."

She was almost shocked. She said, "That's nice to say, but when it came down to it, you wouldn't."

I understand why she had that perspective. Love for one's own children is one of the most powerful human affections. On the other hand, enmity with God is one of the inevitable effects of our fallenness (Romans 8:7-8). Conversion to Christ reorders our priorities—so much that Scripture likens spiritual regeneration to the implantation of a new heart (Ezekiel 36:26).

Shortly after my son was born, I had an experience that made it clearer to me what it meant that God allowed His Son to die for our sins.

When Luke was several months old, Theresa and I decided we

would let him learn to go to sleep on his own. This necessitated letting him cry for a few minutes before he fell asleep. We placed a blanket over his legs and stomach that night to keep him warm. Later, when he started to cry, we were in the other room, and it was breaking our hearts to listen. I went in after about five minutes just to make sure he was okay, but he kept crying. Fifteen minutes went by, and suddenly he started to wail, beyond crying—almost screaming. I said, "Theresa, we've got to hang in there and give it another five minutes. He's bound to go to sleep by then."

In five minutes, it was quiet. I walked from our bedroom into his room and was horrified to see the blanket covering his face, which was why he had been wailing. When I looked at my son and saw that he had been crying out for me to come to him—and I did not come—I was crushed to the core. I could only for a moment imagine Christ on the cross when he said, "My God, my God, why hast thou forsaken me?" (Matthew 27:46). The separation that took place between the Father and the Son and the suffering the Father allowed the Son to undergo—because of His great love for us—suddenly was more clear to me than ever before. When I thought about my little boy crying out for me and my saying "No, I'm not coming to you," I was truly grieved.

Is it unfair that God bestows saving grace on some and not on others?

I was told a story years ago that helped me understand this question from a better perspective.

There was a man walking down the street. Two young robbers assaulted him, beat him up, stripped him of his clothes, took all his money, and left him for dead. They were shortly thereafter caught and put in prison.

When the man who had been robbed was asked to press

charges, he chose to forgive and bestow grace on one of the two robbers. He bailed him out of jail, took him in as a guest in his home, paid for his schooling, and eventually adopted him as a member of his family. He forgave him for everything he had done.

He left the other robber in prison.

He showed grace—unmerited favor—to the one he'd bailed out of jail. But the question is, "Was he unjust, or unfair, to the other robber?" The answer is no. That man got what he deserved. The other one just got undeserved grace.

I've heard our pastor put it this way: "Don't say, 'I just want what I deserve.' You don't want what you deserve. We all deserve hell because of our sin. Whatever good things we have, especially our salvation, we have by grace alone." Many people say, "It's not fair that God would punish some people but not others"—but it is! We all deserve hell! It's just that by His sovereign will, He has chosen to bestow grace upon some people, not for anything they have done.

In damnation, God acts in response to human choice. In salvation, man acts in response to divine choice. God has chosen us to be His children and has showered us with His grace.

Have you kept your first love?

I really want to get personal here. My greatest fear for my own spiritual life is not that I will fall into some worldly temptation. I have been blessed to grow spiritually in a church that teaches sound doctrine, emphasizes bearing fruit and laboring for God, stands against sin and unrighteousness, and desires the glory of God and the advancement of His Kingdom. But in Revelation 2, the apostle John, through the inspiration of the Holy Spirit, records that although the Ephesian church believed strong doctrine, labored to produce good works, exhibited patience, struggled against evil for the sake of Christ, and "fainted not," Christ had something against that church. Those believers had left their first love. Their worship of Christ was mechanical. Their service was heartless. If a church can do that, so can an individual. That is my greatest fear.

I also thought about a comparison in music. You can practice hard, develop a great technique, and study music theory and history. You can discipline yourself and work hard at all aspects of playing the guitar; you can even study with great teachers and play the finest music ever written, but if it's without *heart* and a true love for the music, it's empty. Mechanical. Soulless. Lifeless.

Now that I have been a Christian for many years, I don't want to forget my first love, Christ—how excited I first was about praying to Him and serving Him and reading the Word to learn more about Him. I'm still a long way from where I want to be. But now that I'm a longer-time Christian, hopefully a little more mature in the faith and in doctrine, I still want to know Christ. First John 2:13 says that we start as babies in Christ, then mature to young men, and aim to become spiritual fathers, knowing Christ.

Why pray if God is in control?

Prayer is acknowledging that God is sovereign. We say, "Lord, here is what's on my heart. I don't know what Your will is, but this is what I ask of You in my humbleness." Prayer becomes presumption when it doesn't acknowledge the will of God and the sovereignty of God. Prayer is a mysterious thing; it's possible to ask, "If God is in charge, why bother?" The answer is, "He tells us to pray." Why does He tell us to pray? If for no other reason than to commune with Him, to learn to submit to Him and line up with His will, and to rejoice in that process. Prayer becomes presumption if we don't have the attitude of, "Thy Kingdom come, Thy will be done—whatever will give You the greatest glory, whatever will advance Your name, whatever will give You honor, that's what I want You to do."

An old poem by Marshall Broomhall says it this way:

With peaceful mind thy path of duty run:
God nothing does, nor suffers to be done,
But thou wouldst do the same if thou couldst see
The end of all events as well as He.[5]

What is wisdom?

Fearing God is the beginning of wisdom, and wisdom is the understanding needed to live life to the glory of God. (See Proverbs 1:7.)

How can we balance truth and love with sound doctrine?

The foundation of Christian unity is sound doctrine. Truth prevents love from becoming sappy sentimentalism, and love prevents truth from becoming rigid dogmatism. The main teaching of the short book of 2 John is walking in truth by ordering one's life by the Word of God. According to 2 John 1:6, "This is love, that we walk after his commandments."

What is saving faith?

The Holy Spirit is the One who confirms saving faith. An evangelist might say, "Now I welcome you into the Kingdom of God," to someone who prayed a prayer and walked an aisle, but in fact he doesn't know if that person is a true believer or not at that point. Only the Holy Spirit can confirm whether or not faith is genuine.

A Bible passage that perfectly illustrates this point is the parable of the sower (Matthew 13:3-23; Luke 8:5-15). A seed may sprout and look like it's a Christian. But too many people have come down the aisle, prayed the prayer, and then walked away from Christ. They didn't count the cost, and the cares and the worries of the world choked their faith. When persecution arose, it was too much, and they walked away.

A simple principle of Biblical interpretation
Never generate a doctrine out of an obscure text when no other text in the Bible teaches that same doctrine.

Choosing a church
The primary criterion for choosing a church is biblical preaching. Martin Luther said that the pinnacle of public worship is the preaching of God's word. Worship is acknowledging God for who He is and what He has done. A congregation cannot honor God more than by listening reverently to the preaching of His Word with an obedient heart.

One of the sermons I heard shortly after I became a Christian defined biblical Christianity as teaching and preaching

1. the supremacy of the Holy Scriptures
2. the total corruption of human nature
3. Christ's death upon the cross as the only satisfaction for humanity's sin
4. the doctrine of justification by faith alone
5. the universal necessity of heart conversion and new creation by the Holy Spirit
6. God's eternal hatred of sin and God's love of sinners
7. the inseparable connection between true faith and personal holiness. (Church membership or religious profession is not proof that a person is a genuine Christian if he or she lives an ungodly life.)

CHRISTIAN LIVING

A simple guideline for prayer
At a recent Bible study, I learned a helpful format for praying. The acronym ACTS stands for adoration, confession, thanksgiving, and supplication. I've started to follow that pattern when I pray.

How should we live as Christians?
The Christian life should be characterized by love, excellence, integrity, good works, and a dedication to God's glory.

What is the role of works if salvation is by faith alone?
I have always known that we are saved by grace, through faith alone, not by good deeds. Ephesians 2:8-9 says, "By grace are ye saved through faith; and that not of yourselves: it is the gift of God: Not of works, lest any man should boast." But then what about James 2:17? "Faith, if it hath not works, is dead, being alone."

I love this comparison: Faith and works are like a two-coupon ticket to heaven. The coupon of works is not good for passage, but the coupon of faith is not valid if detached from works. Unproductive faith can't save, because it isn't genuine. Do you have to work your way to heaven? No way! You're saved by grace alone, through faith alone. But if your faith is genuine, there will be some evidence or fruit in your life—your works and deeds.

Who is your captain?
I heard about a mean, crusty old sea captain who was merciless with his crew. After months on the high seas, the crew mutinied, threw him into the bowels of the ship, and appointed a new leader.

One day a crew member was walking past the prison cell when the former captain yelled out an order. Out of habit and routine, the crewman started to obey. Then he said, "Wait a minute. You aren't my captain anymore, and you don't control me. I have a new leader, and I only serve him."

The point is that we don't need to listen to the old, sinful, fallen self anymore. We have a new captain: Jesus Christ, through the Holy Spirit.

Ultimate human forgiveness

The brother-in-law of a friend of mine had a seventeen-year-old son who was shot and killed when he was working in a convenience store. The murderer was caught, convicted, and put in prison, and the father of the boy requested the opportunity to see his son's killer. Through the thick Plexiglas window, he told him face-to-face that he forgave him for killing his son and that he wanted him to hear the precious gospel of Jesus Christ so he could believe and be saved and so they could meet again in heaven.

I've never heard of a more extreme example of human forgiveness, and I can only imagine the peace this father received when he forgave someone else in the way God forgives us. It seems humanly impossible to forgive such a man, but God gives grace at exactly the time it's needed.

When someone wrongs me, shall I not forgive that person? How much less is that than what this man forgave? Luke 6:37 says, "Judge not, and ye shall not be judged: condemn not, and ye shall not be condemned: forgive, and ye shall be forgiven."

A story of faithfulness

Billy Kim, an interpreter for Billy Graham on a Tokyo crusade, told this story a few years ago.

Some North Korean soldiers overran a village. They rounded up two hundred Christians and took them into a church where they nailed a picture of Jesus to the front door. "You are going to go out in single file," they said, "and you are going to spit in your Messiah's face. If you don't spit in His face, you'll be shot in the head."

The first man went up to the picture, spit in Christ's face, and walked out. The second spit on the picture of Christ and also walked out. So did the third and the fourth.

The fifth, a young girl, walked up to the picture, took her dress, and wiped the spit away, saying, "Jesus, I love you, and I'm willing to die for you."

The girl's actions so flabbergasted the soldiers that they said, "Get out. Everybody get out." Then they went outside, took the four men who had spit on the picture of Jesus, shot *them* dead, and let the others go. They said that to be a communist, one has to have great commitment, which these four men did not.

God used the courage of one little girl to save most of this church.

Our eternal glory—which is our capacity to serve God, to serve Christ, to glorify Him, and to praise Him in heaven—is measured out in relation to our willingness to suffer for Christ's sake. The cross, then, is the greatest illustration of how suffering is related to glory. The greatest suffering that ever occurred in the universe occurred on the cross, and the greatest glory that has ever been given was given in response to that suffering. God is not overcome by evil, and neither are His people.

True happiness

Christian joy is an experience that springs from the deep confidence that Christ is sufficient and that God is in perfect control of everything, bringing it all together for our good and for His glory, in time and eternity. True happiness comes from devoting one's life to a great purpose, and what greater purpose could there be than the glory of God and the gospel of His Son, the Lord Jesus Christ?

With Christ, there is blessing, purpose, and joy. I've heard it said that if you find your deepest joy in anything in this life, you are destined for a life of discontentment. Ultimately, we live to glorify God and advance His Kingdom.

Thy will for my life

Sometimes I think of this prayer of consecration, written by Betty Scott Stam, a missionary to China who died there in the 1930s. She wrote it when she was eighteen years old, and it is one of my favorites.

> *Lord, I give up all my own plans and purposes,*
> *All my own desires and hopes,*
> *And accept Thy will for my life.*
> *I give myself, my life, my all*
> *Utterly to Thee to be Thine forever.*
> *Fill me and seal me with Thy Holy Spirit,*
> *Use me as Thou wilt,*
> *Send me where Thou wilt,*
> *And work out Thy whole will in my life*
> *At any cost, now and forever.*

How can we withstand criticism for doing what is right?

Here is a quote I love from an unknown author.

Being About the Father's Business

Keep about your work. Do not flinch because the lion roars; do not stop to stone the devil's dogs; do not fool away your time chasing the devil's rabbits. Do your work. Let liars lie, let sectarians quarrel, let the devil do his worst; but see to it nothing hinders you from fulfilling the work God has given you. He has not commanded you to be rich, he has never bidden you defend your character, he has not set you at work to contradict falsehood about yourself, which Satan and his servants may start to peddle. If you do those things, you will do nothing else; you will be at work for yourself and not for the Lord. Keep at work, let your aim be as steady as a star. You may be assaulted, wronged, insulted, slandered, wounded, and rejected; you may be abused by foes, forsaken by friends, and despised and rejected of men. But see to it, with steadfast determination, with unfaltering zeal, that you pursue the great purpose of your life and object of your being, until at last you can say, "I have finished the work which Thou gavest me to do."

The pleasure principle

When you live in the light of eternity, your focus changes from "How much pleasure am I getting out of life?" to "How much pleasure is God getting out of my life?"

I had to learn the hard way that the pleasures of sin are but for a season (Hebrews 11:25). When that season is over, you pay dearly. "Be not deceived; God is not mocked: for whatsoever a man soweth, that shall he also reap" (Galatians 6:17).

Perfected in weakness

As I mentioned earlier, I heard a sermon based on 2 Corinthians 12:9 (NASB), on the night before my Hollywood Bowl performance when I had a lacerated finger. The text of this passage includes, "My grace is sufficient for you, for power is perfected in weakness." So the suffering that humbles us, the suffering that forces us to God in prayer, the suffering that makes us cry out for grace to endure, is the very source of power in our lives. It is when the Christian has lost all human ability to deal with his difficulty, when he is weak, destitute, without resources, and left totally to trust in

God's power through grace to sustain him that he becomes a channel through which God's power can flow. The trials in our physical lives are what lead us to spiritual strength.

For a Christian, endurance equals the tenacity of spirit that holds on under pressure, while awaiting God's time to remove, dismiss, and reward when the trial is done.

Running to win
Because I needed to protect my hands and fingernails, my high school athletic career was limited to track and field. I went to a small school, where the track coach knew how much I had to practice the guitar, so he allowed me a minimum amount of workout time with the team. I ran events that required speed instead of endurance: the 100-yard dash, the 220, the 440 relay, and the long jump.

One time my school competed against several big-city high schools in the area, and I placed so poorly in the 100 that I figured I had nothing to lose in the 220. I was loose and warmed up, with a "go for broke, don't expect anything" attitude.

When we rounded the first bend, to my surprise I saw that I was in the lead. I kept leading. I saw the finish line just ahead and thought, *I don't believe this. I am going to win!* I focused my eyes on the tape . . . and just a few steps before I crossed it, two guys whooshed past me.

My coach told me later, "Chris, you made one big mistake. You didn't run through the finish line. You ran to it, and your entire stride changed the last few steps. You always must run through the finish line, toward a distance beyond where you're actually running to."

I liken that to practicing a piece of music faster than you'll need to play it in concert. For a fast allegro movement, you don't set concert tempo as your practicing goal. You practice beyond that so that you can comfortably play the concert tempo onstage. Or, to make a spiritual connection, I compare it to looking past your circumstances to Christ as you run life's race.

Hebrews 12:1-2 says, "Wherefore seeing we also are compassed about with so great a cloud of witnesses, let us lay aside every weight, and the sin which doth so easily beset us, and let us run with patience [endurance] the race that is set before us, looking unto Jesus the author and finisher of our faith; who for the joy that was set before him endured the cross, despising the shame, and is set down at the right hand of the throne of God."

Finish well

I pray that God gives me the grace to finish well. I live under a kind of tension, lest I default, so I stay accountable. As Paul put it, "having done all, to stand" (Ephesians 6:13). I also think of 1 Corinthians 9:27: "I keep under my body, and bring it into subjection: lest that by any means, when I have preached to others, I myself should be a castaway." So many have "done it all," yet in the end have fallen to sin and disqualification, bringing shame on the very Lord they represented. Though I am keenly aware of my own sinfulness and need for God's grace, I know that God's grace is greater than our sin.

The king and the charioteers

There's a famous story about a king who was testing his country's finest drivers to see who would become his personal charioteer. He took them to a treacherous, winding mountain road and told them, "If you can't drive with confidence and skill on this road, you cannot be my charioteer."

The first man drove his chariot at breakneck speed around all the twists and turns, coming within inches of the edge. All were amazed at the man's skill and daring.

The second driver, thinking he needed to outdo the first man, drove even faster, steered the chariot's wheels closer to the edge of the road, and brought the chariot back in record time.

A third driver drove very slowly and stayed as far away as possible from every steep edge. As soon as he finished the test course, the king met him and said, "You are my new chariot driver. I want a man whose instincts tell him to stay as far away from danger as possible."

I desire to stay well inside the circle of obedience and not be the kind of person that constantly pushes the boundaries.

Dying to ourselves

Humility is a demonstration of a Christian's spiritual maturity. Self-denial, then, becomes a pattern for life.

When someone holds a grudge against you or you're neglected or purposely set aside, although you sting and hurt with the insult or oversight, your heart is happy and you're content to be counted worthy to suffer for Christ, that is dying to self.

When your good is spoken of as evil, your wishes are crossed, your advice is disregarded, and your opinions are ridiculed, and when you refuse to let anger rise in your heart or to even defend yourself but take it all in patient, loyal silence, that is dying to self.

When you lovingly and patiently bear any disorder, any irregularity, or any annoyance; when you can stand face-to-face with foolishness, extravagance, or spiritual insensitivity and endure it as Jesus endured it, that is dying to self.

When you're content with any food, any offering, any clothes, any climate, any society, any solitude, any interruption by the will of God, that is dying to self.

When you never care to refer to yourself or to record your own good works or to seek commendation; when you can truly love to be unknown, that is dying to self.

When you see another brother prosper and have his or her needs met and you can honestly rejoice with this person in spirit and feel no envy, nor even question God while your own needs are far greater or your circumstances more desperate, that is dying to self.

When you can receive correction and reproof from one of less worldly stature than yourself and you can humbly submit inwardly, as well as outwardly, finding no rebellion or resentment rising up within your heart, that is dying to self.

So you come to Christ with an attitude of self-denial, and you grow from there. Our self-denial isn't perfect; we resurrect our own egos and our own wills, thrust them out, and intrude into the will of God. We have to seek His grace and His forgiveness when we do that. Coming to Christ with an attitude of self-denial is the deepest, and purest, and truest aspiration of our redeemed hearts, even though it's far short of what we would want it to be.

Poverty, prosperity, and suffering

John MacArthur has said this: "In poverty, the heart is easily distracted. In prosperity, the heart is easily divided. Suffering drives out the world and sends us singularly to God."

SERVING OTHERS

A servant's heart

At my elementary school, we always had a class monitor who wore a gold badge and emptied the wastepaper baskets, erased the blackboards, put new chalk on the blackboard tray, and clapped the erasers outside.

One day my third-grade teacher, Miss Carey, asked, "Who would like to be class monitor?" Everybody but me had a hand raised, but I didn't think I had a chance. I was sitting in the back row, just listening and looking up, when suddenly Miss Carey said, "Chris, would you like to be class monitor?"

"Yes," I said, in a tiny voice that wasn't much more than a peep. She had me walk up to the front and pinned the little gold-colored class monitor badge on my shirt. I felt so wonderful, so happy, that I was going to be the class monitor and wear a badge.

That afternoon, I rushed home to my mom and said, "Mom, I'm class monitor! I get to empty the wastepaper basket, erase the blackboard, and put out the chalk every morning for the teacher!"

In my childlike enthusiasm, I was excited about being given the opportunity to serve. It reminds me that the Lord asks this of all of us in Matthew 20:27-28: "And whosoever will be chief among you, let him be your servant: even as the Son of man came not to be ministered unto, but to minister, and to give his life a ransom for many."

There was a very shy man with a withered arm who faithfully worked as a volunteer at my church year after year, putting tapes into albums. No one particularly knew his name, and he didn't get any awards; he wasn't standing up in front of the church preaching or performing, and I never saw anyone give him any special privileges. He had no earthly reward or commendation that I saw, and yet I believe that when he stands before Christ, the Lord will say, "Well done, good and faithful servant." I believe that man will be rewarded more than many well-known Christians.

I also heard about a man in a poor village in India whose heart's desire was to win his neighbors to the Lord. He was so poor that he didn't own a car, just a bicycle. After a long day of hard work, he would ride his bicycle ten miles into the big city and literally sell his blood for money. With the money he earned, he bought a screen, a projector, a portable battery, and a video in his native language on the life of Christ. He would take this equipment to the shore at night and show the film, which would attract nearly all the people in the village. Hundreds came to know Christ through the effort of this humble servant. What a reward he will have in heaven!

How effective are you?

Your effectiveness as a Christian is directly related to one thing: the proximity in which you live in intimate fellowship with Jesus Christ. I believe that the initial attraction of Christianity is the life of the Christian.

What can't we do in heaven?

The book of Matthew closes with the great commission of Christ: "Go ye therefore, and teach all nations, baptizing them in the name of the Father, and of the Son, and of the Holy Ghost: teaching them to observe all things whatsoever I have commanded you: and, lo, I am with you alway, even unto the end of the world" (28:19-20).

Some people go to church for the music, some because their friends are there, some to study the Bible, and some for a higher priority—to worship and praise God. But all of those things you can do better in heaven. The one thing you cannot do in heaven is make disciples for Christ. *So, Christian, if you are not actively involved in making disciples for Christ, in whatever sphere the Lord has placed you, the Lord could take you to heaven tonight, and you wouldn't be missed.* We will have the greatest music in heaven, we will have perfect fellowship, we will have all knowledge (so we won't need to study the Bible), and we will be in a much better state—our glorified state—where we can worship and praise God.

So ask yourself, *Am I advancing His Kingdom? Am I making disciples for Christ?* That concept changed my life and my ministry with the guitar.

How does this life compare to heaven and hell?

For a nonbeliever, this life is the closest thing to heaven he'll ever experience. For a believer, this life is the closest thing to hell he'll ever experience.

A definition of love

Love is sacrificial service without a motive for yourself.

What are your priorities?

Many wonderful ministry opportunities are offered to me as a musician and performer, but sometimes to honor the Lord, I must turn down something in order to spend time with my family. I have had to learn to prioritize my time and not sacrifice my family on the altar of my ministry. The correct priority is this: God first, family second, and ministry third.

CHRISTI'S STORY

Why should you go to heaven?

One day I had the opportunity to share with my eleven-year-old niece, Christi, what it means to be a Christian. I said, "Christi, if you were to die tonight and stand before God and He were to say to you, 'Why should I let you into my heaven?' what would you say?"

"Well," she replied, "I would say, 'Because I've been a good girl.'"

"How good have you been?" I asked. "Have you been perfect?"

"No," she admitted, "I haven't been perfect."

"That's true," I said. "No one is perfect. In fact, the Bible says, 'All have sinned, and come short of the glory of God' (Romans 3:23). But God requires us to be perfect (James 2:10), and who can be perfect? Nobody, right? Nobody can be perfect."

I told her that salvation is a free gift received by faith. Ephesians 2:8-9 says, "By grace are ye saved through faith; and that not of yourselves: it is the gift of God: Not of works, lest any man should boast." I said, "You're not saved by your good deeds; you are saved by grace, and grace means God is freely giving you something you don't deserve."

I also told her the Bible says that God is holy and just. Hebrews 10:31 says, "It is a fearful thing to fall into the hands of the living God." And Exodus 34:7 says that God "will by no means clear the guilty." Since God is just, He will judge those who sin. I went on to say that God is also a loving God. My favorite Bible verse, John 3:16, says, "For God so loved the world, that he gave his only begotten Son, that whosoever believeth in him should not perish, but have everlasting life." God judges those who sin, but in love He gave His Son to die on a cross to bear our sin and judgment.

How can God judge sinners and yet love them? To illustrate the answer, I told Christi a story about a king who was a wise and just ruler of his people.

Someone was embezzling from the king's treasury, so the king issued an edict throughout all the land, saying, "Whoever is guilty, come forward and receive a just punishment of ten public lashings." But no one came forward.

The second week someone was continuing to steal from the king's treasury, so the king set the punishment at twenty public lashings. But still no one came forward.

The third and fourth weeks went by, and the thievery continued.

On the fifth week the king set the punishment at fifty public lashings.

Finally, the guilty person was discovered. The one embezzling from the king's treasury turned out to be the king's own mother! The whole kingdom turned out to see what the king was going to do because they knew that this was a real dilemma: On the one hand, he loved his mother, and he knew that fifty lashes would very likely kill her. On the other hand, he had a reputation for being a just king who would certainly punish the crime.

On the day for the sentencing to be carried out, the king's mother was tied to a stake and a big man was preparing to flog her with a whip. Then the king gave the order: "Render the punishment!" But as he spoke, he took off his own robe, bared his own back, and put his arms around his mother. He then took the lashes she deserved, thereby satisfying the demand for justice.

As I told Christi, that's exactly what Jesus Christ did for us. The Bible says: "He was wounded for our transgressions, he was bruised for our iniquities: the chastisement of our peace was upon him; and with his stripes we are healed. All we like sheep have gone astray; we have turned every one to his own way; and the LORD hath laid on him the iniquity of us all" (Isaiah 53:5-6).

"Who his own self bare our sins in his own body on the tree, that we, being dead to sins, should live unto righteousness: by whose stripes ye were healed" (1 Peter 2:24).

Jesus Christ, by His death and physical resurrection, paid for our sins and purchased a place in heaven for us, which He offers as a gift that may be received by faith. I told Christi, "You have a choice: You can stand before God when you die and say, 'I've been a good girl,' but you will fall short. You could say, 'The good I've done outweighs the bad,' but you will still fall short. You could even invent your own standard for heaven and achieve that, but God's standard is perfect righteousness! Or you can humble yourself and receive the gift that God has described in the Bible: 'Neither is there salvation in any other: for there is none other name under heaven given among men, whereby we must be saved' (Acts 4:12). Jesus said, 'I am the way, the truth, and the life: no man cometh unto the Father, but by me' (John 14:6).

"Apart from the death of Christ on the cross for our sins, no one has access to the Father, no one has access to heaven. That's what the Bible says. True saving faith, then, is trusting in Jesus Christ alone for your salvation—and the response to true faith will be an overwhelming desire to be obedient to the Lord. Jesus said in Luke 6:46, 'Why call ye me, Lord, Lord, and do not the things which I say?' That's what it means to make Him Lord and Savior."

I'm thankful I had the opportunity that day to share with Christi what the Bible says about true salvation. But what about you? Are you willing to humble yourself before God and confess to Him that you are a sinner? Are you willing now to repent, turn from your sins, and receive Christ as your Savior and Lord? If so, you might wish to pray the following prayer from your heart:

Lord Jesus, I know that I'm a sinner. I've been trusting in my own good deeds to save me, but now I'm putting my trust in You. I accept You as my personal Savior. I believe You died for me. I receive You as Lord and Master over my life. Help me to turn from my sins and follow You. In Jesus' name I pray. Amen.

ENDNOTES

1. Walter Arlen, *Los Angeles Times*, January 9, 1966.

2. Luke 6:38: "Give, and it shall be given unto you; good measure, pressed down, and shaken together, and running over, shall men give into your bosom. For with the same measure that ye mete withal it shall be measured to you again."

3. Liner notes, *The Magic of Horowitz*, edited by Thomas Frost, Deutsche Grammophon DG-474334-2, quoted by permission.

4. Arthur W. Pink, "Signs of the Times," *Studies in the Scriptures,* December 1937.

5. Marshall Broomhall, *The Man Who Believed God* (Chicago: Moody Press, 1929).

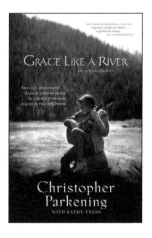

Free Discussion Guide!

A discussion guide for
Grace Like a River is available at

ACKNOWLEDGMENTS

No book comes together without the help of many gracious and talented people, and there is not enough space to thank everyone we would like to. Still, the authors would particularly like to thank these individuals for their valued contributions.

From Chris:

To Theresa, you are the love of my life. I thank you for always loving and encouraging me through difficult times with recordings to make, concerts to perform, and books to write, and for giving me, through the dear Lord, the most precious little boy in the world.

To Duke and Betty Parkening, my dear parents. I can never thank you enough for your love, support, and devotion to my music.

To Terry, you have been a best friend and confidante through thick and thin. I have a special love in my heart for you, my sweet sister.

Sincerest thanks to Dave Thomas, my longtime friend, advisor, recording producer, fishing buddy, guitarist, sound-advisor perfectionist, athlete, and colaborer in Christ. Your friendship is a true gift of God's grace in my life. Your help with this book has been, in a word, *invaluable*. I could never thank you enough.

To John MacArthur, what gratitude I offer to the Lord for sovereignly giving you to me as an earthly spiritual role model, mentor, friend, and beloved pastor-teacher. Your example of excellence, integrity, and character has inspired me to run the race with endurance. You are my earthly apostle Paul.

To Joni and Ken Tada, I am grateful to God for your friendship through the hard times and the joyous times, and during fishing trips, prayer, hymn singing, and barbecues. Joni, I will always think of you when I play "Recuerdos." Your joy is infectious, your writing skillful, your hymn singing uplifting, your paintings lovely, and your life an inspiration to me. Ken, I greatly value your friendship. Thank you for your encouragement to pray for a godly wife—our prayers were answered! Lord willing, we can look forward to many more fishing times together.

Thank you, Sharon Devol, incomparable secretary and personal assistant, for technical wizardry, for always standing on duty, for coordinating everyone involved in this project, and for making sure everything got done. You are amazing!

Particular thanks to Pat Russ. I have been the beneficiary of your talents, wisdom, and friendship in so many ways. You are a blessing to all who know you.

Particular thanks to Scott Bach, for years of valued and invaluable counsel, sympathetic support, and consistently great ideas; for teaching the excellent sound-production workshop for many years at Montana State University; and for setting up this project.

To Jubilant Sykes, with whom I have shared the concert stage around the world. Your friendship and your artistry are a true blessing in my life.

To David Brandon, with whom I have also shared the concert stage for many years. Your talent, wisdom, and friendship have been invaluable to me. Thank you for being best man at my wedding!

Thanks also to Robert Wolgemuth, for sparking the idea for this book, for your generosity and your friendship, and for introducing us to Tyndale House Publishers.

Many thanks to Phil Johnson for kindly checking and double-checking the content and theological accuracy of "Reflections."

To Kathy Tyers, whose friendship, along with Mark's, I will always cherish, whose skill in writing I will always admire, and who picked up fly-fishing as quickly as anybody I have ever seen. Thank you for your graciousness, humility, and patience. Thank you for laboring through all my tangents and silly stories and for desiring to produce a book that will, Lord willing, inspire and encourage young musicians, tell of God's grace, and ultimately—and most importantly—glorify the Lord and Savior we both love so much.

Thanks to a special group of "lifetime achievers," who have inspired me through their accomplishment: Howard and Roberta Ahmanson, Stan Barrett, Kathleen Battle, Elmer Bernstein, Nancy DeMoss, Clayton Erb, Franklin Graham, Michael and Dru Hammer, Kurt Kaiser, Kathleen Kennedy, Frank Marshall, Phil Marshall, Felix Martin del Campo, Frank (Frankie) Moore, Paul Newman, Carole Oeschger, Pepe and Angel Romero, Dorothy Stotsenberg, John Sutherland, Joe and Carol Weller, Kraig Wangsnes, and composer John Williams, among others.

Thanks to Janis Long Harris, Doug Knox, Caleb Sjogren, Sharon Leavitt, Lisa Jackson, Elizabeth Gosnell, Martha Millard, and Andrew Wolgemuth for guiding the authors through the book's planning stages, as well as giving their gracious and craftsmanly editorial support to the very end.

There are, of course, too many people to possibly thank in this space for their gracious presence in my life. Some are mentioned in the text of the book. Thanks also to Chris Amelotte, Muriel Anderson, Tom Beltran, Rob Berretta, Tom Birkner, John Cerullo, Russell Cleveland, Al Dopirak, Dennis Duggan, Tom Evered, Jim Fagen, Steve Ferguson, Mark Forlow, Thomas Geoghegan, Karyn Gross, Gilbert Hetherwick, Ed Hobelman, Gordon Jee, Walt Johnson, Patrick Kavanaugh, Don Kendall, David and Kim Kuo, Michael Kurtz, Edna Landau, Charlotte Lee, Phillip Lester, Gary Lewis, Bruce Lundvall, Patricia MacArthur, Hunter Mallory, Richard Markoe, Guillermo and Eda Martinez, Michal McClure, John Nelson, Rique Pantoja, Belle Godwin Pierce, John Polito, Mary Radford, Amalia Ramírez, Ronald Ravenscroft, Wayne Reynolds, Cecilia Rodrigo, Rick Ruoff, Shirley Russ, Jeff Schroedl, Mrs. Andrés Segovia, Jim Sherry, Harry Spear, Doug Swardstrom, CeCe Sykes, Joanna Thomas, Phyllis Thompson, Ernie Turner, Eve Warren, Mark Westling, Paul and Janet Wilson, and Andrew York.

To Andy Benton, Charlie Runnels, Darryl Tippens, David Baird, and all my colleagues at Pepperdine University who are so wonderful to work with. I appreciate you greatly.

Finally, to the band of brothers—Dave Thomas, Patrick Russ, Scott Bach, and David Brandon—for a friendship that has endured, mellowed, and grown deeper even during the hardest times. Your friendship has been invaluable!

From Kathy:

To David Thomas, for your patience during many hours over the telephone while maintaining a full schedule of concert management and recording production.

To Theresa Parkening, for your gracious hospitality, your consistent and faithful prayers, and your ability to rise to any challenge with a dazzling smile and unwavering faith in our Lord Jesus.

To Terry Parkening Duggan, for your sound advice, empathetic encouragement, and sensitive assistance.

To the memory of my late husband, Mark Tyers, who met Chris during his retirement and "talked fishing, since he didn't want to talk about the guitar."

To Thomas Frost for graciously obtaining permission to quote Vladimir

Horowitz; to Oregon State Archives for kind permission to reproduce the Deschutes River Bridge photograph; to Randy Puhrmann for coaching us on aviation vocabulary; to Mark Rice for taking time out of a busy schedule to write out Christopher's "first guitar piece;" and to Carl Stam for invaluable help tracking down his great-aunt's wonderful prayer.

And to Chris, thank you for the hours of incomparable music, for the years of friendship and inspiration to Mark and me at "Camp Ramirez" and beyond, and for these months of solid, diligent work that are helping to sustain me as the Lord takes my life in new directions.

He shall have dominion . . . from sea to sea . . . from the river unto the ends of the earth (Psalm 72:8).

CHRISTOPHER PARKENING
DISCOGRAPHY

Simple Gifts (originally released as *Sacred Music for the Guitar*), 1982. EMI/Angel Records 0777-7-47525-2-7.

Parkening Plays Bach, 1985.
EMI/Angel Records 0777-7-47191-2-4.

A Bach Celebration, 1985.
EMI/Angel Records 0777-7-47195-2-0.

In the Spanish Style, 1986.
EMI/Angel Records 0777-7-47194-2-1.

Pleasures of Their Company, 1986.
EMI/Angel Records 0777-7-47196-2-9.

Virtuoso Duets (with David Brandon), 1990.
EMI/Angel Records 0777-7-49406-2-7.

The Sounds of Christmas (with Julie Andrews, London
Symphony Orchestra, and Ambrosian Boys' Choir), 1990.
Hallmark Cards, Inc. 620XPR9707.

A Tribute to Segovia, 1991.
EMI/Angel Records 0777-7-49404-2-9.

Joaquín Rodrigo and William Walton Concertos, 1993.
EMI/Angel Records 0777-7-54665-2-2.

The Artistry of Christopher Parkening, 1993.
EMI/Angel Records 0777-7-54853-2-5.

The Great Recordings, 1993.
EMI/Angel Records 0777-7-54905-2-7.

Christopher Parkening Plays Vivaldi, 1994.
EMI/Angel Records 7243-5-55052-2-4.

Angels' Glory (with Kathleen Battle), 1996.
Sony Classical SK 62723.

Stepmom (solo, movie soundtrack), 1998.
Sony Classical: SK 61649.

Christopher Parkening Celebrates Segovia, 1998.
EMI/Angel Records 07243-5-56730-0-8.

Concerto for Guitar, 2000.
EMI/Angel Records 7243-5-56859-2-6.

Grace Like a River, 2006.
EMI/Angel Records 00946-3-56418-2-0.

Jubilation (with Jubilant Sykes), 2006.
EMI/Angel Records 00946-3-56421-2-4.

Original LP Albums by Christopher Parkening

In the Classic Style, 1968. Angel Records S-36019.

In the Spanish Style, 1968. Angel Records S-36020.

Romanza, 1969. Angel Records S-36021.

Parkening Plays Bach, 1972. Angel Records S-36041.

The Christopher Parkening Album, 1973. Angel Records S-36069.

Parkening and the Guitar, 1976. Angel Records S-36053.

Sacred Music for the Guitar, 1982 (rereleased as *Simple Gifts*). Angel Records DS-37335.

A Bach Celebration, 1985. Angel Records DS-37343.

Pleasures of Their Company (with Kathleen Battle), 1986. Angel Records DS-37351.

Music Books, Folios, and DVD

The Christopher Parkening Guitar Method, Volume 1 (in collaboration with Jack Marshall and David Brandon). Chicago: Antigua Casa Sherry-Brener Ltd. of Madrid, 1972. Reissued by Hal Leonard Corporation, Milwaukee, 1998.

Virtuoso Music for Guitar: Romanza. Chicago: Antigua Casa Sherry-Brener Ltd. of Madrid, 1973. Reissued by Hal Leonard Corporation, Milwaukee, 1997.

Virtuoso Music for Guitar: Parkening Plays Bach. Chicago: Antigua Casa Sherry-Brener Ltd. of Madrid, 1973. Reissued by Hal Leonard Corporation, Milwaukee, 1997.

Virtuoso Music for Guitar: Parkening and the Guitar, Volumes 1 and 2. Chicago: Antigua Casa Sherry-Brener Ltd. of Madrid, 1977. Reissued by Hal Leonard Corporation, Milwaukee, 1997.

Sacred Music for the Guitar, Volumes 1 and 2. Chicago: Antigua Casa Sherry-Brener Ltd. of Madrid, 1983. Reissued by Hal Leonard Corporation, Milwaukee, 1997.

The Christopher Parkening Guitar Method, Volume 2 (in collaboration with David Brandon). Milwaukee, Hal Leonard Corporation, 1998.

Christopher Parkening: Solo Pieces. Milwaukee: Hal Leonard Corporation, 2006.

Christopher Parkening: Duets & Concertos. Milwaukee: Hal Leonard Corporation, 2006.

A Celebration of Segovia & Parkening (DVD), Milwaukee: Hal Leonard Corporation, 2006.

The Hal Leonard Corporation (www.halleonard.com) is the exclusive publisher of all Christopher Parkening method books and music folios.

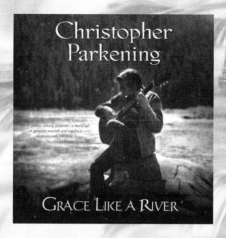

Look for the new Christopher Parkening CD
from EMI/Angel Records.

A stunning collection of some
of his greatest guitar recordings.
A perfect companion to his amazing life story.

❧ ❧ ❧

This audio compilation includes never-before-released live
performances of the spectacular *Koyunbaba* by Domeniconi, and
Castelnuovo-Tedesco's Guitar Concerto in D. It also includes many
favorites such as:
  Chaconne (J. S. Bach)
  Recuerdos de la Alhambra (Tarrega)
  Concerto for Guitar and Orchestra: II. Reflections (Bernstein)

Grace Like a River, 2006. EMI/Angel Records 00946-3-56418-2-0

AUTHOR BIOGRAPHIES

Christopher Parkening is one of the world's preeminent virtuosos of the classical guitar. He has performed throughout the world, and has amassed an extensive discography for which he has received two Grammy nominations. For more than forty years, his concerts and recordings have received the highest worldwide acclaim. The *Washington Post* cited his stature as the "leading guitar virtuoso of our day, combining profound musical insight with complete technical mastery of his instrument." The *Los Angeles Times* noted, "Parkening is considered America's reigning classical guitarist, carrying the torch of his mentor, the late Andrés Segovia."

Christopher is Distinguished Professor of Music at Pepperdine University in Malibu, California, where he chairs the Guitar Department. He has received an honorary doctorate of music from Montana State University as well as the Outstanding Alumnus Award from the University of Southern California "in recognition of his outstanding international achievement and in tribute to his stature throughout the world as America's preeminent virtuoso of the classical guitar." The most prestigious guitar competition in the world has been named in his honor. The Parkening International Guitar Competition will be held every four years, commencing in 2006 at Pepperdine University. Christopher has authored *The Christopher Parkening Guitar Method, Volumes I and II*, which, along with his collection of guitar transcriptions and arrangements, are published by Hal Leonard Corporation. At the heart of his dedication to performing, recording, and teaching is a deep commitment to the Christian faith.

Christopher is also a world-class fly-fishing champion who has won the International Gold Cup Tarpon Tournament (the Wimbledon of fly-fishing).

Christopher resides in Southern California with his wife, Theresa, and their son, Luke.

❦❦ ❦❦ ❦❦

The shadow cast by Andrés Segovia is long, but the mantle of the Spanish master has always rested easily upon the shoulders—or fingers—of classical guitarist, Christopher Parkening.

Chicago Tribune

❦❦ ❦❦ ❦❦

You go to hear Parkening to be completely and overwhelmingly reassured that great musicianship is still one of life's most exhilarating experiences.

St. Louis Post-Dispatch

❦❦ ❦❦ ❦❦

Beg, steal, buy, or borrow a ticket to hear the spectacular virtuoso, Christopher Parkening.

Washington Post

Kathy Tyers, author of two Star Wars series novels in addition to the Firebird Trilogy, *Shivering World*, and several other science fiction novels, also mentors apprentice writers through the Christian Writers Guild.